GRAMMAR SCHOOL BOYS

John Trueman

Best Wishes

Enjoy!

John Trueman

First published by A1
amazon.c

Copyright © J G Trueman 2019

Due to possible memory lapses, some dates in this book may
be slightly askew, but all events described are, as far as my
ancient memory allows, a true and accurate record.

Some names have been changed to avoid embarrassment.

johnnytrueman@yahoo.com

For my very special sons William and Daniel, in order to prove that their loving and dedicated father was once a young person and did not begin life as a grumpy middle-aged tyrant with evidence of his latest meal displayed on the front of his shirt.

Also, for all Old Headlandians, everywhere.

"Floreat Semper schola"

CONTENTS

Prologue		8
Chapter 1:	August to December 1959	13
Chapter 2:	January to July 1960	47
Chapter 3:	August to December 1960	73
Chapter 4:	January to July 1961	94
Chapter 5:	August to December 1961	115
Chapter 6:	January to July 1962	138
Chapter 7:	August to December 1962	157
Chapter 8:	January to July 1963	177
Chapter 9:	August to December 1963	207
Chapter 10:	January to September 1964	230
Epilogue		258

PROLOGUE

Grammar schools (*scolae grammaticales*) have existed as part of the British educational life since medieval times, some schools going back as far as the sixth century. King's School, Canterbury, for example was founded in the year 597. These seats of learning and education were physically and metaphorically attached to cathedrals and monasteries and were established to teach Latin to the sons of the gentry, the wealthy and privileged and, more specifically, the sons of religious leaders as preparation for their almost hereditary rite of passage into the clergy. Recognising that a curriculum consisting solely of Latin was somewhat limited in its appeal, the schools expanded the programme of study to include Ancient Greek. Even this wider range of two subjects didn't satisfy the country's thirst for education and knowledge and so, over time, other subjects were added to the curriculum including music, verse and astronomy – all subjects designed to ease entry into a lucrative religious career.

From this uninspiring beginning, the British education system evolved over the centuries, expanding the range of subjects to include topics which may be of some use in more areas than just religion. Mathematics and English were added along with rudimentary science (possibly consisting of many happy hours attempting to convert base metals into gold). One thing that did not change was the limitation that schooling was restricted to the sons of the wealthy, despite many philanthropists attempting to open education to all boys. Girls, od course, would not be recognised as worthy of education for some centuries yet. Even where the money was available for many less privileged students, their worth to the family as paid labour effectively excluded them from inclusion.

The British educational system progressed sporadically in a generally unstructured and disunited fashion until the Victorian era when the great reformers of the day tried to bring order and uniformity to the edification of British youth. The driving force was the perceived need to civilise the third of the world coloured pink as part of the British Empire before expanding to rule the remaining two thirds. The Elementary Education Act, the Public Schools Act and the Endowed Schools Act in the late nineteenth century formalised much of the system and authorised the term Grammar School to be used for all academically oriented secondary schools, those following a literary or scientific curriculum. There was even a recognition that females may benefit from education, although the places of education were separated and girls' schools could not use the term 'Grammar School', being relegated to more inconsequential 'High Schools.'

As the Empire expanded, the British education system was transported to the colonies; to the Indian sub-continent, to southern Africa, to the Antipodes and, of course, to the Americas. Even now, the majority of formal, modern education across the globe is based on this British model, evolving through the centuries before being exported along with bureaucracy, electoral systems, free speech, cricket and spotted dick.

Although compulsory education for all was introduced in 1880 and augmented by various government acts in following years, the grammar schools remained the major force in classical and scientific education and they were, in many cases, open to all. All, that is, who could afford it.

In the 1930s, the British Government prepared to introduce the Education Act, but its implementation was delayed by the bad-mannered and inconsiderate actions of Adolf Hitler who decided to invade Poland, thus scuppering British plans to reform schooling throughout the country. Not to be put off by the minor inconvenience of a world war, Parliament continued with its delayed plans and, between dodging the might of the Luftwaffe, preparing for the biggest invasion in History, queuing for sawdust sausages and trying to cook omelettes with dried eggs, introduced the act before the war ended. Officially called the Education Act 1944 and presenting the Tripartite System of education, the act was generally known as the Butler Act. It was named after the then Education Minister Rab Butler and ensured that all children would be provided with state-funded secondary education from the ages of 11 to 15. Three types of school were created: grammar schools, secondary technical schools (sometimes described as technical grammar schools) and secondary modern schools. Not all education authorities implemented the tripartite system and many authorities maintained only two types of secondary schools, the grammar and the secondary modern. Admission was decided by an examination at 11 years of age, an early type of IQ test, imaginatively called the eleven plus, although quite what the 'plus' signified is unclear.

Rab Butler himself was a strange looking chap who always appeared to have someone else's lips badly attached and was a pioneer of the comb-over. He also came from an era when the clear majority of politicians were produced from the privileged classes and had limited knowledge of general education, most of them attending public school, followed by university at Oxbridge. Rab himself was the son of Sir Montagu Sherard Dawes Butler of the Indian Civil Service and an old boy of Marlborough College and Pembroke College, Cambridge. Perhaps he was not too well equipped to understand the educational needs of the post war ragamuffins spawned in abundance by sex-starved servicemen, home from six years fighting in France, Africa and the far east. The Establishment probably imagined creating future generations of Biggles' or Bulldog Drummonds, serving in some distant, fly-blown part of our glorious empire, attacking a machine gun nest manned by evil foreigners in the morning, whilst armed only with a pen-knife and a whistle, before scoring a century against the descendants of Australian convicts in the afternoon.

They did not imagine a bunch of ragged-assed council house lads, more intent upon shoplifting ten woodbines or discovering the secret of the mysterious clips on a bra strap than mastering Latin verb conjugation.

The system did, inevitably, produce some notable alumni, generally referred as "Grammar School Boys", a label considered something of a badge of honour. Mick Jagger attended Dartford Grammar School, Sir Trevor Nunn was a notable old boy of Northgate Grammar School in Ipswich, ex-Prime Minister John Major went to Rutlish Grammar School in south west London and Michael Parkinson was famously educated at Barnsley Grammar School. Although, it must be said that Major and Parkinson achieved a paltry five GCE 'o' levels between them, suggesting that their later success in life was despite of their education and not because of it.

My own school, Headlands Grammar School in Swindon notes amongst its alumni Sir Peter Allen, a former Judge in Uganda; Air Vice-Marshal Andy Collier CB CBE; John Eatwell, Baron Eatwell, Professor of Financial Policy and Director since 2002 at the University of Cambridge and, perhaps most impressively, Bob Anderson, the 1988 World Darts Champion.

Grammar schools were controversial from the start, some saying that they were elitist and benefitted only those who passed the eleven plus, at the expense of those who attended secondary modern schools. The contrasting point of view was that the most gifted pupils benefitted by receiving a higher level and more intensive education, whilst the less academic could learn woodwork, sewing and gardening, thus feeding our industrial and agricultural heritage. This debate raged for many years until 1965 when the tripartite system was reformed and the eleven-plus was abandoned. All secondary schools were renamed Comprehensive Schools. That said, Grammar Schools still exist today and are still open to all. All, that is, who can afford it.

Chapter 1 – August to December 1959

- *Ivor the Engine* first aired by Associated-Rediffusion
- General Election results in a record third successive Conservative victory, with the slogan "Life's better with the Conservatives."
- Ronnie Scott's Jazz Club opens in the Soho district of London
- The original Mini is launched

I would imagine that different people remember the past in different ways, but no-one will ever understand how others view events, real, historical or imagined, within the complexities of their minds. Until the day comes, that is, when a genius professor invents a machine that can read a subject's brain impulses, translate the particles, electrons and neutrons buzzing around and project the image onto a televisual screen for all to see and hear. At one time during my school career, I had toyed with the idea of inventing such a machine, however, I spent so much time devising devious ways of using the apparatus that I never quite came around to the hardware or software invention side of the project, otherwise I could now be sitting at home, proudly polishing my Nobel Prize for Inventing.

My own memory recall is reminiscent of watching a mixture of grainy, silent black and white movies, projected somewhere in the recesses of my head, flickering from scene to scene in random order with decidedly flawed continuity. These hazy and fragmented scenes are interrupted by shorter scenes of absolute clarity where the picture is in flawless, in sharp Technicolor with a vibrant surround sound system. My recall of days at Headlands Grammar School are no different, a 1960's kitchen sink 'B' movie, consisting of vague and barely connected scenes, interspersed with clear and poignant tableaux of post-war suburban England.

A vivid scene opens at 09:45, on the seventh of September 1959, three days before my twelfth birthday. My first day at Headland Grammar School, Swindon. My Ex-Pinehurst Junior School mates and I were pushing our bicycles down the long and intimidating drive leading to the school buildings, nervousness exhibiting either silent, unobserved camouflage or over-boisterous play acting. Cycling on school property was strictly forbidden we were warned, on pain of corporal chastisement or, worse, a detention. Although we didn't understand what either punishment consisted of, we adhered to the rule of law.

It was typical late summer, an overcast and muggy day where a drab grey blanket of cloud offered a sombre threat of rain, but which refused to do more than intimidate. Our mood was the opposite. We were bright, nervous, excited and scared, blithely unaware that we were generally considered as the lucky, privileged few about to begin a great adventure in our education. We were simply mindful that we were entering the unknown and would probably be debagged, exposing our underpants, willies and bottoms to the world, or have our heads flushed in the toilets in the very near future. For my age, I was a small lad, short of stature like all my family. My father, our dad, claimed to be five feet seven inches but I think that at least one of those inches was embellishment, and his four brothers were of similar build; short, sturdy Wiltshire farming stock. "I be Wiltshire, born and bred, thick in the arm and thick in the 'ead," as out dad always said, with some kind of misplaced pride. My Uncle George was the tallest of nine siblings, always described as nearly six foot, but no-one ever defined the precise measurement of 'nearly'.

All the new school intake kept within their comfort zones, surrounding themselves with their existing mates from their junior schools. I engineered a position amongst some of my bigger pals.

Derek Windslow was a gentle giant and Pete Griffin an aggressive giant, providing a sound protective cover on my flanks. With Brian Mason in front and Geoff Peaple behind, I felt secure. I glanced at the some of the other groups; the Upper Stratton and Penhill Junior School contingents walking equally nervously but without bicycles, as they lived closer to the school; those from Moredon, Gorse Hill and Old Walcott, like us ex-Pinehurst pupils, pushing bicycles, and two or three large groups from the outlying small towns and villages, Highworth, Blunsdon and South Marsden, who had arrived by bus. By and large, the bicycles were gleaming new models, presented by proud parents as a reward for passing the eleven-plus, and in 1959, bikes were an essential mode of transport. My own vehicle was new to me if not to the world, our dad having bought it from a bloke in Ferndale Working Mens' Club. I had spent several days cleaning and oiling anything that appeared to need cleaning or oiling and carried out general refurbishment such that it was as good as new. More importantly, I had invested my pocket money on a gizmo which attached to the front wheel and acted as a milometer. I proudly reported to my mates that we had travelled 0.92 of a mile to school, although this was not to be broadcast - the official minimum distance between school and home to qualify pupils to cycle was set by the school at one mile. I was just a trifle peeved to see that an old Pinehurst mate, Derek Wall or Wally, had a brand new, drop handlebarred racing bike with ten gears, but consoled myself that he didn't have a gizmo to tell him how far he'd cycled.

A small stream of dark blue flowed gently along the drive, boys dressed in navy blazers with the top pockets emblazoned with the school crest, short grey trousers, grey socks pulled neatly to the knees and black shoes shining from recent polishing, the ensemble topped with a navy-blue cap, also embellished with the school badge. The girls were similarly clad in blazers, which covered blue gymslips over white blouses and topped with blue berets. The uniformity was exaggerated by the fact that almost all the uniforms were a size or two too large, giving us "room to grow." Any protests by the incumbents to parents that the outfit was too big was simply answered with, "You'll grow into it." Indeed, many did grow into their uniforms but many, particularly smaller pupils like me, never grew quickly enough to catch up with their uniforms. The clothes were worn and threadbare long before they would fit. Even then, our replacements would again be selected with more room to grow. I was in my late teens and working before I managed to buy anything that fitted at the time of purchase. My scrawny neck poked out from my oversized shirt collar like a tortoise searching for a lettuce leaf, and my navy-blue tie with stripes of red and yellow was pulled tight in a vain attempt to constrict the over-large shirt collar, but it refused to stay in place and continually disappeared under the left wing of the shirt collar. My blazer, though purchased some months before, was at least two sizes too big, as were my short trousers which reached my knees and flapped like sails in the morning breeze. My socks refused to stay up despite wearing elasticated garters and my cap had a mind of its own, never quite moving in the same direction as my head. The only clothing which could in any way be described as smart were my shoes which our dad had polished the night before using his army spit and polish technique using plenty of Cherry Blossom and real spit, which he obtained by making a particularly obnoxious sound from the back of his throat before gobbing slimy phlegm onto my shoes and buffing with the back of a spoon.

Each pupil also carried a satchel. These were far from uniform and varied in design and manufacture from standard backpacks in canvas or plastic offered by the school supplier to impressive leather briefcases. Kiffer Carter had a World War Two gas mask case. Most satchels were carried on the pupils' backs with straps secured around the shoulders. My own was a very smart case made from thick, unyielding leather, which was larger and better quality than most and would have been most impressive had I been of greater stature. As it was, I looked like a miniscule Sherpa with a month's supply of equipment and chattels to transport up Everest. I'm quite sure that Sir Edmund Hillary would have selected me to aid his historic conquering of the mountain. Quite where our dad supplied the satchel from, I cannot be sure, but there were some slight signs of wear and a stamp saying *GWR-BD Shop Office* on the inside of the flap.

We approached the large and intimidating building, two stories of red brick, which were a rather ugly brown brick, with little or no character and looking more like a Victorian prison block than a seat of learning. The cyclists were diverted by a large, hand-painted sign saying *First Year Bicycles*, which confused many as it was unclear what we were being told to do with our bicycles. From the confused group, a brave cyclist decided that he would follow the direction indicated on the sign. We followed the leader, reaching a large area of bicycle racks protected under a cover of corrugated iron. These were the famous bike sheds that new boys' older brothers had informed us were reserved not only for storing our transport but were the designated area for snogging and feeling up girls. Why anyone would want to snog a girl behind a bike shed and what feeling up consisted of was somewhat baffling to me.

As we parked our trusty steeds and returned to join the pedestrian pupils at the large main doors to the building, I began to feel uncomfortable. Something was amiss, but I couldn't quite identify what the problem was. I looked at the other pupils, smartly clad in their oversized navy-blue and grey livery and glanced down at my own outsized blazer. I could feel by face burning as I blushed and tried to hide my embarrassment. My blazer was a different shade of navy-blue to the other new pupils' uniforms.

Throughout my time at Pinehurst Junior School, it had been assumed that I would pass the eleven-plus and go to grammar school. This was not wishful thinking or arrogance but just plain common sense and logic. It was usual for around fifteen to twenty pupils from Pinehurst to pass the eleven-plus each year, about ten percent of the fourth-year population, and I had always been one of the top four pupils in the top class. Until the final examinations of the final year, I had always been in the top three, competing with Brian Mason who lived just across the road from me, and Stuart Battersby who lived in the MAP bungalows at The Circle, for the top spot. We shared the spoils in each of the seven end of term tests we had taken. That is, until the last exams of the last term when an interloper usurped the three wise men and blasted his way to the top spot. When announcing the examination results, our teacher, Mr Moore, expounded at some length that Derek Wall's rise to prominence was the result of sheer hard work and showed just what could be achieved by dedication and commitment. I was shattered, particularly as Wally – pronounced to rhyme with brolly - had previously been given the position of football captain in the school team, a role that I coveted I felt that I should have been awarded...and he lived in Moredon and should not have been in Pinehurst School in the first place...and he had a brother who played football for Swindon Boys.

Our mum was always on the lookout for a bargain and decided that, as I was bound for grammar school, it made sense to buy my uniform several months in advance at the January sales. Against my better judgement and with a degree of grumbling dissent, we caught the bus to town and headed for Foster Brothers in Swindon's Fleet Street to try on a navy-blue blazer that our mum had seen in the shop window, marked down to half price. Why I had to try this garment on remains a mystery as its dimensions and mine were incompatible, but we bought it anyway. Foster Brothers were not the official school outfitters but, after all, a navy-blue blazer is a navy-blue blazer. Except that, unknown to our mum and me, there are different shades of navy blue and my first day embarrassment was caused by the fact that my blazer was a shade lighter and bluer than everyone else's. I could live with oversized apparel as most other newcomers were in the same boat (or same coat), but a different coloured blazer, especially one where the school badge had been rather obviously and carelessly tacked on to the breast pocket, rather than being an integral part of the pocket, was too embarrassing. Although I tried to conceal myself between Pete and Derek, I was sure that unknown lads from unknown schools were staring at my sartorial indiscretion. One particularly large boy seemed to be staring more intently and turned to speak to one of his comrades, perhaps to point out my blazer, and so I came out from my hiding place and pushed the big lad.

"What you looking at, Fatty?" I growled as deeply as my unbroken and squeaking child's voice would allow.

The boy looked confused and shrugged. "Um. Nothing. I'm not even looking."

I remembered our dad's advice in such situations. "Always get your retaliation in first," so I pushed big lad harder and swung a wild punch which may or may not have landed somewhere near his left ear. He just stood looking more confused and, happily, more embarrassed than me. My diversionary tactic appeared to have worked.

"You better not," I warned as my opponent turned to his mates holding his palms outward and shrugging his large shoulders with a look of sad confusion spreading across his chubby pink face.

The contretemps was quickly forgotten as the double doors to the school burst open and a tall skinny man with a teddy boy quiff burst through, his arm held firmly to his back by a shorter, stocky man who ejected the teddy boy from the building, telling him in no uncertain terms not to return. This was our first encounter with Tarz, the feared school caretaker. The way that he disposed of the taller and younger fellow was both exciting and frightening and the reason for the ejection was never disclosed. I don't believe that I ever never knew Tarz's name. He was always just Tarz and no-one challenged his authority.

Moments later, the door reopened. A troupe of older pupils emerged and stood proudly on the school steps and stared at the assembled throng of nervous young newcomers. We gaped in awe of these people. They were adults in school uniforms much like our own, except that the boys were wearing long trousers and the girls were attired in smart grey skirts and white blouses. Their ties were also different, a silky maroon with the school badge printed in a regular pattern running their length and, on their lapels, was a large shiny blue badge proclaiming *PREFECT* in gold embossed lettering. They did not look the fiends who, we had been warned, would remove our trousers or flush our heads down the bogs, but we were aware that looks can be misleading. The new boys and girls were divided into groups and led by a prefect to changing rooms within the depths of the intimidating building. Here, we were told to leave our satchels and change into our daps. As part of the instructions prior to the first day, all parents were ordered to provide their child with a pair of white plimsolls and a bag, with a draw string, in which to keep the footwear. To us, they were daps and the bag was always a dap-bag, having never before heard the term 'plimsoll.' Although the wearing of a school uniform, including white daps, was designed to ensure that we were all appeared uniform, differences in social structure was reflected in the footwear. Those pupils from the poorer council areas, Pinehurst, Penhill and parts of Stratton, tended to have very basic white daps from Woolworths while, for the better off, mainly from the outlying villages, slightly more robust gym shoes from Stead and Simpsons were *de rigueur*. Those from the private housing estates of Old Walcott, The Lawns or Whitworth Road donned heavier, sturdier gym shoes akin to modern trainers and purchased from Blaylocks, purveyors of ladies' and gents' footwear in Swindon's Old Town. I, naturally, fitted in to the Woollies dap camp. I was lucky to fit into any camp as, up until the previous week, my parents were inclined to send me with a pair of brown bumpers purchased for the summer and whose sole had detached itself from its upper which was now secured with an Elastoplast. It was only continual moaning and pleading that convinced our mum to buy the regulation white daps and a tin of Blanco White Cleaner.

We had been randomly divided into groups of around ten pupils and assigned to our prefect. The Pinehurst old boys managed to keep in the same group and we were allocated to a lanky youth with greasy hair and a face that, as our mum would say, "Only a mother could love", decorated with an interesting diversity of spots and pimples. Our tour of the school was thorough and well-scripted, but of absolutely no use. We were rushed up and down identical staircases, through a warren of identical corridors with identical doors, having no idea of the orientation of the maze. We were corralled into science laboratories which amazed and confused us, a gymnasium which was simply too grand to comprehend, music rooms, libraries, workshops, art studios, drawing offices, common rooms and teachers' offices, which all blurred into one huge and confused labyrinth. The one area that did stick in our minds was the location of the tuck shop. Amazingly, this was an actual shop counter within the school, selling tuck - crisps, sweets, chocolate, biscuits; in fact, everything and anything seemingly selected to be of little nutritional value and designed to rot teeth. That was a location on the first floor was worth remembering. Our minds spinning, the excited groups were finally taken to the huge, impressive and intimidating assembly hall and ordered to sit.

On the equally huge, intimidating and impressive stage before us were half a dozen grown-ups, we assumed to be teachers, wearing strange black gowns, which most of the group had wrapped around themselves as they sat like a and stared down at the new intake like a venue of vultures waiting for their next victims (us) to die. They did not speak. We dare not speak. After a few moments, the doors into the hall opened behind us and we could hear footsteps clacking briskly towards the front. No-one risked turning around, but the teachers shuffled to their feet and our prefect leaders indicated that we should follow suit. Passing us and climbing the stairs to the stage, was a tall, straight-backed gentleman, his cape flowing behind him like a huge pair of wings, a hooked nose and piercing eyes giving the impression of an enormous head vulture. The imposing figure turned and faced the assembly. The teachers sat, we followed suit. This was Thomas Symmons Magson MA. The headmaster. Forever known as The Boss.

The Boss welcomed us to the school by explaining its objectives and our role in maintaining the standards expected from this eminent and noble institution. He outlined some of the school rules although I, and I guess most other recruits, were far too overawed to take in much of what was said. Discipline, hard work, walk on the right, education, teachers are Sir or Madam, examinations, no chewing confection, always wear school uniform, respect, honesty, fountain pens at all times, plimsolls must be worn, no talking, stand up for adults, justice, pride, no running, blah, blah, blah, play up! play up! and play the game! When I told our dad that we had to call the men teachers Sir as if we were in the army, he said, "Just because you've got to call 'em Sir, you don't have to mean it…and it don't mean they're better than you." He tapped the side of his nose as if passing on the meaning of life.

The Boss also explained the school motto, clearly exhibited in Latin on our blazers and caps. *Omnia expire bona contine.* He explained that this means we should experience everything and continue with the good. I wonder if he would have approved of the motto years later when we were experiencing shoplifting, alcohol, cigarettes, and undoing bras with one hand, most of which we deemed as pretty good and worth continuing.

As his final part of the introduction, the Boss clarified the houses to which we had been allocated. As part of our parents' pre-term joining instructions, they were told what house we would be joining as each boy was to have a rugby shirt – a soccer shirt would not do – and sports socks in the colour of his or her allocated house, so we already knew in which house colour we belonged. He explained that each house with its defining colour was named after a prehistoric monument near Swindon: Silbury House (yellow) was named after Silbury Hill: Barbary House (blue) after Barbary Castle: Kennet House (green) after Kennet Long Barrow and my house, Rockley (red) after something prehistoric which escaped me then and escapes me now.

Shell-shocked, we were then divided into our forms, based on our scores in the eleven plus. At the top was 1U for those deemed university standard; then came 1A for no other reason than A was the first letter of the alphabet; those in midstream were in 1M denoting middle, medium or mediocre perhaps; the two lower forms were divided into 1B for boys and 1G for girls, although quite why this gender division was necessary was never made clear. I had been placed in the top class, 1U, which I had expected because, after all, I had previously found schoolwork relatively simple. What I had not realised at that point was that rudimentary Maths and English, upon which our schooling had thus far been based, covered but a small percentage of our future education and, from now on, ability in other subjects plus the requirement to study and learn would overtake any natural aptitude for basic subjects. As the names were called out for each form, we assembled behind our new form teachers before being led to our new classrooms.

We followed our form teacher, Miss Bushby, to our new home base and staked a claim to a suitable desk. I grabbed a corner desk next to Brian Mason, my friend and close neighbour from Pinehurst Juniors. My joy at such a prime spot was short-lived as

Miss Bushby re-allocated desks based on sex and alphabetically by surname. I ended up in the front row of desks, almost immediately under our new form teacher's eyes. We were surprised to learn that the Christian names we had been given at birth by loving parents and used at home and in school ever since, were now superfluous and all the boys would be known solely by their surnames for the next five or more years. By contrast, the girls had given up all rights to their surnames and would be known solely by their Christian names. This probably came as a relief to Clarence Jackson and Jennifer Pratt, but to most of the peer group, the loss of a name was a traumatic blow, if just in the short term. Ed Balls would have been devastated.

Each pupil was presented with two exercise books, one of normal size labelled *GENERAL WORK BOOK* and a small pocket-sized book labelled *HOMEWORK*. The next hour or so was spent having the Boss' school rules reiterated plus receiving direction in new rules: always record everything you are told in the exercise book labelled *GENERAL WORK BOOK* unless it is a specific subject in which case we should record everything in the specific subject exercise book, and all homework must be recorded in the small exercise book labelled *HOMEWORK*. I wondered if I should record the fact that we should record everything in the exercise book labelled *GENERAL WORK BOOK*, in the exercise book labelled *GENERAL WORK BOOK*, but no-one else was writing anything, so I sat and allowed my mind to wander, catching just the few odd words – walk on the right, no talking, cover books in brown paper, no ball pens, stand for adults, blah, blah, blah.

A loud bell disturbed my daydreaming and all my classmates stood and began filing out of the room. Apparently, it was dinnertime and we could leave. I followed Brian whose name had now changed to Mason, and we arrived at the bike racks at the same time as other old pals, now in different classes. We cycled home in buoyant mood having survived our first morning without being too stretched and without losing our trousers or drowning in a lavatory. On our return two hours later, I was a little disappointed that we were given real lessons and were expected to learn stuff – I was far happier being told a few rules and daydreaming.

I made an inauspicious start to my further education. By coincidence, Miss Bushby was also our French teacher and our first proper lesson was in this mysterious new language. The rules were clear that whenever a teacher, in fact any grown up, entered the classroom, we were to stand. As Miss Bushby entered the room, my mind was wandering and, although I was vaguely aware that my classmates were smartly standing to attention, I stayed seated for a moment before realising my mistake and jumping to my feet. Miss Bushby glared at me. "Do you understand the rules, Trueman?" she quietly and politely demanded.

"Er, yes Miss," I squeaked.

"Miss what?" she enquired.

"Miss…" I had forgotten my own form teacher's name. "Miss…Miss Busby," I squeaked again.

"Bushby. Miss Bushby. Please sit," she stated firmly. I sat, aware of the sniggers behind me. I never confused her name with that of a gnarled old Manchester United football manager again.

We were issued with French textbooks and informed that we should take them home that evening and cover them in brown paper, clearly marking the subject on the cover and our name on the label inside the front cover. The label showed all previous, temporary owners of the book and the school year in which they had taken ownership. I was unsure whether my abandoned Christian name was allowed but, after referring to previous owners, included it under 1959/1960 to record legal title. I became a little excited when I found Brian Mason's older brother Robert had owned this very book four years previously and couldn't wait to tell

Brian who was now Mason. The remaining part of the forty-minute lesson was spent in trying to understand the rules and nuances of what Miss Busby described as the beautiful language from the beautiful country of France, which surprised me a little as our dad had always said that I should never trust the French as they were cowards who smelt of garlic. And the country smelt of piss because they piddled in the street. Nonetheless, I tried hard to concentrate on what was being taught, even attempting to replicate the French nasal accent, without once drifting away to my own private world.

At the lesson's end, we were given homework which I meticulously recorded in my new homework book, carefully dated and neatly written with my new fountain pen and underlined using my new ruler. That evening, I left school with my satchel bulging with exercise and textbooks, ready to show my parents just what a conscientious and studious grammar school boy I was determined to become. After tea, I opened my satchel and removed the contents, laying them out on the dining room table, and asked our mum if she had any brown paper with which to cover the textbooks. Our mum looked confused and said that no-one had told her about brown paper, but she would see what she could find. After several minutes, she returned with some large brown paper bags and said that they'd have to do, and no-one would notice the few greasy marks from our dad's cheese sandwiches.

I was a bit put out that we had received two pieces of homework from our French lesson that day. Not only were we expected to cover the textbook, but we had been set the onerous task of learning all the members of the family in French. I glanced through the French textbook: *père, mère, fils, fille, grand-père, grand-mère*. It seemed straightforward and not worthy of much study, particularly as Mick and John Paines from across the road were just off down the brook with a football. And, as our mum said,

"French is easy. Just learn the words then put them back to front to make the sentence." So, I joined the footballers down the brook.

Two days later, we had French again. Miss Bushby smiled sweetly and said that she was sure that we had all learned our family members well, but just to recap she would ask some pupils to translate. Out loud.

"Mason, what is 'daughter' in French?"

"*Fille*, Miss Bushby,"

"Ann, what is 'grandmother' in French?"

"*Grand-mere*, Miss Bushby."

My mind was blank. I could feel my face burning with anticipated humiliation as I tried to sit lower in my chair and stare at my desk in the hope that I would not be noticed. Miss Bushby scanned the room, her gaze alighting on this little red-faced, guilt-ridden boy in the front.

"Trueman, what is son in French?"

Panic set in as I went through what I thought I had learnt in my head, 'Mare, pair, er...f f f', the word was stuck somewhere. I was sure that started with an 'f' but that was all I remembered until I managed was a rather weak, "*F, f, fils*, Miss Bushby," with a somewhat exaggerated nasal inflection. Whilst correct, my nervousness and panic had caused the sound emitted to be more like someone with a cold clearing a blocked nose.

Our teacher appeared taken aback, her eyes staring as the rest of the class burst into laughter. I shrunk even lower, blushing more deeply, my embarrassment made more intense by the thought of what my classmates would say. The faux-*pas* was never mentioned openly, although I thought that I heard exaggerated nose-blowing behind my back several times over the next few days. A valuable lesson had been learnt and one which I vowed would not be repeated.

During the first week, the class was given its first Biology lesson. We trooped cautiously to the Biology laboratory and were amazed by the exhibits on view: a full-size skeleton stood guard in the corner, cabinets were full of bottles containing suspended dead frogs and mice, rows of drawers were mysteriously labelled with terms we did not understand. We took our seats behind large work benches, wondering if the knowledge gained here would allow us to dissect animals, handle internal organs, perhaps even gain an understanding of the mysteries of the female reproductive system. And who knows? Perhaps this could be the first step to becoming a renowned surgeon. The teacher, Mr. Stewart (whom we later learned was known as "Turd", the origin of which remained a mystery throughout my time at school) introduced the subject to be studied that term: The Wildflowers of Britain. We were not beginning a career of brain-exchange to create Frankenstein-style life-forms after all, but learning how to distinguish a bluebell from a daffodil. The subject was less than enthralling but we busied ourselves learning about stamens, sepals and stigmas: about saxifrage, snowdrops and sorrel. It took every bit of concentration and discipline I could muster not to organise an escape attempt from the lab. When homework was set, however, I was determined not to make the same mistake as the earlier evening and meticulously recorded in my homework diary, *Describe characteristics of common woodland flowers*, before I rushed out to cycle home.

Pupils who had passed the eleven plus had their names proudly printed in the Swindon Evening Advertiser, "The Adver." This not only filled the parents of successful children great pride, but unwittingly alienated families whose children failed the examination, helping to build a wedge between Grammar School and Secondary Modern pupils, a wedge which did not need any help in its construction. The published names also offered an opportunity for unscrupulous salesmen to call on proud parents offering a set of encyclopaedias, which they assured the naïve mums and dads were essential to the continuing educational success of the child and could be purchased for a small sum down and easy weekly payments on the never-never or "glad and sorry" as our mum called it – glad that you own the article but sorry that you couldn't pay for it. The fact these tomes bore no relation to the school curriculum was lost on our mum and many like her.

Armed with my new encyclopaedias, I retreated to my bedroom determined to produce an outstanding piece of homework on the woodland flowers of Great Britain. After searching through the relevant section of my new source of knowledge, I discovered the passage which would make me a star pupil and banish the embarrassment of previous shoddy work. I wrote:

Forget-me-not. In 15th-century Germany, it was supposed that the wearers of the flower would not be forgotten by their lovers. Legend has it that, in medieval times, a German knight and his lady were walking along the side of a river. The knight picked a posy of flowers for his lover, but because of the weight of his armour he fell into the river. As he was drowning, he threw the posy to his loved one and shouted "Forget-me-not." The flower was often worn by ladies as a sign of faithfulness and of enduring love.

I proudly placed my Biology exercise book in Turd's pigeonhole where homework was left for marking, confident in the knowledge that meticulous research and accurate recording would reap its just rewards. The next Biology lesson took place the following week and I sat proudly as the exercise books were returned. Eagerly opening the book, I was dumbfounded to see that my effort was graded *D* with a comment *Interesting, but not Biology*, an observation that I did not understand. Having returned all the books, Turd congratulated the class on excellent homework, "With one or two exceptions," he added, looking at me. Again, I blushed deeply hoping that no-one noticed my colour but sure that the heat I was generating could not go unnoticed. Turd then selected one particular piece of homework for praise, produced by

Andrea, a swotty-looking girl with glasses that I had barely noticed before, and he actually held her exercise book up in the air for the class to see before reading, *Bluebell. Has blue, bell shaped flowers on a leafless stalk. Cowslip. Wrinkled green leaves are covered in hairs with a cluster of 1-30 yellow flowers. Cow parsley. Has large, flat umbrellas of small white flowers, and large, fern-like leaves…* and so on until, an age later, *Wood anemone. Each stem has a single, white, star-shaped flower, often flushed with pink or purple.*

I was amazed. I accepted that Andrea's submission had included many more flowers than my single entry, but how can reporting that a flower has blue petals, especially when it's called as bluebell, be more impressive than a German knight falling in a river and being drowned to death. I vowed that, in future, I would ensure that I understood exactly what the teacher was expecting and record the requirements more accurately in my homework diary. But I still felt peeved.

Latin was a subject that I found difficult and at which I was, quite frankly, utterly and absolutely useless. The Latin teacher, Mr. Furber, was an officer in the Air Training Corps and a very serious and humourless soul. He was aware that Latin was often perceived as both complex and of little practical use and had obviously felt the need to allay such perceptions early. After a rudimentary overview of the subject, he set homework of identifying English words with a Latin derivation. I scribbled the requirements in my homework diary and, that night, carefully turned again to my encyclopaedias. I found a page entitled *English Words with Latin Derivatives* and set to work. The first word in the list that I recognised was *anus* which I decided was too rude to include, so I continued my search and wrote:

Axis, camera, circus, focus, mucus, omen, pauper, pollen, radius, stimulus.

Ten words meaning exactly the same in Latin as in English. Ten. A good round number and the homework completed in five minutes. I was confident that a commendation from Mr. Furber was coming my way. The homework was duly handed in and I waited expectantly for the next Latin lesson. As the exercise books were returned on the Friday, I opened mine with a sense of excited anticipation: this was to be my moment: just recognition at last.

I could scarcely believe that my list of words had been desecrated by another big red *D* and the words, *See me*, a phrase that I would come to know all too well in the future. In my confused and wounded state, I was barely aware that Wing Commander Furber was enthusiastically extolling the virtues of the class homework and how well pupils had done, 'With one or two exceptions.' He then read out a good example of how well we had fared. He picked up bloody Andrea's exercise book from her desk and read aloud, "Dislocation, local, locality, locate, location, locative, translocate, translocation, locomotive, locomotion are derivatives of *locum*. Alliteration, alliterative, biliteral, illiteracy, illiterate, literacy, literal, literary, literate, literature, obliterate, obliteration, transliteracy, transliteration, trilateral are derivatives of *littera*..."

Little wonder that my weedy list was not recognised as a work deserving of great reverence. It wasn't my fault that I didn't know what a *derivative* was and, anyway, Andrea's parents must have helped her and I bet she had a better set of encyclopaedias than me. But three sets of homework and three disasters taught me a valuable lesson - that I was better off not doing my own homework. Through skill, subterfuge and bribery, I became quite expert at copying other pupils' homework each morning, selecting just enough excerpts from their efforts to pass muster.

Those first days continued in a blur of new subjects, new classrooms, new friends, timetables and homework. Junior school subjects had been changed, sometimes beyond recognition. Spelling and Composition became English Language and Reading was now English Literature. Sums had moved on to Mathematics, broken into three subjects of Arithmetic, Algebra and Geometry. What was previously lumped together as 'General' was now separate subjects of History, Geography and Religious Instruction. On top of these changes there were the new science subjects of Chemistry, Physics and Biology. Most onerous of all, to me at least, was our introduction to languages, Latin and French. I was continually excited and stimulated by my new environment, yet confused and overwhelmed. Where I had been used to being a star pupil, one of the elite, clever boys and top of the class, I found my new classmates to be generally brighter than me, grasping the fundamentals of the new subjects with ease, while I struggled to adapt to both the rigid discipline and the academic changes. But in the bewilderment and turmoil there was one area that shone through, one subject in which I excelled and would raise my profile to compensate for the relegation amongst the murky also-rans. I had a natural ability for sport and, as it turned out, especially rugby union. We had been previously lectured on the correct terms that we should use for games at school. Football, we were told was a generic term for all ball games which involves any kicking and we must, therefore, differentiate between games. Football, as we knew it, was association football and should be called soccer - oddly, a shortened version of association - to distinguish it from rugby football, which we should call rugby or, better still, rugger.

Our introduction to the game of rugger came on a cool and cloudy Wednesday morning under the tutelage of the games master, Bomber Brown. Bomber was an archetypal games master, a stocky, rugged and muscular man who believed that sport was an essential element in education, not just from a fitness viewpoint, but in the development of the very character of a person. He considered a pupil's education incomplete with academic training alone. Participation in sports and games would offer the opportunity for each of us to grow up to be Tom Browns, bravely thrashing the cad, Flashman, or Alf Tupper, the Tough of the Track, winning gold medal after gold medal despite the cheating Johnny-Foreigner's chicanery. Bomber's main preoccupation was rugby union. Soccer, cricket and athletics were just about acceptable as games but to prove oneself worthy of being a true sportsman, it was essential to risk life and limb being trampled underfoot by a pack of overweight thugs in rugby boots.

All streams from the first year's male intake were released to take games together for two consecutive periods of forty minutes each week, our previous separation temporarily abandoned. After excited chatter as we changed into the requisite kit and assembled, as instructed, beneath the huge rugby posts on a pitch furthest away from the changing rooms. We stood, waiting nervously, resplendent in our bright red, blue, green or yellow rugby shirts, the majority a size or two too big, looking like a colourful group of outsize garden gnomes. We then heard the heavy thuds as the infamous Bomber Brown thundered toward us and I am convinced that the ground trembled. After a brief introduction to the basic rules of the game – pass backwards, kick forwards, scrum down, line out, no biting, scratching or punching - Bomber declared that the game was not about running quickly with the ball but about passing the ball swiftly by hand and he would prove that passing was faster than running. He selected half a dozen or so of the nearest pupils and set them in a straight line about three or four yards apart. He asked for a volunteer to who could run fast and, though my hand shot up, despite our dad's advice to, "Keep your 'ead down and never volunteer for nothin'," two other lads pushed someone forward saying he was the fastest runner they knew and Wally reluctantly and modestly stepped forward to thwart my ambitions again. Bomber then explained that he would prove that passing the ball is more effective by racing the passed ball against the runner over the twenty yards or so of the line.

Bomber shouted, "Go!" and passed the ball the few yards to the first boy in line whilst Wally set off. The first boy dropped the ball and Wally reached the end of the line. They tried again. The first boy caught the ball and stood proudly without passing it on. Wally reached the end of the line.

Bomber changed the order of the boys and bellowed, "Go!" once more. The new first boy looked on in amazement as the ball hurtled toward him, hit him cleanly in the belly and dropped to the ground as he gripped his midriff, gasping manically. Wally reached the end, turned and jogged quietly back to the beginning of the line and took up his position for the fourth attempt. What Bomber did not know is that he had, by chance and accident, selected six of the more academic, but most unsporting lads in the group, boys who had never kicked, thrown, caught or passed a ball before and, indeed, never would. After several changes of personnel and more attempts, where the ball was dropped, bounced off heads, bodies and arms and tossed manically in the wrong direction, and with Wally beginning to look worn out having run and won several sprint races in succession, the ball finally reached the last member of the line. Wally had slowed down and arrived a split second after the ball, whereby Bomber punched the air in triumph, exclaiming, "There, I told you so."

He abandoned any hope of more trials or coaching and divided the assembly into two teams and started a game. Immediately I felt at ease and confident. From my allocated position as a centre - thankfully, I was too small for the forwards - I ran, tackled, passed and touched down, revelling in the game. As we left the field, I was elated, especially as Bomber caught up with me and asked if I had ever played the game before. I truthfully replied in the negative, but Bomber looked at me as if he didn't believe it.

I was euphoric as I sat in the changing room. I wanted this feeling to last forever, until Bomber stepped inside the room. "Showers. All of you. Now."

I had never showered in public before. In fact, I had never showered before; a quick rub with a damp flannel each morning and a weekly bath had always completed my ablutions. Now, I had to stand in a communal shower, with lots of other boys, all of us naked. The only people who had ever seen me in the nude were my parents, and then not for some years. At the swimming pool, I was always covered by a towel, secreted in a cubicle or in a quiet corner. And now I would be exposing my willie to all and sundry. I had no choice, so I quietly sneaked into a corner facing the wall to remove my kit, sidled into the shower, washed quickly and returned to my place covering myself with my towel. No-one seemed to be taking any notice of me and many were sharing my embarrassment, but my awkwardness was amplified as I saw some of the others' towels. They were huge, fluffy sheets which wrapped around the owners several times; mine was a small hand towel, somewhat threadbare, which barely covered my private areas. Fortunately, no-one seemed to notice and I felt a little better, especially when I noticed that Kiffer Carter's towel was printed with a map and the words *Present from Weston-Super-Mare*.

I survived the first week's academic toil intact, although secretly disappointed that none of the new intake had had his head flushed in the bogs or had trousers ceremoniously removed. I cycled home with my mates on Friday afternoon happy to have lived to tell the tale but dissatisfied with my performance in most areas.

I continued to find Maths and English relatively straightforward, but was feeling a little lost in other subjects, particularly in languages, so made a personal commitment to study harder and definitely, definitely brush up my efforts with homework. That weekend gave me the ideal opportunity. We had received heavy and varied assignments to be completed before Monday's return and I pledged to myself that I would really concentrate and find the time to produce exemplary work. It was a busy weekend with much sleep required to recover from the week's educational excesses, interspersed with games of football down the brook, hanging about in the street and generally doing anything but schoolwork. Without warning it seemed, it was Sunday evening: the weekend was almost over and my satchel was unopened. Perhaps I could report the satchel stolen or say that the dog ate the contents, or the books had spontaneously combusted. Having spent some time formulating plausible and implausible excuses for not completing my homework, I realised that there was nothing for it, but to do the work. I retired to my bedroom and took out my books including the homework diary, which I opened and read what I had to do. Some entries made sense, but others meant little. What did I mean by *Learn noun declensions - a us um etc*, for Latin or simply *Describe towns* under History. This is most unsatisfactory I thought, reiterating the teachers' description of my work, and I was determined to do something about my persistent dilemma. With that thought, I took my homework diary and headed each page with the date for the following few weeks. I divided each page horizontally into three, neatly drawing a line to separate the sections. I was pleased with the neatness and order that it gave the diary but decided that it could be improved. On the top of each section, I neatly wrote *Subject*, carefully underlined using ruler and pen. Delighted with this improvement, I added the word *Description* at the top and *Complete by* at the bottom of each section. I decided that completing this enhancement should stop at Christmas, so I worked diligently until 24th December was reached, remembering to exclude Saturdays, Sundays and holidays. All in all,

I considered my efforts an excellent job, although it was now too late to complete any of that week's homework assignments. No matter, I concluded, there will be plenty of time in the morning.

That first week set the tone for the rest of the term. I never quite got to grip with languages and never got to grips at all with homework. I was always too busy to sit down and study especially as my bedroom overlooked the street and the Pinehurst Secondary Modern lads had free evenings and weekends. The street became a sports pavilion hosting whatever sport was prevalent at that time, or became a base for other games, hide and seek, knock door runaway, marbles and kick the can: or it was the perfect base for simply hanging about. The draw of simply hanging about was very difficult to resist.

I was also building up a reputation as the class bad boy. Although much of the notoriety was accidental, caused by my lack of understanding, I played on the reputation and was forever hatching small and futile plans to undermine the authority of the teachers. I had watched *The Colditz Story* where John Mills made the Nazis captors' lives difficult with continual subterfuge and I felt that my tricks were in the same vein, fighting back against the authority of our prison guards. Removing chalk from the teachers' desks, sketching crude, coded messages on the blackboard, making silly noises and passing rude notes to friends to make them laugh in class were played out on a daily basis. I had competition in the role of class clown with a lad from a different junior school, delightfully named Raymond Plunkett. When miss Bushby called the register each morning, we were instructed to reply, "Present, Miss Bushby," and Plunkett and I hatched a plan to respond with, "Pregnant Miss Bushby." Alongside words like penis, intercourse, breast and virgin, *pregnant* was considered a very daring and risqué word and would illicit furtive giggles when used. The morning came and Miss Bushby began calling the register, girls names first, followed by the boys, in strict alphabetical order of surname. She reached, "Plunkett?". There was a slight pause before the response came as, "Pregsent, Miss Bushby." A rather feeble attempt to produce a hybrid retort which the teacher appeared not to notice. I was only a couple of names after Plunkett and I heard, "Trueman?". I replied with an obvious if rushed, "Pregnant, Miss Bushby." She paused, stared at me for a second, then carried on to the remaining couple of names. Despite my daring, I knew that my face was bright red and I was sweating profusely. The incident soon became the number one item on the first-year jungle telegraph but, disappointingly I was simply considered stupid by my peers, an opinion ignited and fanned by Plunkett. Miss Bushby never mentioned the incident and future plans to answer, "Present Miss Bushbaby," were abandoned.

The term ended with swathe of examinations, for which I had abandoned street football for a few weeks and managed to do some swotting, even paying passing attention my previous homework, most of which had been prepared by my classmates. The exams went without incident, except in Music. Our teacher Norman Gilbert was a scary and ferocious individual, who never failed to fill me with an illogical fear. I have recently found this description of him:

Norman Gilbert grew up in Yorkshire and was a student of Sir Edward Bairstow at York Minster. During the 1930's he held positions at St. John's Church, Halifax and St. Paul's Church, Llandudno. Shortly after release from war service, he was appointed Music Master of Headlands Grammar School in Swindon, Wiltshire. 'Veni Spiritus Whitsuntide' is the 4th of his "Pieces for Four Seasons," the other three being for Christmas, Lent, and Easter. Published by Novello in 1959, this is No. 17 in "Novello's Organ Music Club" series.

Knowing this, it seems disrespectful that he was universally known as Green Gilbert, schoolboy slang for a bogey, when he was a classically trained, well-known and respected composer. That said and fear apart, I quite enjoyed music lessons. We could sit quietly, listening to tunes written mainly by chaps with foreign names like Beethoven, Mozart, Brahms and Chopin whilst Green Gilbert waxed lyrically about things I never understood. On other occasions, we would be asked to sing together: *Oh My Darling Clementine, Greensleeves* or *Scarborough Fair* were favourites and, so long as one's miming skills were up to standard, this caused no problems. And there was no homework. I was somewhat taken aback, therefore, when Green Gilbert announced one day that the following two lessons were to be reserved for end-of-term tests and that we should learn a verse or two of a favourite song and be prepared to sing in front of the class. My favourite songs, *It Doesn't Matter Anymore* by Buddy Holly and *Livin' Doll* by Cliff Richard were out of the question, so I investigated folk music which was acceptable, and came across *What Shall We Do with The Drunken Sailor*, the words to which I thought were outstanding and had quite enjoyed bellowing out during a couple of previous lessons. I briefly scanned the words to the shanty but was confident that I knew enough to get by. I worked out that the two examination lessons equalled eighty minutes and with a class of thirty-five pupils, with time taken to call each pupil, announcing the song, comments from Green Gilbert and other administrative duties, each pupil would have at most ninety seconds, more likely just one minute, in which to sing. By the time I had asked what to do with the drunken sailor, hoorayed, up she rose and put him the brig until he's sober, my time would be over. There was no real requirement to learn any more verses.

The days came and I was horrified to learn that the pupils who were in the school choir - I didn't even know there was a school choir - would not need to sing for the exam as they had already taken the test. This rule excused most of the girls and some of the boys - strangely, those who had dropped the rugby ball earlier in the year - which left only about fifteen of us to sing in front of the class. Over two lessons and excluding the administration, we would each have about four minutes of performance time. I tried to keep calm and quite enjoyed watching the torture of the first lesson, although it was akin to a public visit to Bedlam. The boys squeaked, grunted and generally made strange bellowing noises to unrecognisable tunes, with the baying crowd looking on, before being mercilessly criticised by Green Gilbert for failing to project, whatever that meant. I put my own pending exposure to ridicule at the back of my mind, trusting like Mister Micawber that something would turn up to save me. By the time that I was sitting in the classroom the following week awaiting my turn to be pilloried, I knew that Micawber was wrong. I trembled in fear. I recalled my only other experience of singing in class, when I was in Pinehurst Infants School and the teacher asked for volunteers to sing for the class. I jumped up and sang one of the only two songs that our dad had taught me.

> *Oh dear, what can the matter be,*
> *Three old ladies locked in the lavatory,*
> *They were there from Monday 'til Saturday,*
> *Nobody knew they were there.*

I was told that this was not the sort of song that children should sing so moved on to my second rendition.

> *I can't get my winkle out,*
> *Isn't it a sin.*
> *The more I try to get it out,*
> *The further it goes in.*

I did not understand the outrage expressed by the teacher, nor why I was sent home with a letter for our mum and dad, but I do remember our dad laughing loudly when he read it.

In what seemed an obscenely short time, Green Gilbert called out my name. I sat and refused to budge. I was very scared and, as I sat there building up the courage to move to the front, words came out of my mouth that surprised me. "No Sir," I politely explained, "I can't sing."

Despite Green Gilbert's insistence that I stand and sing, I stood, or rather sat, my ground and refused to sing. The impasse was broken when Green Gilbert offered me the choice of singing or a detention, I chose the detention and was sent from the room and told to wait in the corridor. The detention never materialised.

About one month before the end of term, we were told that games lessons had been cancelled and the whole year was to meet in the gymnasium for dancing lessons in preparation for the school *soiree*. Headlands school had a strange habit of using French to complicate simple terms. The Christmas party was a *soiree* and there was a *vestibule* and *foyer* to identify the hallways at the school entrance, although I was never sure which was which. The news of the change in syllabus was greeted with something less than enthusiasm amongst the boys and a coy excitement by the girls. Shirley said that we would probably dance together. In fact, she insisted that we dance together. Shirley was a girl from Pinehurst Junior School who also passed the eleven plus and attended the grammar school and with whom I was having an irregular, secret and illicit affair. I liked Shirley. She was very tall, balancing the fact that I was very short, and she had an infectious giggle which I found exciting and titillating. She reminded me of Vivian Vance who played Lucille Ball's sidekick Ethel in the *I Love Lucy* television show and who, strangely perhaps, I found very attractive. Our informal and clandestine relationship consisted solely of occasional meetings outside school or cycling to and from school when my mates weren't watching, where we just talked about school, family and friends or feelings, the sort of topics that I could never talk to a mate about for fear of being labelled a cissy or, worse, a nancy-boy. But now, it appears, we were to become dancing partners.

The lads reluctantly assembled in the gym, heads down and not daring to look up towards the girls whilst the maidens, in contrast it seemed to me, were all smiles, giggles and fluttering eyelashes. Shirley stood out a head above most of the others and gave me a shy smile and a barely noticeable wave. I shrugged. The sexes were ordered to stand on opposite of the hall whilst unfamiliar music was played and Miss Wildman, the girls' games mistress, demonstrated the waltz with Bomber. Miss Wildman was a forty something spinster with a body like Terry Downes and legs like Billy Wright. She could politely be described as plain, yet she glided across the dancefloor like a track-suited Ginger Rogers, tightly gripping Bomber, himself transformed into a slim and suave Fred Astaire. The music stopped. Bomber stopped and shook Miss Wildman loose from her leech-like grip. He announced that each boy must, without fail, cross the hall and ask the girl of his choice to dance. Realisation hit us like I imagine being hit by Miss Wildman would feel: we not only had to speak to a girl in public but speak politely AND dance with her. Added to that humiliation was the fact that each boy had to select a partner, whereby everyone would know which girl he fancied. After some encouragement by Bomber in the form of a booming order to do as we were told or else, the lads inched slowly across the floor. Happily, Shirley stepped out from the crowd and grabbed me, saving me from the shame of asking her for a dance. All boys were soon paired up leaving the few unselected girls to dance together and we stumbled around the hall in a shuffling, shambling, untidy throng. I held on to Shirley, not having a clue what I was doing but being clutched closely to her body – I could well have been suffocated by her bosom, had she had a bosom. After three weeks of training we could just about manage a clumsy version of a waltz plus an even more cumbersome Gay Gordons and Valeta, although, again, I simply held on as I was twirled around the floor by Shirley.

The soiree itself, held on a Saturday a week or two before Christmas, was a repeat of the dancing lessons, but with orange squash and fish paste sandwiches. We were even instructed to wear school uniform, complete with white daps. I continually gasped for breath, suffocating at the place where Shirley's bosom was soon to be, and I began to wonder if I should end our secret, platonic relationship, but thought it too late. And anyway, it was better to be permanently seconded to Shirley than suffer the humiliation of asking another girl to dance. Besides, all the girls now smelt of orange and fish paste.

The last school days were taken up with long and worrying rounds of examinations intertwined with periods of study. Much as I tried to study, my mind had a mind of its own and refused remain focussed on the subject at hand, wandering off to football matches, cowboy gunfights or the ladies' underwear page in our mum's Kays catalogue. I found that I had the ability to read a whole page of script, inspecting and understanding every single word yet not retaining anything I had read. Where the information went, I have no idea, but it was definitely re-routed before it made it into the filing cabinets of my brain.

Our report books were handed out on the final day of term and I was quite pleased to see that I had somehow attained four 'A' grades and seven 'B's. A pretty solid performance all round, I thought. That is, until I saw that I had finished twenty-seventh out of thirty-five in the class and fiftieth out of one hundred and thirty-eight in the year. The comments from the teachers were kind, some even saying that I had made a *Good beginning, Sound work* and that I could *Work well,* but there was also the ominous *He must learn his work more thoroughly, Could improve* and *Rather disappointing,* which were a precursor to my future terms' report comments. I had no grade and no comments against Music. Along with my report, I was given a note to tell our mum that I would be in the 'A' stream in the following term. It's a good job that she never quite came to grips with the form labelling convention and thought that I'd been promoted to the top class.

I liked Christmas. I liked the anticipation on Christmas Eve, I liked Christmas Day with presents, I liked Christmas dinner, I liked Christmas tea and I even liked Christmas television. Whilst I would never admit it to my friends, I especially liked being indoors with my family with no competitiveness, no acting tough, no trying to impress: just our sister, Rae, our mum, our dad and our nana. Our Rae was fifteen months' older than me and we got along very well, considering that we had nothing in common except our parents. I loved sport, she hated it. I liked comics about soldiers and cowboys killing each other, she liked comics about pop music and handsome couples kissing each other.

Our nana always arrived for the holiday and took over our dad's chair next to the fire, sitting, smoking and watching television for the entire festive season. Our dad drank a lot. Even when he wasn't drunk, the aroma of stale beer often permeated the air around him. He was continuously working long shifts as a watchman in Swindon's famous British Rail factory or attending the pub for other long shifts, so we didn't see too much of him. Our mum was always at home, cooking, cleaning, washing, ironing, sewing, drinking tea, smoking and watching television. But at Christmas we all interacted within the confines of a comfortingly traditional and time-honoured routine.

As tradition had it, our Rae and I would always wake early to open presents, the exact time theoretically dependant on our dad's shifts. If he was on earlies, he would wake us at five o'clock before he went to work: if on nights, we would be roused at five o'clock when he came home. Any other shifts or if he had time off, he would wake us at five o'clock just because it was Christmas day. Our presents were stuffed into a pillowcase and left on the end of our beds, the contents included the usual mix of toys, games, books and, if we were very unlucky, clothes. Our nana always made a separate presentation of her gifts after breakfast and it was always the same. A box of fudge for me and a box of Cadbury's Chocolate Fingers for our Rae.

Our nana also brought a Rowntree's Dairy Box each year – the selection was cheaper than Cadburys Milk Tray or Nestles Quality Street - the only time that we ever had a box of chocolates in the house. It was a mixed blessing because our nana was always first to open the box on Christmas Eve, and test the contents. She had never quite mastered the description of the centres on the box lid, specifically as to which centres were soft and which were hard. She only liked the soft centres. It was the norm to find several of the chocolates with teeth marks where our nana had tested them for their hardness and, if they didn't pass the test, they were returned to the box for the next consumer. I didn't mind as I liked the hard toffee or nutty centres far more than the coffee or orange cremes, and the odd bitemark from our Nana's dentures never impaired the flavour.

This year, our dad was working most of Christmas Day, obviously taking a quick refreshment break in the nearest pub or club to see a man about a dog and enjoy a celebratory drink at work during the afternoon. He was a bit unsteady on his bike and his rocky on his feet when he returned home at six o'clock.

"What's it like out?" our mum greeted him with her usual question.

"Black over our mother's and cold enough for an umbrella," he replied, with a straight face.

When we had our standard sandwich, trifle and Christmas cake tea, our dad had his Christmas dinner. The only time that we ever had wine in the house was the bottle or two of sauterne our mum bought for Christmas and our dad had emptied a bottle while he finished his dinner. He then started on any other alcohol he could find in the house, usually our nana's sherry, before falling asleep in front *High Noon*. How anyone could sleep in front of Gary Cooper and Grace Kelly was a mystery to me, but I could understand how a twelve-hour shift starting at five a.m. including beer, whiskey, sauterne and sherry would be a little tiring.

On Boxing Day, he was again working the early shift from 5 o'clock, but finished at 1 o'clock. He rolled home at about three o'clock after calling in at the North Swindon Club to see another man about a dog. "Cold enough for a walking stick," he said before being asked. Boxing day dinner was cold chicken and pickles, a salad which no-one ate, mince pies and more Christmas cake. Our dad finished another bottle of sauterne and the rest of our nana's sherry before we retired to the sitting room. He was barely comprehensible as he laughed and joked in his alcoholic haze, then he quietened down for half an hour before speaking.

"Our tank got blown up in the desert," he stated in a very matter-of-fact tone. "Eleventh Hussars, Prince Albert's Own. That was us. About October 1942. We'd 'ad an easy time of it 'til then. Fort Capuzzo, Sidi Barani, even Tobruk was no problem. Except we never knew where we was. We just got orders to move and we moved where we was told. Sometimes we was chasin' Jerry, sometimes Jerry was chasin' us. Went on like that for nearly two years. We was under Montgomery. Mad as a March 'are, Monty. Met him once when 'e give us a pep talk. Talked nonsense and never made no sense. Then bloody Rommel comes along and blows our tank up at El Alemein. Only two of us got out. I still got the shrapnel in me shoulder. Others burnt to death. Good crew. Good mates too. Couldn't get out. And what for. A bit of sand in the desert. Never worth it. North Africa. All camel shit and flies."

Our dad sat quietly with a glazed look in his eyes, sighed and up went to bed.

Chapter 2 – January - August 1960

- American rock and roll singer Eddie Cochran, 21, is killed in a car crash in Wiltshire
- Francis Chichester, arrives in New York aboard *Gypsy Moth II* having made a record solo Atlantic crossing
- The Grand National is televised for the first time. The winner is Merryman II
- Soviets shoot down an American U2 plane. Pilot, Francis Gary Powers of the CIA is captured.

I lived in Pinehurst, a sprawling council estate in north Swindon, split into two distinct sectors, divided by the Infants, Junior and Secondary Modern schools. The Eastern section is a pre-war estate of red brick semi-detached houses, in eight streets radiating from a large central hub, a circular, eight-acre, grassed recreation area, imaginatively named *The Circle*. The streets on the spokes of the circle are named after trees, including Cherry Tree Grove, Acacia Avenue, Maple Grove and Sycamore Grove, addresses which conjure up visions of wide, leafy suburban boulevards with professional gentlemen leaving home each morning in their sparkling Morris Minors or new Ford Cortinas, waving farewell to a pretty young wife and 2.4 children. The truth is a little more down to earth. Although many of the homes and gardens were well-tended, some houses were run down, the fathers generally being manual workers, often out-of-work manual workers, and the only car in situ was likely to be a rusting pre-war Austin 7, rotting amongst brambles in an overgrown front garden. Many houses were inhabited by families who had been in the area, and occasionally in the same house, for many years with no ambition to live anywhere else. It was a tough but close community, the residents proud of their working-class roots, proud of Swindon and proud of Pinehurst.

The western estate was built just after the war to house serviceman returning home after vanquishing the Hun in North Africa and Normandy or subjugating the Japs in Borneo. All houses on the estate were BISF, a British Steel framed house, designed and produced by the British Iron and Steel Federation, as part of the new, post war Ministry of Works Emergency Factory Made Housing programme. The main structure of the house was of steel, with the framework of the building made from tubular steel columns. The framework was clad on the lower storey with rendering on metal lath. The outer cladding of the upper floor was of steel trussed sheeting fixed by angles to the steel columns. The area was known throughout Swindon simply as Tin Town.

In keeping with the time, the streets were named after war heroes of the recent conflict. The main arterial road was Montgomery Avenue, named after our dad's leader, Field Marshal Bernard Law Montgomery, 1st Viscount Montgomery of Alamein, KG, GCB, DSO, PC. Wavell Road was named after Field Marshal Archibald Percival Wavell, 1st Earl Wavell GCB, GCSI, GCIE, CMG, MC, KStJ, PC. Alanbrooke Crescent after Field Marshal Alan Francis Brooke, 1st Viscount Alanbrooke, KG, GCB, OM, GCVO, DSO & Bar. My own street, Pound Lane, was in memory of the delightfully named Admiral of the Fleet, Sir Alfred Dudley Pickman Rogers Pound GCB, OM, GCVO.

We were told that the streets were named after some soldiers.

I once met Sammy Burton, the burly Swindon Town goalkeeper and local hero, when I was with our dad in Swindon's covered market in the town centre. Before the meeting I had not known that Sammy and our dad even knew each other, but they appeared to be the best of pals and our dad had never bothered telling me. This was the first time that I had heard his standard response whenever he met someone he knew. Sammy asked, "'Ow are you, Jack?" Our dad replied, "Poor but 'appy Sam, poor but 'appy." This was a baffling response to me as I never considered us a poor family. We lived in a three-bedroomed semi-detached council house with a large garden. We never went hungry except Thursdays when money ran out and were always relatively warm, except in winter. Probably because of the government's wartime 'make do and mend' campaign, we were decently clothed, patched trousers and darned socks being the norm, if not *à la mode*. To us kids, poor people were those few families on the estate whose children smelt of pee and wore heavy hobnail boots which, we were told, were donated by the government to deprived families. If hungry, we could always fill up with bread and dripping or, my favourite, sugar sandwiches. "Good for energy," our mum always said, blissfully unaware that my teeth were rapidly rotting with each mouthful and with an addiction which may well have ended with diabetes. We were used to living without central heating and, during cold spells, simply huddled around our only source of heat, a coal fire. This same fire was designed to heat a boiler at the back of the flue which operated two ugly radiators, but was a costly and inefficient method of heating and therefore rarely used. My bedroom, the small box room at the front of the house, was the coldest part of the home and I would often require a variety of blankets to keep warm at night, but no blankets could stop my breath rising in plumes of white vapour unless I hunkered down under the bedclothes. Each morning during the frequent cold spells, I would awake to spectacular ice sculptures created overnight on the window, landscapes of beautiful frosty ferns hiding in a mystical frozen wonderland. I would often draw open the skimpy curtains and lie in bed inventing stories of wicked pixies and mischievous elves creating mayhem in the enchanted woodland created by Jack Frost. At weekends, I would wrap blankets around me and kneel on the bed, breathing hard on the frozen window to clear a patch in the ice in order to see the paper boy deliver the Sunday papers. I would rush downstairs and grab The People so that I could study the previous day's football scores and see which celebrities had been caught with their trousers down.

We may have been continually broke, hard up or badly off, but we were never poor.

The Christmas holidays were over far too quickly, and I restarted my classical education in the lower class, relegated ignominiously after my poor exam results of the previous term. My resumption in a different class was not as traumatic as may have been expected. The shift in personnel was far-reaching, with many pupils promoted or demoted as the academic leaning of pupils and classes began to sort themselves out. My new class of 1A contained several of my previous classmates, some old mates from junior school and many acquaintances that I had made in the previous term through human osmosis. As such, I felt quite at home and settled in quickly. I was pleasantly surprised to find that I was in the same class as Shirley. She was a conscientious student and I immediately began to see the opportunity of easing my homework load.

The new form teacher was, according to my report book, a lady called A M Harris who made such an impression on me that I have little recollection of her except that she wore glasses and seemed at best stern, at worst hostile towards children. I don't know if she was young or old, fat or thin, tall or short. I have no recollection of her taking lessons but apparently, again according to my end of year report, she taught the class Latin. I guess that separation from the fearsome Mister Furber was a pleasing relief and I could look forward to a new year and a new class without the humiliation experienced during my initial exposure to classical education. But the greatest advantage in joining this new class was Shirley. In return for my attentions as her clandestine escort, she offered unselfish input to my written homework. We would meet in the classroom before school on most mornings and I would hurriedly copy her conscientious labours from the previous evening, a ruse which saved me from continual chastisement and earned me decent marks, but dismally failed to help in the process of knowledge absorption. Of course, the ploy offered no advantage at all if the homework was based around the retention of new facts or revision of previously absorbed information.

Following the term's first assembly in the main hall and a lecture from The Boss about the great opportunity that we were privileged to have been offered, the initial morning of our return was spent carrying out administrative functions: finding our new classroom, meeting our new form teacher, receiving another lecture on how lucky we were and drawing up a lesson schedule. We were instructed to copy the master timetable from the blackboard under the almost forgettable AM Harris's incorrect assumption that this would make the timetable stick enduringly in our young brains. We were also to select new form captains, one for each sex, and I was duly elected as boys' representative. Quite why I was chosen, I have no idea except that perhaps my rebellious acts of the previous term had become well known and the other boys looked up to my daring, gung-ho approach to work and discipline. I think, however, it is far more likely that they saw me as an easy scapegoat for any classroom wrongdoings. Whatever the reason, I proudly assumed the title and wore my new badge which announced my status, *Form Captain*, with what I considered to be dignity, pride and honour, but was probably more a display of intolerable arrogance.

It was a cold, windy and especially wet start to the new year, making our twice-daily cycle commute to and from school an extremely unpleasant challenge. I was seemingly permanently wet, sitting in rain-sodden clothes in the classroom and drying out just in time to get soaked again cycling home for dinner. Here I would dry out as I ate, before cycling back to school in the rain for a damp and shivery afternoon. Relief from our sodden existence came in mid-January when the rain and cold winds dropped, and we were blessed with a sprinkling of snow. Under normal circumstances, a layer of snow, albeit a thin layer, was a sign for jolly japes with our chums, snowmen built and colourfully dressed, snowballs gathered and playfully tossed at one another in merry and good-humoured spirits. A true winter wonderland where we could almost hear Perry Como singing, *Sleigh bells ring, are you listening, in Pound Lane, snow is glistening* as we mounted our bicycles and began our daily shuttle to school. On the first day in our snowy utopia, the ex-Pinehurst Headlands lads were cycling past Pinehurst Junior and Senior schools in Beech Avenue, when it occurred to me that the bright-eyed and pink-cheeked young Pinehurst scallywags were up early that morning and had prepared piles of snowballs stored by the roadside. I thought what an innocent and gleeful time they too were having. Some of our old pals waved and we slowed to acknowledge their cheery greeting, a strategic error of General Custer at Little Bighorn proportions, as snowballs suddenly rained down on us from all angles. I turned and saw a few of my best mates, the Paines boys, Micky Kell and Spuddy Taylor hurling snowballs in our direction, most with unerring accuracy as they splattered into our bodies and faces. In our panic, we began a frantic attempt to escape, bicycles skidding dangerously on the slushy road until we finally managed to obtain a grip in the sludge and peddle furiously away. All was well for about five hundred yards until we triumphantly reached The Circle at the top of Beech Avenue, well out of range, and raised a communal shout of joyful relief to accompany an instinctive display of 'V' signs directed at our adversaries. Our joy was short-lived as we realised that a second ambush had been planned, this time by the more violent boys from The Circle. As the snowballs fizzed around our heads, it became obvious that these were far more dangerous weapons than before, mainly, we soon realised, because the weapons were more firmly compressed making them far harder and icier. Perhaps more relevantly, each snowball was wrapped around a stone. After a short but frantic cycle dash, the getaway was finally achieved to loud, mocking cheers from our erstwhile school mates. Luckily our pride was hurt far more than our bodies, but it was a lesson learnt.

Pete Griffin was all for rounding up a posse for the homeward journey to exact revenge on our attackers, but Derek Windslow – always the practical group member - persuaded the rest of us that cowardice was the better part of valour and we detoured via a round-about route to avoid Beech Avenue and Pinehurst schools. Strangely, I was out playing football in the street with the Paines boys the following weekend and none of us mentioned the battle.

As long as flurries of snow remained, we continued to cycle the long way around to avoid being bombarded with ice and stones, whilst school resumed much as before. Maths was always a relatively strong point with me and I looked forward to meeting our new Maths teacher, Mr. Grog Evans. There was a television comedy series called *Please Sir!* in the late sixties, where John Alderton played a lovable but hapless teacher trying to control a class of twenty-five-year-old actors, pretending to be fourteen-year-old students. It was a popular but unremarkable series, the one shining light being the portrayal by jobbing actor Richard Davies of Mr. Price, a Welsh teacher with stereotypical teachers' uniform of a sports jacket with elbow patches, worn over a knitted cardigan, checked shirt and knitted tie. I am convinced that writers and the casting director of the show based the character on Grog Evans.

He too was Welsh, speaking with the same lyrical accent, was physically similar, dressed identically and carried out his teaching in the same dutiful but mournful way. Quite why he was called Grog is unknown and we never questioned the reason. I guess that it just seemed to suit him.

I had a very mixed relationship with Grog. I loved Maths and was good at it, but I was unruly and disruptive. One minute Grog was singing my praises, the next he was chastising me like a hellfire and brimstone chapel preacher. I found the use of numbers stimulating, the strange logic of the way mathematical formulae can be used to resolve problems or how numerical peculiarities can throw up strange consequences. Why is the square of the hypotenuse on a right-angled triangle always the sum of the other two sides squared? And how did Pythagoras discover this, particularly as the ancient Greeks used a strange and alien numbering system? Who could not be fascinated by the fact that for all multiples of 9, the digits add up to a multiple of 9. For example, 18, 27, 36 etc. An almost magical fact that also applies for far higher numbers: 108, 207, 477, 4122, 21366. How is it that 111,111,111 times 111,111,111 equals 12,345,678,987,654,321? My fascination with numbers was such that I would often fall asleep working out how many days I had lived (365 X 11 + 250 for this year so far and leap years = 4265). I once peed into a measuring jug and worked out how much urine I'd produced in my life…about one third of a pint, six times a day equals two pints per day, times 365 equals 730 pints per year times for 11 years made 8030 pints, just over 1000 gallons or 125 bushels of pee. Now that really *is* interesting.

During the day, I was busy trying to impress my new classmates with my unruly antics during lessons, which exasperating a patient Grog, until one day he broke. Quite why we fell out, I cannot fully remember except that I was muttering something in class, probably rude, facetious or both, when he demanded to know what I had said.

"Nothing, Sir," I replied, doubtless in a cocky manner, playing to my audience.

"I will ask you once again, Trueman, what did you say?" he asked, obviously becoming frustrated with my discourteous behaviour.

"Nothing, Sir," I repeated.

"Then you will take a detention, Trueman, where you will write an essay on 'nothing.'"

My smugness disappeared. I was the first in the class to collect a detention, an award which was not received with pride, and I was very worried how our mum and dad would react. A detention involved taking home a note describing the offence, the note to be returned with a countersignature from the Parent or Guardian. When I arrived home that evening, I sheepishly passed the note to our mum fearing the worst but need not have worried. Our mum signed the chitty without comment and decided that our dad had no need to see it. A detention meant staying late in school on the following Thursday evening for an extra hour and carrying out a demeaning and meaningless written task. In most instances as I was soon to discover, this involve "lines", whereby the miscreant was compelled to write an ameliorating phrase, usually one hundred times, in the hope that the phrase would brainwash the writer into better behaviour. I failed to see how writing *I must not project elastic bands in class* one hundred times would convince the troublemaker that he would no longer project elastic bands in class. Particularly as the lines were usually completed vertically rather than horizontally by writing all the *I*'s first, followed by the *musts*, then the *not*s and so on.

I nervously found my way to the classroom where the detention was to take place and sat alongside a dozen or so other miscreants who had transgressed in the previous week. I began to write my essay on *Nothing* for Grog, which was better than lines but not as easy. After two or three futile attempts to write something expressive and profound, a metaphorical lightbulb sparked to life in my head and I had a brainwave. I wrote:

Nothing is the opposite of something. Examples of something are sausages, wellington boots, motor cars, haircuts, fingers, plates, chocolate, towels, squirrels....

and so on for a complete page. I turned the paper over and wrote:

Examples of nothing are   ,   ,   ,

,

,   ,   ,   -   ,

covering the whole page with commas and remembering to end with the grammatically correct;   ,   *and*

.

I was quite proud of my ingenuity until I handed the essay in to Grog, who looked at the paper, turned it over, smiled and firmly stated, "Very amusing Trueman. You will go back next week and complete a proper essay on defining nothing...and you will return each Thursday until I am satisfied." A lesson learnt, I never had to go back for the third time and showed Grog a good deal more respect from then on.

The other new teachers were also absorbed into our lives with little effort and the term progressed in a steady but unspectacular way. The new French teacher was small man called Hickman, who was English but insisted that we called him Monsieur 'Ickman in class. Over years of teaching French and visiting France, he seemed to have developed the characteristics of the archetypal Frenchman, just requiring a striped jumper and beret and to carry a string of onions to complete the caricature. He was the epitome of the Crazy Gang's Eddie Gray and was, quite naturally, called Monsewer. Foreign languages and language

Page   56

teachers left me less than inspired and I generally paid little attention to what was happening in class, preferring to daydream about sport or trying to figure out how constantly teaching French had genetically changed Monsewer 'Ickman into a Froggie. And, of course, I knew full well that my homework would be more than adequately covered by the ever-dependable Shirley.

Geography was a highlight of the week, where were tutored by a young teacher called Bennett, another Welshman, who went out of his way to make things interesting, incorporating little known facts into his lessons. For this term, we concentrated on the physical Geography of South America, although concentrated did not really apply in my case. Between absorbing the general facts about population, rainfall, mountains and forests, we learnt that the Angel Falls in Venezuela were the highest falls in the world and named after an American called Jimmie Angel: that Chile's Atacama Desert is the driest place on Earth: in parts of Brazil, fishermen use dolphins to help catch fish: the Andes is the longest mountain range in the world. These simple facts helped bring the countries to life, although I did once report that the Amazon had sixty-nine estuaries and a tributary that was over two hundred miles wide. A simple mistake, I thought, and there was no need for Bennett to read my *faux-pas* to the rest of the class. Bennett was also prone to insert silly jokes into his lessons for added interest, once advising us with some seriousness that Macu Picchu was named after an Inca chief who sneezed when asked by explorers the name of his holy place, and that Chile was so named due to the cold east winds which blasted in from the Pacific.

English was easy if a trifle dull, History and Biology were interesting but too time-consuming to really appreciate. I quickly realised that I could do just enough work to hold my own, without over-stretching, which produced adequate if not outstanding results.

Sport was a different ball game. The rugby season finished and most of us lads were looking forward to re-igniting our soccer careers. The term *lads* of course excludes those who failed so spectacularly to catch a rugby ball at the start of the previous term. At Pinehurst Junior School, I had played for the school team which won the Swindon Junior School League and I still remember the team: Dave Simpson, Dave Reese, Les Hedges, Leroy Hedges, Mick Kell, Derek Wall (captain), John Trueman, Graham Taylor, Dave Corbett, Brian Mason, Phil Hunt. Reserves Stuart Battersby and Dave Rowlands.

Of these, Dave Simpson, Derek Wall, Brian Mason, Stuart Battersby and I went to Headlands, which boded well for the coming season. Our dad said that Headlands should always win the local schools' leagues as football was a game where intelligence was foremost, and we were intelligent because we went to grammar school. He explained that the game of football is about thinking quickly, identifying opportunities, selecting the right pass and effecting the move – like a game of chess. Only the intelligent, he hypothesised, could play football well. I wonder what he would have thought if he could have listened to some of today's multi-millionaire footballers mumbling incoherently through an interview on *Match of the Day* or repeating hackneyed platitudes when employed as an "expert" TV pundit. That said, Headlands had never in its history had the opportunity to test our dad's thesis as teams were not entered into Swindon's schools league competitions. The school convention and tradition defined that we should play rugger from September until Christmas and soccer from New Year to Easter, which precluded entering football leagues where fixtures began in September. It was also the school ethos that sport should be played for honour and glory, to play the game for the game's sake and not for anything as tasteless as league positions, cups and medals.

Whether Bomber Brown had remembered the debacle of his attempts to train us in the finer points of rugby, or whether he simply couldn't be bothered with football, I know not, but he took little interest in the post-Christmas games lessons. He simply ensured that opposing teams were selected, blew his whistle to start the game then wandered around disinterestedly, appearing to be dreaming of refereeing the All Blacks and the Barbarians at Twickenham or preferring to watch Miss Wildman in her navy-blue knickers gracing the hockey pitches. He randomly blasted on his whistle to signal free kicks, corners or goals and, in moments of distraction, a knock-on or scrum down. After two or three lessons, I was called to see him at the end of the lesson alongside two other lads, John Bailey and Ian Melrose, both of whom had shown footballing ability in the games lessons. Thinking the worst, I was pleasantly surprised to find out that we three had been designated to select the school team for an upcoming game against Commonweal Grammar School, Swindon's only other Grammar School and based the Old Town. We were told to pick the team plus reserves and to nominate a captain. We accepted the task with due gravity and diligence, meeting one playtime to make our selection. We agreed the team and reserves, which we neatly transcribed onto a sheet of A4 in two-three-five formation, the only formation ever played at that time, and began discussions on the captaincy. I held back, fully expecting to be nominated and imagined myself modestly accepting the role, perhaps after a mild protest that I wasn't totally worthy but would accept the onerous role for the good of the school.

Bailey spoke first, "I think that Wally, would be the best captain. He's the best player and he was captain of Pinehurst last year when they won the league."

Ian agreed enthusiastically nodding and adding, "Good idea, John. Time to get back to lessons anyway."

And so it was that, once again, Wally had somehow managed to appropriate my rightful place as team captain. He wasn't even present during the selection process and I was, which added to my irritation.

We three selectors were given our instructions. We were to hand out a team shirt to each of the selected players on Friday and instruct them to be at Commonweal school at ten o'clock the next morning for a ten-thirty kick off. How the players were to reach Commonweal, some four miles distant from our school, was left to the individual. Although there were busses and taxis and the odd car-owning parent, most lads chose to cycle. Having arrived, we were somewhat surprised and disappointed that bestowing the list of instructions was the end of the involvement of the sports staff from Headlands. No teacher turned up on the Saturday and it was up to a bunch of twelve-year-olds to try to organise everything from shirt distribution, arrival at the ground, changing into our kit and playing the game itself. Bomber called it "character building," but we weren't convinced. We won the game comfortably enough, but the gloss was somewhat taken off a fine performance by the task of ensuring that the dirty, sweaty shirts were to be taken home, washed and returned to school on the Monday. And, predictably, by the fact that Wally scored the best goal of the game.

The term passed slowly, brightened only by the increasingly long days allowing groups of friends to extend their street games into the evenings. Pound Lane was a small street of just twenty-eight semi-detached houses, but those few abodes contained some fifty children within a five or six-year age range. This is perhaps not surprising as the houses were built in 1948 and immediately occupied by young couples, often separated by the years of the Second World War and the grim immediate post-war period. Suddenly, they had spacious, warm homes with large gardens and almost ten years of pent up lust to release. And the ladies had, perhaps, been expertly primed by the large number of American troops in the area during the war, offering cigarettes, chocolates and stockings in return for some friendly company. The only wonder is that there weren't even more kids about. The street itself was our park and social area, with the constant clamour of a playground. Away from school, daylight hours were spent on various sports – whichever sport was in vogue at that time of year. In winter we played football, where the goals were marked by drains either side of the road, connected by an untidy line in chalk. The drains were supplemented by the renowned 'jumpers for goalposts', with clothing discarded as bodies warmed in the frenetic action. The goalposts were named after the families of the houses they were near. In the middle of the street, the posts were outside of our house and the Paines family who lived opposite and were universally known, in Pound Lane at least, as Trueman's drain or Paines's drain. This ragged line between them usually marking one goalmouth, with another line joining Harris's drain to Smart's drain identifying the opposing goal.

In Swindonian speak, where a surname ended in 's', it was normal to add an extra 's' to signify ownership, hence Paines's drain. Each Summer. we waited for the van to come around selling Walls's ice cream, although occasionally we would be treated to a Lyons's. Many people worked in the cigarette factory in Colbourne Street, producing Woodbines for Wills's. We also ate Hales's fruit pies and meat from James's butchers, whilst a Mr. Iles ran a well-known Swindon Jeweller, always known as Iles's.

Girls did not play football. They skipped, played hopscotch or sat in the gutters chatting, whilst the boys were competing for the FA Cup. In the late evenings, when it was too dark to see the ball, the sexes joined together to play hide and seek or Jack Jack shine your light until called in by parents for supper and bed. We also had rest periods of simply hanging around outside, often under Church's lamp post or by one of two "green things." At both the top and bottom corners of the street were green metal boxes, perhaps three feet high by three feet wide and about two feet deep. No one knew what they contained or what they were there for, but it was generally thought that they were something to do with electricity. They were simply known as green things, so we would often meet on Carter's green thing, which was directly and conveniently adjacent to Coale's lamp post offering a comforting light during cold and dark winter nights.

Football was a real passion amongst all the boys in the street and, whilst we all had leanings towards the bigger first division clubs (my own allegiances were to Wolverhampton Wanderers or Tottenham Hotspurs – whichever team was higher in the First Division), Swindon Town was a unifying passion. I would never miss a home game since attending matches with our dad as a youngster of six or seven. Too young to ride my own bike, I was perched on a small saddle attached to his crossbar and off we would set, leaving home at midday for a three o'clock kick off. The early start was to give our dad time for a few pints in the Southbrook Inn on the way, although our mum thought for years that games of football started at twelve thirty and lasted for four hours. Whilst our dad was building up his strength for the cycle ride to the County Ground with several pints Courage bitter, I was temporarily abandoned, sitting in the entrance porch on a cold stone step, being fed the occasional bottle of lemonade and bag of crisps. At two thirty, we would begin the hazardous journey into Gorse Hill (pronounced Gorsill as the leading 'h' did not exist in Swindonian) and through County Road, my chauffeur drunkenly weaving in and out between other bicycles and the occasional car until we reached the County Ground. Here, we would swerve into the back alleys behind Shrivenham Road and our dad would park his bike in one of the many private garages opened by enterprising householders. Carefully stacked, each garage could hold perhaps thirty bicycles and, at threepence a time, was a nice tax-free earner for someone whose gross wage for a forty-hour week in the Great Western Railway factory was under ten pounds.

Now that I had started grammar school and owned a brand-new second-hand bike, I was able to cycle to games with my mates, still using the same garage as before to store the vehicle. I enjoyed the independence but rather missed the pop and crisps, if not the aching and frozen buttocks from the stone steps of the Southbrook Inn. I would call for Brian Mason or Geoff Peaple, hoping that the door would not be opened by one or other of their parents. I held my friends' parents in great esteem and not a little fear. It was always a short and simple, yet awkward and stilted conversation.

"Hello Mister Mason. Is Brian in please?"

"Hello John. I'll call him. How's school?"

"OK Mister Mason, thank you."

"Off to the County Ground?"

"Yes, Mister Mason."

And all the time I would be looking at the ground, thinking please go away Mister Mason, I don't want to talk to you. Grown-ups were always addressed as Missis or Mister and I could never imagine addressing them in any other way even as I grew into adulthood. I once met Brian Mason's father in a country pub, years later when I was married with children of my own. The conversation was similar.

"Hello John. Enjoying a pint then?"

"Yes, Mister Mason."

"Why don't you call me Jim."

"Yes, I will, Mister Mason."

That season at the County Ground had started with great optimism. The Town had a new record signing, Jimmy Gauld at £6,000 and a free-scoring, rugged centre forward David (Bronco)

Lane, but by the time that the new year had arrived and we had been dumped out of the FA Cup at home to the might of Walsall and thumped three nil at home by Southampton, most fans had settled for our usual mid-table finish. A few years later, it was revealed that Jimmy Gauld was the ringleader in a betting scam which also involved Bronco Lane and other Swindon favourites, Jack Fountain and Walter Bingley. The ruse required placing bets on the outcome of Swindon matches and a degree of bribery encouraging our beloved Robins to throw matches. Had we known that at the time, perhaps we wouldn't have been so complacent about the team's pedestrian and error-strewn performances.

As the football season and the school Christmas term came to a disappointing close, Easter arrived to a surfeit of chocolate and was over all too soon before returning for the summer term. The monotony of lessons didn't change, but the term was again uplifted by the games lessons. For the first Wednesday morning allocated to my favourite subject, the boys were asked to choose between cricket and athletics. Quite naturally, many of the boys, particularly those selected to pass the rugby ball during our first term, had never held a bat or ball, or run or jumped, putted or thrown in their lives. They had no idea which sport to choose and were directed to one or other based on levelling the numbers between the two groups. I chose to play cricket. I had been a dab hand at street cricket in Pound Lane, where the bats were fashioned from anything that could be used to club the ball, from old tennis racquets to roughly shaped pieces of wood discovered in gardens and sheds. The fact that I had never actually played real cricket with a real cricket ball or real bat on a real cricket pitch, did not deter me. Teams were selected and, using my powerful position as form captain, I assumed captaincy for one of the teams. Quite naturally, I selected myself as opening bat. I strapped on the oversized pads provided and selected an oversized bat before striding out to the middle with my partner, carefully scanning the fielding positions as I had seen Peter May do in the West Indies on television. The pads were far too large and began to slide to the side of my legs and the bat, which was almost as long as I was tall, began to feel somewhat heavier than an old tennis racquet but, undaunted, I decided to face the first ball. After all, had I not hit a six from Church's lamp post, over Micky Millmore's dad's garden and into Montgomery Avenue, using a bat crudely carved from a portion of old timber during the previous Easter holidays? I stood at the wicket and took one last look at the fielding positions before rearranging my genitals, a compulsory activity for all the batsmen I had also noticed on television, and faced the bowler, a tall, skinny kid from 1B, whom I had seen around but didn't know well. As he ran forwards, I patted the wicket confidently with my bat. As I looked up, the thought passed through my mind that he was running very quickly. I saw his arm turn in a blur but did not see the ball leave his hand. I swung the heavy bat with all my strength and the ball thumped into my ribcage with a loud thwack and excruciating pain. I was amazed at the speed that the ball must have reached, to hit me in the guts before I had even caught the merest glimpse of it. I was even more amazed how hard the ball was, so much harder than the balding tennis ball I slogged for six over Mickey Millmore's dad's garden. I gritted my teeth and tried not to show the pain in my side as the ball was returned and the bowler started his second run. Again, I saw nothing but a blur as his arm turned and I swung wildly again before hearing the wickets being skittled behind me. I dejectedly walked off, dragging my bat behind me, not knowing then that the bowler was one Robert Charles (Bob) Anderson who would use that same powerful right arm to become a national javelin champion and the world darts champion some years later. I decided to transfer to the athletics track from the following week, although I proudly showed off the vivid bruise on my side for weeks as it changed from red to blue to yellow. "I didn't hardly feel it," I lied.

That term limped to a close with my performance in lessons ranging from mediocre to average and most of my homework plagiarised from Shirley's original efforts. I hadn't made a positive commitment to be lazy or disinterested, it was just that there seemed to be too many other things which grabbed my attention and schoolwork did not appear in my top ten of priorities, lagging way down the list behind playing sport, watching sport and daydreaming about sport. The end of term examinations reflected my lack of effort although the results and teachers' comments were certainly a mixed bag. In English, I was *Unpredictable*. In History *Rather disappointing* and in French there was apparently *Much more effort needed*, yet I miraculously managed fourth place in Latin and seemingly *Answered well in class*. Although I achieved top position in Maths, I was surprised and disappointed that Grog Evans had written that I *Must make a more serious effort*. How could I be top of the class in a core subject, in probably one of the only two subjects that really mattered, the only subject that I really enjoyed and was good at, and be told that I *Must make a more serious effort*? Typical bloody Grog Evans – bloody vindictive Taffy, I thought. Perhaps our dad was right when he told me never to trust a Welshman, "After all, their talk similar is to German," he explained.

I was *Good* in Biology and top of the class in Gymnastics and Games with a double A and a *Congratulations – keep it up*. My Geography result was an excellent A but I felt that I could have improved my position had I not believed Mr. Bennett when he told the class that cattle in Argentina were raised on corn, which is where the term corned beef comes from: a fact that I proudly made the cornerstone of my answer about farming in South America in the end-of-term exam.

Almost-anonymous Form Teacher Harris's comment on my report stated that I *…must work harder next year*, which was fair enough. I was determined that that was exactly what I would do. Before leaving school on the final day of term, I loaded my satchel with a carefully selected sample of exercise and text books with and promised myself that I would spend a minimum of one hour each day of the summer holiday revising, specialising in those subjects in which had been highlighted as requiring more effort – History, French, Geography, English and Maths. I worked out that, allowing for weekends off and no work on our annual seaside break, I could reserve twenty-five days for study at one hour each day for five subjects, each subject would receive five hours of revision over the course of the summer. This was a convenient division of effort and more than enough to cover the previous year's work. I'd even managed to include Maths as I *Must make a more serious effort*, although I was pretty sure that I would abandon this session when the time came.

Our dad was a watchman in the British Rail factory, for which Swindon was rightly and proudly world-famous. Being employed as a watchman *inside*, as the locals described anyone working in the factory, offered many advantages. Protecting the railway buildings and property against thieves and gypsies offered a great opportunity to borrow tools and equipment on a permanent basis, which explains why our house was a treasure trove of railway memorabilia – wheelbarrows, buckets, various tools, cutlery and crockery were often stamped *GWR* or *BR(W)*. That said, so was the property in half of the houses in our street and it was not unusual to see bedroom mats and curtains emblazoned with similar motifs. There were other perks in our dad's job: a free uniform, flexible working hours, almost unlimited overtime and no supervision for much of the time, allowing regular refreshment breaks to be taken at local hostelries. One of the legitimate perks of all BR staff was that they were given several free rail passes each year, for use by themselves and their families. When the passes had been used up, staff were allowed an unlimited number of Privilege Tickets or Privs, which were heavily discounted. The free and cut-price tickets meant that journeys by train were the most common means of travelling any distance and opened up the country for BR employees. Each summer, the Trueman family would pack up and set off on a rail journey to exotic seaside locations for two weeks' holiday of sun, sea and sandwiches.

Our train journeys had traditionally taken us to seaside destinations somewhere on the south coast, for many years to Weymouth. The previous year, however, our mum and dad had been very adventurous, and we travelled west across the Welsh border to Barry Island. My parents had caught the travel bug and, this year, had booked two weeks in far off Cornwall at a small village called Hayle on a beautiful estuary near St. Ives Bay. Rather than the usual couple of hours travel to Weymouth or Barry, this journey was scheduled to take around five hours, so our mum made up fish-paste sandwiches and a flask of Camp coffee to sustain us, and our dad was planning where he could grab a quick pint or two on the way. The excitement mounted as we boarded the steam train, particularly as this year we were not going bed, breakfast and evening meal in someone else's home, nor were we to be confined to a small and uncomfortable caravan: we were to stay for two weeks in a chalet. We had never experienced the luxury of a chalet before, but in one of our Rae's illustrated books about Heidi, she discovered a picture of a rather grand wooden lodge, with a large balcony overlooking a deep and spectacular gorge and surrounded by snow-capped mountains and pet goats. This was described as a chalet.

The five-hour journey was exhilarating: for the first hour or so, after which our Rae and I became fractious and irritable until placated by fish-paste sandwiches. We happily turned down the offer of the Camp coffee. Our dad also became fractious and irritable when we changed trains at Exeter as he was too busy lugging suitcases from platform to platform to find time for a pint in Exeter Station Buffet. Arriving at Hayle Towans chalet camp by taxi from the station, our Rae and I were somewhat disappointed to find that, rather than the grand and luxurious wooden lodge we had imagined, our holiday accommodation turned out to be a shed. It was a big shed, but a shed, nevertheless. We stumbled into our temporary home, excited but tired and began to explore. It didn't take long to explore two rooms, so we went outside while our mum unpacked. Our dad had already gone out to see a man about a dog.

We couldn't find the toilet and I was bursting for a pee. We searched inside and outside the chalet and finally discovered the basic facilities in another small shed attached to the big shed. Inside was a large oil drum with a rough-hewn wooden toilet seat above and a toilet roll on a piece of looped string attached to the door with a rusting nail. This was to be the family lavatory for four people for two weeks. I'd heard our dad pee at night when he came home from the pub and it sounded like I imagine a huge waterfall would sound: I had serious worries about sleeping with Niagara crashing into a steel drum next door and had doubts that the receptacle, big as it was, would last us a fortnight. I reckoned that our dad would fill it on his own in a couple of days. My worries were assuaged the over the next few days when we saw a tractor towing a huge metal storage tank bumping its way round the site. It stopped at each chalet and a scruffy man in wellies jumped down, entered the chalet toilet, carried the oil drum on his shoulder to the tank where the foul brown waste was emptied, before the drum was returned to its shed. I was fascinated by the man whom we named Dan Dan the Lavatory Man. Our dad cracked a joke about him earning time and a turd. I got that one.

It was an untypical seaside holiday as, it seemed to me, it rained almost non-stop and I spent most of the time in the chalet reading comics. Each morning, our dad looked out of the window and declared, "Looks like it's goin' to clear up and be wet." The camp had a small shop and post office, where I would wander each day, dodging the rain, to spend my holiday money. I remember little else of the holiday except that I spent my daily shilling pocket money, saved over the previous year and augmented by Christmas gifts and half a crown from our nana, in the camp shop. I studied small toys, sweets and ice creams but invariably chose an American comic book, my favourite being *Buffalo Bill, Scout and Frontiersman (Illustrated in full color),* and a Hales's fruit pie.

On the one fine day, our parents decided that we would walk to Carbis Bay via Porthkidney Sands, a pleasant stroll along the ocean's edge. I was wistfully happy, splashing in and out of the sea as we ambled along, when my attention was directed at something odd in the sand on the tide line. On close examination, I was overjoyed to find a complete top set of dentures. What a find! I could imagine the reaction at school as I casually drew them from my pocket, nonchalantly saying, "Look what I've got." The other boys would be so jealous that I owned such a treasure. Our dad didn't see it that way, however, and insisted that the teeth be turned in to the local constabulary. I was very disappointed that evening as our dad carefully wrapped my treasure in toilet paper and set off for the police station. I waited patiently reading how Buffalo Bill singlehandedly wiped out the Native American population of the western states of America, for our dad to return, in the vain hope that the police would refuse to accept the dentures. He wasn't home by the time that we went to bed although we heard him come crashing in and make the waterfall noise, so we knew that he'd been to the pub. I had to wait until the following morning to find out about the teeth. Our dad explained that, by pure coincidence, the man who had lost the dentures was in the police station to report them missing and was so grateful to get them back that he insisted he buy our dad a beer or two. As our mum said, "I might look like a cabbage, but I'm not that green."

On return home to Swindon, I briefly thought about my pledge to study. I had missed the first two weeks of the break as I needed time to recover from the hard grind of the school year, missed the third week as I was too busy preparing for the Cornwall trip, obviously could do nothing whilst in Cornwall which meant that all the cramming was to be crammed into the final two weeks of the holiday. Five subjects multiplied the promised five hours each was still twenty-five hours' work but now just ten days left (weekends were obviously excluded). As I pondered how best to divide the available hours by the effort required to allow a revision timetable to be created, the Olympic Games began in our street and it was obligatory to take part. There were now just five available study days left. After due consideration, I decided that this was insufficient time to make any difference to my education and so the plan was abandoned: but I would definitely, certainly, positively and without doubt work harder next term.

The Olympics were held in Rome that year and the flickering black and white television pictures showed a packed stadium, bathed in scorching sunshine and athletes dripping in sweat as they concentrated the last four years training into this one great occasion. But it was as nothing compared to the Olympics in Pound Lane, where we could have several finals of the sprints, 100, 200 and 400 metres on the same day, every day. The programme was only interrupted when Sergeant Salter of the local constabulary was spotted on his outsized bicycle, patrolling the area. Salter considered that stretching string across the street as a finishing tape and several kids running hell-for-leather towards it constituted a danger to traffic. That we never had any traffic did not deter him from halting the events, which restarted immediately he moved on to the next street.

I was doing pretty well in the shorter sprints, winning several imaginary silver and bronze medals and a brace of gold. I struggled with the longer distances particularly the 1500 metres, which we changed to a mile race. This amendment was brought about by necessity as the gizmo attached to my bicycle wheel would only measure distances travelled in Imperial units. This showed that round the block four times taking in Pound lane, Cunningham Road and Montgomery Avenue measured exactly one mile, although there was some doubt as to the accuracy of the measurement when Tyrone Moody broke the four-minute mile barrier twice in one day.

Don Thompson was a British athlete who won the only athletics gold in Rome that year. A small bespeckled man called Il Topolino, the little mouse, by the Italian press, he became a national hero and everyone in the Pound Lane Games wanted to emulate him. The slight issue was that he had won the 50-kilometre walk. In respect to the great man, we held only walking races for several days albeit over the full range of distances. I failed to claim even a bronze, but there was a distinct rumour that some competitors should have been disqualified had any of us had understood the rules of competitive walking.

Chapter 3 – September - December 1960

- In Hamburg, four long-haired musicians perform their first concert as The Beatles.
- Penguin Books is found not guilty of obscenity, in the case of D. H. Lawrence's novel *Lady Chatterley's Lover*.
- The first episode of soap opera Coronation Street is aired on ITV.
- The last man is called up for National Service, as conscription ends.

One year down, only four to go. The Pinehurst grammar school pals battalion were in buoyant mood as we set off on our bikes for the first day of our second year. We had all survived the first year pretty much intact: no-one had been suspended or expelled: no-one had been debagged or had their heads flushed in the toilet: no one had been beaten or bullied. And now there would be younger children in the school whom we could, should we feel inclined, debag, flush, beat and bully, although we knew that we wouldn't.

We shuffled down the school drive, chatting excitedly with long-standing Pinehurst estate mates and catching up with those from other estates, boasting loudly about imaginary exploits and adventures over the summer holidays. As experienced and worldly-wise students, our satchels were no longer carried on our backs but suspended from our bicycle crossbars, our uniforms were worn to a satisfactorily shabby degree and some students had almost grown into the clothes: caps looked slightly faded and no longer rested on our ears, short trousers no longer ended below the knee and blazer sleeves no longer completely covered our hands. We were obviously not new boys. And we agreed that those first-year kids had just better watch out, or else.

I had maintained my position in the A stream despite apparently not trying hard enough, and most of my classmates were those from the previous term. Having changed into my now grey white daps, the previous year's first day baby-sitting was abandoned and we were expected to find our new classroom ourselves from a complex list pinned on the school notice boards. On eventual arrival in the correct room, I was pleased to see Shirley there and we exchanged friendly glances and perhaps even smiles, until I was distracted by a friendly wrestling contest with Bernie Wirdnam. Bernie or Reggie or Barnie was a long, gangling lad from Moredon with a penchant for mischief, who was to become a lifelong friend and influence on my life, a relationship possibly initiated by an intellectual meeting of enquiring minds, but more likely by mutual predilection towards disobedience and tomfoolery.

A shadow appeared in the classroom doorway and all pupils scattered to find a desk, automatically selecting similar positions to those that we had left at the end of the previous term. We were conditioned to present ourselves in alphabetical order. We stood behind our desks as the new form teacher entered and I was left open-mouthed and stunned, a feeling of impending doom spread throughout my being and my head spun as if in a nightmare. I recreated Edvard Munch's *The Scream* as Grog Evans entered. I could imagine nothing worse than having Grog as form teacher and the *must make a more serious effort* comment competed with the sound of a thumping pulse in my head. Although a written comment, I still heard the remark with Grog's lyrical Welsh inflection, followed by an imaginary *look you boy*.

After settling down and listening to the now familiar new term pep talk, the class began the process of electing form captains. I had found the position somewhat onerous the previous term and decided to reject any calls to stand again. Having given my all as leader and achieved great things, I thought it honourable to stand down and allow someone else to take on responsibility. Besides which, no-one proposed me this time.

At the end of the Second World War, Prime Minister Clement Atlee and his Minister of Education, Ellen Wilkinson, an anti-poverty champion, persuaded Parliament to pass the Free School Milk Act, which gave every school child under 18 the right to a free one-third of a pint of milk each day. It lasted until 1968, when the Labour Government, headed by Harold Wilson, removed free milk at all secondary schools. In 1971, Margaret Thatcher became the 'Milk Snatcher' making herself even more unpopular than before with certain sections of the populous, following her decision to withdraw milk for all children over seven years of age. But in 1960, free school milk was still very much part of school life and our education process. Again, ignoring our dad's advice about volunteering, I agreed, with Bernie, to undertake the arduous role of milk and straws monitors. Bernie accepted the senior position in charge of milk distribution, whilst I was to manage the inventory management and distribution control of drinking straws. Apart our joint vocation in answering a calling to provide our classmates with much-needed nutrients, we had previously observed that milk monitors were given time off to collect the crates of milk from the delivery point, carry them to the relevant classroom and distribute the bottles to the class, with complementary straws. After the milk had been consumed, it was the duty of the same team to collect the empty bottles, re-crate them and return them to the collection area. Twenty minutes a day at least would be spent messing about with milk bottles rather than attending lessons, which seemed to us a fair exchange of time and effort. And we could have any unconsumed bottles of milk for ourselves.

After school that afternoon, all pupils were divided by gender and house to attend meetings called to organise the house hierarchy for the coming school year. Although many pupils took this as a good excuse to go home early, I attended the meeting of Rockley House. After reading the previous year's minutes, the outgoing House Secretary declared that attendees were to nominate and elect the new House Captains for upper, middle and junior schools. Obviously as a consolation prize for not becoming Form Captain, I was duly elected to act as Rockley Junior House Captain to represent the first and second year boys. I was proud of the honour yet disappointed that I was not given a badge – I liked wearing badges and was a tad miffed when my request for a badge proclaiming "Milk Monitor" was soundly dismissed by Grog – and, as yet, I had absolutely no idea what I was supposed to do with my new status. At the conclusion of the meeting, the three House Captains, the Senior Vice-Captain and House Secretary were asked to remain whilst everyone else was dismissed. This was not a good start to my elected role as I wanted to go home for my tea. The Senior House Captain explained that my role was to select rugger, soccer, cricket and athletic teams for the house matches, captain the selected teams and set an example to all junior house members. I felt proud and honoured to undertake the responsibility and was determined to undertake the role with dignity, honesty and integrity, but I would have been much happier with less responsibility and a badge.

Two weeks into the term, I was selected as captain of the school's Under-13 Rugby team and life was good. Junior House Captain, Under 13 rugby captain, deputy milk monitor and straws monitor. This was more like the Tom Brown's schooldays that I had imagined when I was first selected to attend grammar school, the only blemish being the mandatory attendance of lessons and copious amounts of homework.

As we settled back into the mundane routine of school life, few incidents light up the murky existence in the flickering movie of my school life. It seems that it was one long grey slog of lessons and homework, interrupted only by the joy of games lessons and weekends of representing the school at rugby on Saturday mornings, watching Swindon Town's first team or reserves at the County Ground on Saturday afternoons and kickabouts all day Sunday before rushing in to make rudimentary efforts at homework Sunday evenings. Then, it was back to the gloomy slog on Mondays. That said, odd incidents cropped up at school to relieve the mundanity. I continued to struggle with French as it required a substantial amount of study – grammar, declensions, conjugation, nouns and adjectives, verbs and adverbs, noun genders and a multitude of new words to translate. One morning, without warning, a ray of light illuminated the dreary rounds of verb declension. Monsewer 'Ickman introduced a charming and beautiful French lady to the class, a student from gay *Paris* who would be supervising our French lessons for the next month in an exchange deal with an unidentified young English teacher exiled to pee-smelling France. Monsewer made a grave error of judgement when, after a brief introduction, the mademoiselle was abandoned, alone with a gang of unruly children. It was an opportunity not to be missed. We boys, led by Bernie who had a French mother and, therefore, a smattering of the tongue, included as much coarse language into the course as possible, mistranslating as much as possible. On introducing ourselves, Mademoiselle learnt that Bernie liked football and liked to play with his balls (*J'aime le football et j'aime jouer avec mes balles*), that Carter had a dog called Shagger (*J'ai un chien appelé Shagger*). I opted for a simpler phrase and explained (I hoped) that my uncle was a homosexual security officer (*Mon oncle est un homo de sécurité*). This taunting continued for about half an hour with mademoiselle becoming more and more vexed before she left the classroom in tears muttering something in French which we didn't understand, but could well have translated as *ignorant little shitbags*. A few minutes passed before Monsewer stormed into the room and read *l'acte d'émeute*, but our angelic faces portrayed absolute innocence and Mademoiselle's exchange duties were confined to the senior A-Level pupils who took learning languages somewhat more seriously. It was a fine example of shooting ourselves *dans le pied*, as lessons continued with extra vigour and discipline under Monsewer 'Ickman.

At the beginning of the term, we were introduced to Woodwork, a basic but complex subject where I could not be described as a natural. My only previous experience in carpentry was watching our dad making rabbit hutches in the back garden. We started with one rabbit donated by our Auntie Ivy and Uncle Arthur who had inherited Snowy from another relative. We thought that Snowy looked lonely, so our Rae and I agreed to save up her pocket money and buy Snowy a friend. We were soon the proud owners of a black rabbit we called called Sooty – we tended not to be too imaginative with pets' names in Pound Lane - from Hinders' pet stores (pronounced 'Inders' to rhyme with cinders). We weren't to know that Snowy was a male and Sooty was female, so it wasn't long before they were breeding like, well like rabbits. Our Rae and I rather liked the idea of keeping livestock, so more or her pocket money went on two guinea pigs. Our dad couldn't keep up with the hutch building to hold the growing menagerie, so the guinea pigs were housed together and turned out to be another amorous couple. They too bred like rabbits – or guinea pigs. As we dismally failed to sell any of the offspring, our dad was kept busy making hutches. The wood was donated by British Rail, as were nails, screws, hinges and chicken wire, and our dad became a dab hand at knocking up desirable rabbit town houses in a sought-after location with extensive views across the garden to Jeff Moody's dad's house and garden. He explained that screws should be hammered home with a large BR hammer, which is why the screws had flat tops, and the groove was there only if you needed to take extract them. Then, and only then, should you use a screwdriver. That was my only experience of woodwork before being released into the school workshop under the supervision of a man with a bald head and a brown coat whose name, escapes me, if indeed I ever knew it.

After a preliminary lecture about the joys of wood, the thrill of woodworking, different types of wood, and the dangers of wood in the workshop, all boys were asked to select what item they would like to skilfully construct over the following term. We were offered three options; a pencil box, a foot stool or a kitchen stool. I could see no use for a pencil box as I only owned one pencil, which didn't need its own container, and I didn't really understand what a foot stool was, so I opted to spend the term constructing the kitchen stool. After all, we had a kitchen at home, although it never occurred to me that it would be next to useless as there was no room for a stool in a council house kitchen: strangely, the builders never considered installing a breakfast bar. Bernie was equally as confused and also selected the kitchen stool option, so we were paired together, sharing a workbench to begin our first sensual adventure with timber. I was immediately perplexed. The wood to be used was clean, rough and virgin unlike the worn, pre-painted planks that our dad brought home from work for the construction of rabbit hutches. There were no rusty nails or screws to extract. No old paint to scrape off and no mysterious numbers and messages such as *BR11842* or *To Carry 10 Tons*. We were told that we should cut the timber to size with a saw and smooth it with a plane. Our dad had several saws in his shed, all marked GWR, and I had seen him use them in his wooden constructions, but I had no idea what a plane was or how it would be used. Secondly, we had illustrated plans to follow. Our dad had built several rabbit hutches, a lean-to bike shed and a coal bunker, all using wood, without illustrated plans. Finally, the plans showed that we were to

Page 79

use mortise and tenon joints with glue and without a nail or screw in sight. Our dad had housed half the rabbit population of Pinehurst without a mortise, a tenon or glue. After weeks of careful measuring, tedious sawing, planing and chiselling in line with the illustrated plans, Bernie and I were ready to assemble the thirteen constituent parts of our stools, four legs, eight struts and a seat. I felt uneasy about the thirteen parts. Although they appeared to fit when paired together, I was not confident that the whole could be assembled to create the solid and attractive piece of furniture in the illustrated plan. Unlucky thirteen perhaps, I thought.

The assembly went better that expected. We were instructed to complete the construction to ensure that all constituent parts fitted before disassembling and finalising the construction with glue the following week. Apart from the fact that some joints were loose with the mortise too big for the tenon (or was the tenon too big for the mortise?) which could be fixed with a little chiselling or some carefully placed wood shavings, and a couple of joints that were too tight (another quick chisel with the chisel would fix that), all seemed well and Bernie and I carefully stored the constituent parts of our masterpieces for the following week's lesson. Perhaps I should have been even more careful with the storage or secured the parts more securely, but for whatever reason, once assembled and firmly glued in place, my stool refused to stand up. The main cause of the instability appeared to be the fact that one of the stool legs was about half an inch longer that the other three. My first reaction was that Bernie had, by some subterfuge, swapped one of my legs for a less than perfect creation from his stool, a charge firmly denied by the accused, after he had managed to stop laughing at my misfortune. This may well have been an unfortunate error, but no matter: the resolution was simple. All I had to do was shorten the longer leg. Except that the exact adjustment turned out to be somewhat more complex than expected and after several attempts at measuring with a rule and by eye, I decided that I should leave the problem until the following week by which time an easier solution to the problem may have dawned or the leg may have miraculously shortened itself.

By the following week, I had not managed to devise a satisfactory solution and I was disappointed to find that my stool still refused to stand firmly, so I had no option but to begin surgery. Bernie was of little help, taking great delight at my misfortune and offering unhelpful advice – soak the long leg for a while and it might shrink or nail a small chunk of wood to the three shorter legs or drill a hole in the floor for the longer leg to sit in. For a brief moment, I considered the last suggestion as a serious option before dismissing it as a little impractical. The adjustment appeared to work well as the longer leg was shortened in line with my painstaking measurements. But the stool refused to stand resolutely. I had been somewhat over-enthusiastic with the saw and the surgery meant that the previously longer leg was now shorter than the other three. More measurements were taken and more adjustments to leg lengths were made: and more: and more, until I finally had a stool which stood steadfastly on the floor without the faintest suggestion of a wobble. I had proudly produced a strong, usable piece of furniture. The one slight issue was that my stool was not the planned height of twenty-four inches but was a mere sixteen inches on one side and fifteen and a half inches on the opposite side. Not only did my short stool slope quite significantly but, on more careful examination, the legs did not sit squarely on the floor, the mortise (or is it the tenon?) showed obvious and untidy signs of packing and glue exuded from every joint in ugly yellowing blobs. That said, I was still quite proud of my Frankenstein stool as it was the first tangible article that I had ever created under my own steam. I was not quite so proud when the teacher in the brown coat said that he was speechless but continued his speech anyway to say that he could not allow the stool to leave the school and I could not take it home. I was bitterly disappointed and shelved my preliminary plans to build our mum a wooden breakfast bar at home to accommodate the stool.

I rarely used the school tuck shop. I would wander past and stare at the salty or sugary treats on view, but rarely had the cash available to squander on such indulgencies. Some lads, particularly those from the wealthier private estates were given a daily tuckshop allowance, enough for an Arnott's Wagon Wheel and a pack of Burton's Potato Puffs perhaps, but most of my close mates made only the occasional purchase. If our mum was particularly flush, and by that, I mean if she had a couple of bob left at the end of the week, she would slip our Rae and me a few coppers or a thruppeny bit, but otherwise we had to make do with our weekly allowance of sixpence. Men working inside were traditionally paid in cash on Thursday evenings and their wives had usually run out of money during the preceding day or two. I was often asked to go the local Co-op on Thursday evenings to spend the last of our mum's housekeeping money on food, awaiting our dad's return from work/pub/club with what was left of his wages, providing our mum could scrape up enough coppers from the dark corners of her purse. This was a chore I did not relish as balancing two pounds of potatoes on my handlebars was not easy and the time taken would be better spent playing football in the street. One Thursday evening, as I left the Co-op and was loading the bag of potatoes, a glint caught my eye by the front wheel of my bike. I looked down and saw a coin which I immediately snatched up and slipped into my pocket, jumped onto the bike and, gripping the potatoes tightly, pedalled quickly away. Before reaching home, I stopped and studied by booty – a huge, new, shiny half-crown: two shillings and sixpence: half a dollar. I thought long and hard about my lucky find. Perhaps the coin had been lost by a really poor, deprived neighbour, maybe an old age pensioner who could be starving, relying on this very coin to save them from the workhouse or an ignominious death by starvation. Perhaps there was a famished baby sobbing for food at this precise moment as its mother scraped around for any scraps to satisfy its hunger. There was no doubt in my mind what I should do as a moral and caring person. I realised that I should take the cash back to the Co-op and hand it in. It would be difficult, but it was the only decent thing to do. I put the half-crown in my pocket and rode home, reminding myself that I was needy too and it is finders-keepers after all. I studied my newly acquired wealth that evening, planning what I could do with such a fortune and decided that I should be prudent. I would save some to help our mum out at Christmas and may even buy her a nice present. I could almost see her face light up in a beautiful smile as I handed over a box of her favourite lavender-scented Cussons Imperial Leather. I could buy our Rae a better Christmas present than usual, perhaps a new rabbit or guinea pig or even a fluffy new kitten. I was still planning my benevolent actions the next day at school, smugly overwhelmed with my own generosity and full of a sense of righteousness, until I went to the tuckshop and spent every last penny on Smiths crisps, Burton's Potato Puffs, a Nestles' Caramac and Milky Bar, a Cadbury's Bar Six and a Rowntrees' Nux bar. Of course, I shared my ill-gotten gains with my mates and made sure that they all realised what a kind and generous fellow I was. The investment was disappointedly wasted as I never received the anticipated return on investment.

I arrived home that dinner time not in the slightest bit hungry, a situation which was abnormal. Like most families, we had dinner at dinner time in the middle of the day, tea at tea-time on arriving home from school in the afternoon and supper, always consisting of cereal, just before bed. Dinner was meat and two veg. every day, without exception. The meat varied daily: often left-overs on Mondays then faggots, mince, steak and kidney pie or pudding, chops, sausages, casseroles or stews. The meat was accompanied by boiled or mashed potatoes, Bisto gravy and one other vegetable which, for me, was always Farrow's Giant Processed Peas. This was the only vegetable I would consider, and our mum had given up trying to make me eat anything else. I suppose that she thought that something green is better that nothing, even if the green colouring of processed peas seemed to have been created at the Dulux paint factory. Our dad always said that, "Dinner's not dinner without a puddin'," so a pudding was always provided. Apple pie, Jam poly-poly or spotted dick, all served with Bird's custard were favourites, although rice and macaroni were considered acceptable. Naturally, ice cream was out of the question as we owned neither fridge nor freezer.

Our dinner was always accompanied by the BBC Light Programme. The wireless was switched on before breakfast in the mornings and stayed on all day until it was replaced by the television later in the evening. It seems that there were only two programmes ever playing at dinner time. The first was Workers' Playtime, a residue from the 1940's when it was broadcast from various factories around the country as a morale booster for factory workers during the dark days of the war. It featured some of the great radio personalities of the day such as comedians Charlie Chester, Arthur English and Ted Ray, singers Anne Shelton and Dorothy Squires, and variety acts like impressionist Peter Goodwright, who managed to sound the same no matter who he impersonated, and Percy Edwards who did impressions of dogs barking and wild birds twittering. My own favourites were a west country comedian called Billy Burdon who always finished his act by saying that he had to go because, "It's a long walk back to Dorset," and Ken Platt who began his act by saying, "I'll not take my coat off, I'm not stopping." It was good, clean fun which represented the spirit of post-war austerity. The second regular accompaniment to dinner was the Billy Cotton Bandshow. Billy was a cockney band leader character who started each show with the cry "Wakey-Waaake-aaaay!", followed by the band's signature tune "Somebody Stole My Gal." Regular entertainers included singer Kathie Kay and pianist Russ Conway, but the resident singer was a crooner called Alan Breeze, who sang the hits of the day with the band's backing. Mr Breeze was fine when singing melodious hits by Matt Monroe or Perry Como, but never quite cut the mustard when replicating the new Rock and Roll of Elvis Presley or Cliff Richard. But fair play to Alan, he gave it his best shot, even though he never hit the target.

I felt very guilty that I hadn't spent some of my fortune on our Rae as she deserved something to cheer her up. A couple of weeks earlier on a Sunday evening I was lying in bed, drifting off to sleep, when there was a huge commotion from downstairs. Our Rae was crying, our mum was begging our dad to stop whatever it was he was doing and our dad was shouting, so I naturally went down to see what was causing the fracas. It was a chaotic scene with our dad holding centre stage bellowing something about our Rae being late home, a cock and bull story, must have been a boy involved, what was she up to, keep your nose out. What I gathered was that our Rae had caught the bus to visit our gran, our dad's mum who lived on the new Walcott estate, and was on her way back home when a small puppy followed her to the bus stop. It looked so forlorn that our Rae didn't catch the bus but stayed and tried to find the puppy's owner, missed the next bus and had to walk home arriving long after the curfew set by our dad. He went mad, imagining that she was "up to no good", whatever that entailed, and our mum had intervened. As I arrived, he was threatening to give our mum a good hiding so jumped between them. "Don't you dare touch our mum," I bravely declared.

"I've already give 'er a belt," our dad shouted, "What you gonna do about it?"

I had to admit that it was a jolly good question. I had no idea what I was going to do about it, as I certainly wasn't going to fight our dad. He was a foot taller than me and double my weight, had been his regimental light-middleweight boxing champion and beaten the Germans almost single-handedly in North Africa before expelling them from Italy. What could I do? I stuttered something about, "You better not, that's all," before our mum took me by the hand and led our Rae and me upstairs with a comforting, "It's OK. He'll be all right now."

We went to bed and heard nothing more, but our Rae deserved a little treat and I never gave her any of my chocolate, for which I was most remorseful. And our dad never spoke to any of us for the next few months, for which I was most grateful.

Back at school, lessons must have been running fairly smoothly as I remember little or nothing more of that year, though I guess that I was doing just enough to get by and, woodwork apart, keeping my head above water. My report is good enough, although I am now struck at how useless the teachers' comments are. Amongst the meaningless, *Has worked steadily and is a capable worker*, there are inept comments by largely anonymous teachers. For example, what can be gained from a comment by the English master or mistress – *I expected a better Literature result?* Does this mean that I was doing superbly in class but simply did not perform to my full potential in the end of term exam or that I was capable and did not do enough work to merit a better mark? In Chemistry it says, *He could improve on this result.* Was the result good, bad or indifferent and how could I improve? In handicraft (woodwork) the man in the brown coat wrote, *Could do better that this.* No, I couldn't. I tried my utmost but was useless at woodwork, so what did I need to do to improve? The one bright spot was, surprisingly, from Grog Evans who not only turned out to be one of the best teachers that I remember but complimented me on my Maths - *A good result. A steady, capable worker* and, as form master, stated that I was *a very pleasant boy*. I wondered if he would have written that if he knew that I didn't give our Rae any chocolate, but I supposed that my role as deputy milk monitor and my sterling work in managing the logistics of drinking straw control and distribution won him round. That said, I had improved my overall position and even the Boss wrote that I had made *pleasing progress*. Things were looking up and so was I.

If the academic and sporting side of my school life was reaching its apex, then my grasp of extra-curricular activities took a short but traumatic nosedive. In Swindon town centre near its magnificent but run-down nineteenth century town hall stood a large and impressive building, the Baptist Tabernacle. To Swindon's everlasting shame, this inspiring edifice, built from Bath stone and fronted by six imposing pillars, is now broken in pieces and laying in a farmer's field some miles outside of the town. In the sixties, however, the building was used for regular religious services and it was here that the pupils of Headlands Grammar School were summonsed just prior to Christmas to attend a carol concert. We were instructed to appear there one cold December morning and school uniforms were, of course, mandatory. As I waited beneath the pillars having cycled into town with the rest of the Pinehurst contingent, stamping our feet and blowing white clouds of breath into cupped hands in a vain attempt to keep warm, there were a few good-humoured hisses and boos as a trio of prefects arrived and entered the building. I naturally joined in and characteristically took things too far by bellowing out a loud and aggressive catcall, much to the amusement of my peers. I was feeling pretty pleased with my daring when one of the prefects turned and marched up to me.

"Is that supposed to be funny?" he asked in what I thought was an unnecessary and over-aggressive manner, "And where's your cap?"

As I was stuttering and wondering which question I should answer first, the prefect added, "You'd better see me outside the Prefects' Common Room tomorrow at twelve sharp. Understand?"

That was now three questions and I was tempted to answer, "Yes. In my pocket. Yes." But all I managed was blank stare. In fact, I didn't know that the prefects had a common room or, indeed, what a common room was.

The following day, I ascertained the whereabouts of the Common Room and duly turned up a minute or two after mid-day and waited in the corridor. I waited for a few more minutes as prefects entered or left the room. It was the first time that I had noticed the behaviour of senior pupils and it occurred to me just how unlike the lower years these young men and women behaved. They strolled in and out confidently, almost happily, chatting and smiling as if they were enjoying the whole school experience. I even saw boys chatting with girls as if they were friends. At that time, I was unable to talk to a girl, except our Rae and Shirley or the girls from Pound Lane, without doing a rather accurate impersonation of a profusely sweating beetroot.

After twenty minutes or so, as I was waiting patiently to be debagged, caned or toasted in front of the common room fire, one of the senior girls approached and asked who I was waiting for. She was lovely. It was like talking to Doris Day in Calamity Jane – the part when she dresses in a smart white blouse and sings under a tree – and my head was swimming with adoration and embarrassment. "I think that you've waited long enough now. Run along and I'll make sure that it's OK," she said gently as *Once I had a secret love, that lived within the heart of me played* serenely in the background of my brain. I floated down to the bike sheds and

Page 88

pedalled furiously home for dinner. On returning to school, Derek Windslow asked if I had turned up at the Common Room and whether that was the reason I didn't cycle home with the rest of the lads. "No," I lied, "If he wants me, he'll have to come and get me," in an attempt to sound like Howard Keel as Wild Bill Hickok.

A few incidents apart, my lack of recall about the anonymous teachers and indistinctive lessons certainly did not apply to the festive season. Our dad had managed to arrange his shifts such that he was off work on Christmas Eve and Christmas day, which offered the obvious opportunity for a good drink, which he would not turn down. He had arranged to meet with his siblings and their families in North Swindon Working Men's Club on the evening of the twenty-fourth December for a family get together. Our dad left home at five thirty that afternoon for six o'clock opening time, to make sure that we reserved the best table, whilst we stayed at home to prepare for the occasion by donning our best bib and tucker. Throughout the day, I had been feeling a bit rough with a mild headache and my nose had started to run, but I never mentioned my condition to our mum as I didn't want to miss a night out at the club. I had to wear a silly dickie bow tie which was attached by elastic around my neck and our Rae was allowed to wear a little make up, as she was approaching fifteen. We had had a bath although it wasn't a Sunday and, at about seven o'clock, our mum and our nana led us on the mile walk to the club. Our mum was not too happy as she was not looking forward to an evening of Trueman boozing. She didn't drink alcohol, didn't like being in pubs or clubs and certainly didn't like any of the Truemans. Our dad always said that the trouble with our mum was that she didn't like enjoying herself. Once in the club, we joined the family seated at three tables in one corner of the bar. There were our dad's brothers Bill, George, Frank from Gloucester and Snobby, with their formidable wives. The exception was Uncle

Snobby who was never married because, as the family always said, "After all, 'e's a cripple with a gammy leg." Also present were our dad's sisters, Aunties Sis and Lorna, with their husbands. Only Auntie Edna and Uncle Don were missing because they ran a pub in the City in London and could not take time off on Christmas Eve.

By the time we arrived, the party was in full swing, for the brothers anyway. They had all queued up at the club door before opening time to get the best tables, and there was a fog of cigarette smoke above them mixed with the smell of beer and port and lemons. I had a glass of lemonade and our dad put a little beer in the glass to make a shandy and make me feel very grown up. Our Rae had her lemonade topped up with a drop of port and even our mum joined in with a Babycham, although she drowned the alcohol with some of my lemonade, displaced to make room for my added beer. Our nana ordered a port and lemon, "But not too much lemon." All was winging along merrily as the music duo took the stage for the evening's entertainment. There was a pianist with hands like bunches of bananas who could, nevertheless, knock out recognisable tunes, and a drummer who seemed to restrict his input to brushing one drum with what looked like a large paint brush, making a moderately rhythmic swishing sound. After the first number, the drummer introduced the duo. "Good evening laygennulmen," he announced, "We are the Symbolics. And I am Sym." This caused much laughter, particularly on our tables, although I had no idea what was so funny.

The evening was progressing well and I was engrossed in watching banana-fingers and the swishing drummer when there were shouts and a crash as one of our tables was knocked heavily and beer and glasses seemed to be flying around me. I turned to see our dad being held by Uncle George and Snobby being held by Uncle Frank as they strained to get each other, hurling insults as more glasses crashed to the floor. Aunties screamed and shouted, all the men bellowed at the same time and everyone in the club stood to get a better view of the action. I slipped under the table. After several minutes of bellowing and posturing, the scuffle calmed down and, following a few more strong and ungentlemanly words and another session of shoving and pointing, we were gathered up and ushered out of the door. What caused the rumpus I never found out but suspect that it something to do with our Rae wearing make-up and Snobby making an inappropriate remark. A family with a violent nature and an excess of alcohol may also have played a small part. As we walked home, our dad was in obvious distress, "I should have thumped 'im," he repeated several times, "But you can't. Not with 'im being a cripple with a gammy leg. But I should 'ave thumped 'im … and we're going 'ome before closing time," he bewailed.

I was feeling worse when we arrived home, now suffering from a sore throat, headache and runny nose and I ached from head to toe. Our mum called it feeling like a wet dish rag. She had been an auxiliary nurse during the war and had gained a comprehensive knowledge of medicine and medical practice. She knew how to cure any illness, so she packed me off to bed with a hot water bottle and two Phensics. She also made me swallow a spoonful of Vaseline to cure my sore throat. Luckily, another of her cures, a plentiful dose of hydrogen peroxide into my ears to clear any wax, was not required. I also avoided her cure for heat bumps, whatever heat bumps were, which was a liberal application of Sarsens vinegar. All stings were to be treated with a Reckitt's blue bag, but this too was deemed unnecessary. I blamed the illness on the fact that our Rae and I had not received any inoculations as our mum said that we could be infected by rusty needles. I surprisingly felt better in the early hours of the morning, probably despite our mum's cures rather than because of them, and managed to wake to open my presents after forcing down two more Phensics and a spoonful of Vaseline, before collapsing back into bed for the rest of the morning. I awoke and heard our dad leaving the house at a quarter to twelve to see man about a dog. Clubs and pubs could only open for one hour on Christmas day but each establishment could choose between opening from midday until one o'clock or one o'clock until two. Our dad and his mate Les Wiltshire would cycle casually to the North Swindon Club for twelve o'clock opening and, at closing time, cycle frantically to the Southbrook Inn which opened at one, thus ensuring two hours of drinking. I had managed to drag myself out of bed and was waiting in my dressing gown, feeling very sorry for myself when he arrived home, red-faced and unsteady at half past two.

"What's it like out?" our mum asked.

"Black over our mother's," our dad replied as he swayed a little, took off his overcoat and sat down to await dinner and his bottle of sauterne. Later that afternoon, as we were starting on the fudge and tooth-marked chocolates and our dad was finishing our nana's sherry, he suddenly reiterated his mantra, "Just because you've got to call 'em Sir, you don't have to mean it…and don't think they're better than you."

Our Rae and I looked at each other and shrugged. Our mum shook her head, our nana carried on smoking and watching the television.

"May 1940. We was stuck in the middle of nowhere in northern France, waiting for orders," he continued. "My sergeant had just managed to find a few eggs in a farm 'ouse and we was frying 'em up on an open fire in the yard, when a big car pulls up. Four officers gets out and says we've got orders to retreat to Dunkirk. Leave them eggs and get going immediately. Sarge says which way's Dunkirk, then? Officer says address an officer as Sir, sergeant. Dunkirk is south. And they drove off. Just like that. Left us all there to find our own way back while they sped off in a blooming' big car. Never trusted an officer after that." He looked directly at me, "Never trust anyone who wants to be called Sir," he stressed and tapped the side of his nose twice.

"Took us three days, walking' at night," our dad continued, "Sleepin' in ditches, Jerry strafin' us from their planes. A few of our blokes copped it. We just 'ad to leave 'em there in the ditches at the side of the road. Couldn't 'elp 'em when they was dead. Then when we gets to Dunkirk, not an officer to be seen. Not a single one. Took priority on the boats, they did. While we was on the beach getting strafed and bombed again and again, they was 'ome in Blighty 'avin' bloody tea at the bloody Ritz."

"Language, Jack." our mum said. Our dad just nodded, got up and went to bed without another word.

Chapter 4 – January - August 1961

- The farthing coin ceases to be legal tender.
- Betting shops become legal
- Tottenham Hotspur win the double of the league title and FA Cup
- Britain applies for membership in the EEC.

The new year and new term started well. The ructions of the Trueman's Christmas Eve celebrations made a great story for my mates, especially when embellished to make our dad a heroic saviour of the family's honour against a band of treacherous and villainous brothers in the family feud, and in which I played a full and brave part. The weather was cold, wet and windy, but thankfully free from snow and its incumbent battles with the Pinehurst Mafia. I had received a reasonable report after having a reasonable term and was confident that, at last, I had mastered the right mix between school work (do just enough to get by), homework (plagiarise wherever possible) and social life (don't let schoolwork stand in its way).

Sport was, as ever, highest on my personal list of priorities and the wet weather had resulted in cancellation of games for most of the month, much to the boys' chagrin and the relief of our mums, who were spared the weekly chore of washing and ironing screwed up, mud-encrusted kit and sopping, filthy towels. Most mums had never seen a washing machine, let alone used one, and all clothes, towels and bed linen were washed by hand or with help from an ancient boiler. As the family bathed only weekly, excluding the forced shower after games at school, this was a far from pleasant task. Our boiler was a large, ugly wash tub with a wringer attached and, as far as I understood the machine, simply boiled the clothes producing a fog in the kitchen that could be cut by a knife and a foul smell something akin to mixing urine, sweat and Brylcreme with Omo or Daz washing powder. The laundry was boiled for several hours, helped by the occasional poke with a large wooden stick, bleached white by years of submersion in boiling water. For reasons which escape me, this instrument was referred to as the copper stick and was always used as a threat to bring us into line, as in, "Do that again and you'll get the copper stick." After boiling, the clothes were removed from the boiler with a large pair of wooden tongs and passed through the wringer, two wooden rollers turned by a large handle which squeezed grey, sludgy water from the laundry, before hanging the washing on the line in the back garden. This took place every Monday without fail and the smell finally dissipated by the following Friday.

Whilst frustrating that no school football was played for a month, the minor compensation was that we were herded into the school hall, or any other available space, where we were ordered to study. This meant, of course, that we could catch up on the homework that we had missed earlier in the week. It was a fine line in deferring homework and still allowing the work to be presented in time, but with careful planning homework never had to be completed at home.

Write a story of 250 words with a twist at the end. That was the task set as composition for English Language homework and which, unusually, sparked my interest. I read constantly at that time, mainly comics and football reports, but my reading list also included cowboy books that our mum borrowed from the library to keep our dad amused whilst guarding British Rail's valuable rolling stock. I liked the idea of writing a story and worked on the idea both at home at school during the cancelled games lessons, until I had produced what I considered to be an amusing tale of intrigue and innovation. Quite what the story involved I no longer remember except that it involved cowboys and finished with the line, *He had been misled and things had gone awry.*

So proud was I of my novella that, when the teacher asked for a volunteer to read out their work, my hand shot up almost of its own volition. This was a surprise to the teacher and, indeed, to me as I had vowed to adhere to our dad's advice about volunteering, but perhaps my resolution was assuaged by success as deputy milk monitor and straws monitor. I stood as tall as possible for a shorty and loudly delivered my story. It was going superbly, with the class appearing to be enraptured with my cowboy tale of mystery and suspense: until I delivered the punch line …*He had been misled and things had gone awry.*

As I looked up from book, smugly grinning in anticipation of appreciative applause, there was a hush and atmosphere of confusion in the class, then a few whispers followed by giggles and finally riotous laughter with included barely stifled guffaws from the teacher. I felt my face burning, a sensation worsened by the teacher's explanation. How was I to know that *misled* wasn't pronounced to rhyme with fizzled or *awry* to rhyme with gory? I had theatrically announced that, "*He had been mizzled and things had gone 'oary.*" I had previously read both words many times and knew what they meant, but no-one on our estate said them aloud. In Pinehurst, people were not misled but were conned or shafted, and things never went awry, they went to cock or tits up. The one saving grace was that I changed the line at the last minute and had not included the fact that it had been a mishap.

In early February, possibly buoyed by my heroic support in hiding under a table on Christmas Eve, our dad announced that we were going to London by train, just the two of us, to watch a football match: Tottenham Hotspur versus Leicester City at White Hart Lane.

Overjoyed, delighted, ecstatic. I'm not sure that the English language, as rich as it is, has an adjective to describe how I felt. I was going to White Hart Lane to see my favourite team play.

I could, and almost sixty year on still can, name the team without thinking: Brown, Baker, Henry, Blanchflower, Norman, Mackay, Jones, White, Smith, Allen and Dyson or Medwin. It is amazing to think that in their historic double-winning year, Spurs used only seventeen different players, with ten players taking part in over forty games and four players being ever present with forty-nine appearances. And they only lost seven games that season. Even more amazing was that I was going to see my heroes. In 1961. The double year. The first team in modern times to achieve this feat.

I remember nothing at all about the game. I know that Leicester inflicted a rare defeat on the Lilywhites by three goals to two, but the contents of game are a complete blank. All I remember is that there was a man outside selling roasted peanuts who shrugged when our dad shook his head as we passed and said in his strong London accent, "Nobody wants nuffunk," a phrase which amused my father and which he often repeated, well into his eighties. What I do remember well is the journey home. Of course, we took advantage of a free pass or priv ticket for the outing and travelled by train. We took the main line from Swindon to Paddington, then underground to White Hart lane via the Hammersmith and City or Circle lines, changing at Liverpool street to what is now the London Overground, but then was what? I cannot find mention of White Hart Lane on any old underground maps, so how our dad found his way is a mystery. Besides, I never saw him look at a map before or during the journey, but we arrived safely at the ground. Perhaps it was homing instinct as he found his way to The Bricklayers by one o'clock, where I found myself standing in the pub doorway with my usual bag of crisps and a bottle of lemonade, feeling somewhat self-conscious and conspicuous in my red and white Swindon bobble hat and scarf amongst the dark blue and white of the Spurs' supporters. I was fortunate the game was not against Arsenal.

After the game, we made it back to Paddington, again without reference to any maps or timetables, just as it was opening time at the Load of Hay, a rough-looking pub situated just outside Paddington Station. I was getting cold and would offer this advice to anyone: standing in a pub doorway at six o'clock in early January, drinking cold fizzy pop is not an experience to be relished. Luckily, our dad only had a quick one and we retired to the station buffet for his next pint or two. I'm pretty sure that we missed at least one train bound for Swindon, but the joy was that I could sit in the warmth of the buffet, munching my crisps and sipping warm lemonade. When it was time to go, our dad grabbed my arm and we dashed to the platform where the Swindon train lay waiting. I was surprised that we hurried half the length of the platform, passing many empty and apparently suitable carriages, until our dad stopped at one carriage, ostensibly identical to those we had passed and said, "This un's airn," and we boarded the train. He was also very particular that we sit on the right-hand side of the carriage. The reason for the careful selection of our position became apparent as we pulled into Reading station. The carriage he had carefully selected, *airn*, stopped directly outside of the Reading Station Buffet. Our dad checked his watch and said, "Just time for a quick one before the connection from Guildford gets in. You stay 'ere."

So, stay there I did, for about ten minutes watching our dad rush into the buffet and down a pint before leaping back into the carriage just as the train was about to pull out. After arrival at Swindon station, we caught the Pinehurst bus home, but our dad jumped off before we reached our stop, to take advantage of the last hour's drinking at the Ferndale Working Men's Club, whilst I continued my journey alone. The logistics of this operation continue to impress me. No reference to maps, no reference to timetables, yet our dad had timed the journey perfectly so that he had managed four or five pints on the journey home and made it

Page 98

to the club with another hour's boozing time left. Little wonder that he maintained that school learning was a waste of time.

This memorable trip was a rare variation from my standard Saturday mornings, which were almost always spent in one of four activities. The top priority was playing football or rugby for the school team. If there was no game or during the summer months, I would join with the other Pound Lane lads and lasses and either go to the pictures at the Palace in Gorse Hill or the Savoy in Swindon's Regent Street. Alternatively, we may have decided to go swimming at the baths in Milton Road. To enjoy these activities, it was generally accepted that all the kids were given one shilling by their parents, which covered sixpence entry fee to whichever entertainment was selected and tuppence each way bus fares, leaving tuppence for sweets. It was then debated whether we should walk and save the bus fares, leaving a small fortune of sixpence for sweets, but the generally accepted compromise was to bus to the venue and walk back, with four pen'oth of sweets.

The trips to the Savoy were a particularly exciting experience as the cinema had a balcony. The young customers were seated in the order that they had queued, starting from the front row of the stalls. When downstairs was full, they were directed upstairs to the balcony. It was a fine line positioning ourselves in the queue such that we made it into the balcony - get it wrong and the cinema could fill up and we would miss the film. Mickie Mason, Brian's older brother had the queuing off to a fine art and we inevitably made it to the balcony, from where we could bomb those below with sweet wrappers and anything else at hand. As we shuffled about in the queue to get prime balcony position, we had to evade the attention of the commissionaire, a tall and intimidating old boy in full uniform and sporting a magnificent large red nose, hence his nickname of Rudolph. Whether caused by his nose, I know not, but Rudolph also had a speech impediment and was always met with shouts of, "Rudolph," from various unseen positions in the line. He was guaranteed to respond with his usual mantra, "You boys be'er look ow. I knows where you lives". Which was met with gales of laughter and more shouts of, "Rudolph."

This pleasing and enjoyable routine was broken occasionally by the requirement to collect a bag of coke from the Gas Works in Gorse Hill. How this activity was coordinated was a mystery but, by accident or design, most of the families requiring coke would send their children off on the same day. A motley assortment of vehicles would assemble with an even more motley assortment of grubby children, and we would set of for the Gas Works. Each set of siblings would gather with their coke wagon, usually a modified pram, sometimes as basic as just the four wheels with the carriage removed or perhaps replaced by a new carriage, roughly built with second-hand British Rail wood nailed or tied to the axles, and sometimes the complete pram, buckled, tattered and torn after years of baby and coke toting. There would often be as many as four or five families together plus other members of the street gang who just went along for the adventure. The ramshackle caravan, with the younger children sitting comfortably on the empty coke sack in the vehicle, would travel down Montgomery Avenue, across the allotments, through the horses' field, down Gorse Hill to Gypsy Lane and the Gas Works. It was not unusual to meet other, similarly ragged nomads from other streets on the way, such that the convoy would expand as we neared our goal.

The highlight of the trip occurred when it was our turn to have our sack filled. After buying a ticket at the pay station and queuing to reach the filling station, a coke-blackened worker would hold our sack under a huge shoot, pull a handle and the coke would rush down to fill the sack in a great cloud of black dust. The sack was loaded onto the makeshift wagons and we would push, heave and strain as the heavy trucks were trundled through the streets back to our respective homes. Of course, the shilling saved from not going to pictures or swimming was not paid but perhaps we would be given a few coppers to invest in making Messrs Barratt, Cadbury and Nestle even richer and to sustain us in our labours.

In the rough and derelict grounds of the gas works was an abandoned air raid shelter constructed, we assumed, to protect our brave gas workers from the bullying terror of the Luftwaffe. After collecting our bags of coke, the Pound Lane kids would sometimes furtively enter the dark and dank shelter and imagine that German bombs were exploding above ground. Our talk was always of the war, in which I could take a leading role as our dad was a real Desert Rat and had several war medals, and shrapnel in his shoulder. During one debate about the evil Bosch, the conversation drifted on to the question of religion, specifically why God allowed the war to happen. The general consensus was that there must have been a good reason for God to allow Hitler to carry out his wicked and murderous campaign or, as an omnipotent deity, He would not have allowed the carnage. I listened to the arguments, becoming increasingly confused, even suggesting that perhaps there could not possibly be a God and surely the whole story of Jesus may be a fairy tale. I'm not sure that I believed what I was saying and was certainly nervous that my outspoken views would reap a dreadful revenge from on high, but I was at that age when the urge to question generally accepted views, the instinct to establish my individual identity and the natural inclination to be a big-headed, know-it-all kid, merged to make me an argumentative windbag. But, as I questioned how any reasonable God would allow all the disastrous happenings of the world such as flood, famine, pestilence (whatever that was) and war; if this particular God was that *all-seeing* and *all powerful*, how come the world was in such a state: if God created the world and everything in it, why did he create poisonous snakes, cancer and

Adolph Hitler. And, if He could make the lion lie down with the lamb, why doesn't he do that, instead of making lions eat any innocent lamb that happened to cross its path? As I expounded my theory, everything that I had ever learnt at Infant and Junior School, at Sunday School and now at Grammar School was being questioned and my fellow debaters had no answers to my questions except to repeat, "Because it says so in the Bible," which, to be frank, I did not see as a compelling argument. As we scrabbled out from the dark, damp shelter into the bright Spring sunshine, I had mixed feelings of confusion and fear. I wanted to believe that we were being cared for by a superior spirit and had been brought up to believe that the Holy Trinity was a fact (even though I had once prayed to the Father, the Son and the Holy Goat). Yet, through sheer obstinance, I had managed to place serious doubts in my own mind.

I pushed my rickety trolley with its sack of coke home, confused and brooding on how to resolve the conundrum.

At school the following week, the doubts were still foremost in my mind. I decided to seek guidance in the weekly Religious Instruction lessons with George Holroyd, known to all as Holy Joe. Holy Joe was a devoutly Christian man, who believed not only in the Holy Trinity as if they were real people living amongst us and with whom he could converse, but that the Christian God really did create the world with his own hands, molding it to shape, adding the sea, rivers, mountains, deserts and plains: making all the animals and constructing the first man, Adam, in his own image, although from what he was constructed was unclear. His wife Eve was made quite literally from one of Adam's ribs. Holy Joe had also written and published a book of bible stories which we used as our class textbook. This book, understandably considering Holy Joe's conviction, reported bible stories as historical facts. We were taught that a young lad called David killed a nine-foot giant with a pebble before cutting off his head. So much for peace on Earth and for forgiveness. We were taught that another young fellow called Daniel was thrown into a den of hungry lions and the wild hungry beasts refused to see him as dinner and let young Danny sit down with them in peace. We were taught that three more young lads with the strange names of Shadrach, Meshach and Abednego were tossed into a furnace and never suffered even the slightest of burns, although their restraining ropes burnt off completely. Holy Joe believed every word of these stories literally, *because it says so in the Bible*.

It was a few weeks before I could question the Bible stories in Religious Education lessons as I was determined to prepare my case thoroughly and wait for the right opportunity. I was genuinely confused and was seeking spiritual direction, not confrontation. That time came one fine Tuesday morning when Holy Joe re-introduced the story of Noah and the flood. We followed the tale from his textbook, with its black and white woodcut illustration showing a variety of animals queuing patiently to board the ark. They were tidily assembled in pairs as Noah carefully oversaw the boarding operation and his sons shepherded the passengers on board, looking as if they were checking the passports and tickets. I waited patiently and nervously before Holy Joe asked, as he always did, if there were any questions. My hand shot up almost of its own volition and I asked how Noah had stopped the lions and tigers eating the sheep and goats. The reply was the usual homily about God making them chummy for the trip. I was tempted to ask why then, did he not retain this atmosphere of friendship and wellbeing once they had left the ark, but thought that irony (or was this sarcasm?) would be lost on Holy Joe. As my follow-up question, I asked what the carnivores ate, and what did the herbivores eat and why did the birds not fly away and how did he know he'd collected all the animals and what about those he left behind and what about microscopic bugs? I was genuinely worried about my misgivings and seeking a logical and credible explanation, yet every answer Holy Joe gave was based on the dubious fact that God could do whatever he felt apt and the Bible says so. Frustrated as he was, I must give Holy Joe credit for trying to answer the impossible questions as honestly as his faith allowed, until my final question, for which I had studied and planned. "How Sir," I asked, "Did Noah mange to get all the animals to the middle east where, presumably, the ark was built? Kangaroos only came from Australia, which hadn't been discovered at that time, and lions only came from Africa and tigers from India and what about penguins and polar bears?"

Holy Joe smiled patiently but there was a distinct look of annoyance on his face as he leaned across my desk and stared me straight in the eye and very firmly told me that obviously the world was very different then and countries were in different places on the globe and that animals were different because God had designed the world to change and progress and why should I doubt what extremely intelligent theologians and historians had written two centuries before and was accepted as the truth by half the world's population and that it was a matter of faith without which mankind is nothing and I was just a silly trouble-maker trying to be clever and he was no longer going to waste his time on me and any more childish questions and I would be given a detention. I was firmly put in my place and was embarrassed at my naivety, thinking that perhaps Holy Joe and everyone else was right after all. The God-fearing re-conversion lasted for as long as my embarrassment and, as we moved on to our next lesson, I was more confused than ever. My perplexity was exacerbated when the girls in the class huddled into groups and would not look at me as we hurried along the corridors, alarmed, I suspected, that they would be turned to pillars of salt. The boys seemed that they simply did not want to be associated with me, fearing that they would be tarred with the same anti-God brush. The exception was Bernie of course, who simply said, "You're bloody stupid arguing with Holy Joe. It's just not that important" So much for resolving my uncertainty.

Our dad and I had become very chummy since the trip to Tottenham and had spent more time together. I had voluntarily accompanied him to his allotment and helped in the preparation of the plot for that spring's planting. This inevitably finished with a trip to the Southbrook Inn for a couple of pints for him and my usual crisps and pop. Our dad's violence seemed to have subsided after the dog and the Christmas Eve incidents and the whole household had slipped seamlessly into a harmonious version of the post-war nuclear family, with our Rae and I morphing into slightly older, working-class versions of Janet and John. I half expected our dad to exchange his roll-ups for a pipe and our mum to appear in a pretty frock and heels instead of a worn pinnie and slippers. Our dad also somehow managed to give our Rae and me a portable radio each. Our Rae was given a small transistor radio, whilst mine was a large Vidor portable valve radio, purchased second-hand from a bloke at work or down the pub. It was only really portable to a fit and strong weightlifter, otherwise it was an effort to move it across the room, but to me it was a wonderful gift and opened up a new world. It looked more like a small attaché case than a radio and was switched on by opening its lid. The two dials, one for tuning and one for volume control, were augmented by another switch to change the wavelength which meant that I could listen not only to the Light Programme but a crackling Radio Luxemburg. I began tuning in each evening in my bedroom as a catalyst to homework, imagining that pop music playing in the background would help my concentration. Predictably, listening to Keith Fordyce and Muriel Young presenting songs by Del Shannon, Eden Kane and the Everly Brothers had the opposite effect. I spent more time lying on my bed singing along with *Halfway to Paradise* than I did studying English clause analysis.

School slowly plodded on with nothing remarkable happening: a round of dreary lessons and homework, interspersed with the light relief of sport. I was selected for the school football team and had, by now, switched from my previously favoured outside right position to right back. In the 1960/61 season, whilst Tottenham Hotspur were creating their record of winning the double of the league and F.A. Cup, another revolution was taking place at Swindon's County Ground. Under manager Bert Head, Swindon Town had introduced several very young, local lads into their team and they were making waves in the old third division. Along with teenagers Mike Summerbee, Ernie Hunt, John Trollope and Cliff Jackson was a hard-tackling seventeen-year-old right back called Terry Wollen. He was not only a cultured and skilful defender, but was tall and handsome with a superb Tony Curtis quiff. He became my hero, hence my change in position. There were some similarities between us: we both played right full back and I combed my hair into a quiff, but there, I'm afraid, the resemblance ended. He was a truly magnificent footballer whereas I was never as good as I thought I was, or somehow convinced others that I was.

The term ended with the arrival of Easter and, thankfully, there were no school reports at that recess. I had been cruising for the whole term, despite my pledge to put in more effort. But no matter: I still had the Summer Term to rectify my idleness and pull up my socks before the exams, so I entered the Easter break with a sense of nervous relaxation.

For the first and possibly only time, our Rae and I spent a full week at Easter at our nana's bungalow in Chippenham. It was a strange week: a mix of boredom and bus trips around North Wiltshire interspersed by huge slices of fruit cake.

Mooching around the bungalow one dreary afternoon, I gazed idly in our nana's bookcase. One title leapt out at me, *Lady Chatterley's Lover*. The previous year there had been a long and well publicised court case when the book was the subject of a watershed obscenity trial against the publisher Penguin Books. Penguin won the case, the book found not to be obscene and it quickly sold 3 million copies to people who wanted to read something obscene. The book soon became notorious for its story of the physical relationship between a gamekeeper and his master's wife (his mistress in both ways), with its explicit descriptions of sex, and its use of previously unprintable words. The newspaper reports used titillating descriptions of the book, whilst carefully steering clear of repeating the actual text. Of course, all the boys at school would have given their eye-teeth for a copy and some lads even claimed to have read passages, but refused to divulge the contents, obviously because their claims had no foundation. But there it was, *Lady Chatterley's Lover* in our nana's bookcase. I surreptitiously removed the volume and carefully tidied the remaining books to disguise the void, before hiding my prize in readiness for perusal at my leisure. That night, when our Rae and I were tucked up in our make-shift Z-beds in the front room and our nana was in bed snoring loudly, I retrieved my stolen treasure and, by the light from a small table lamp, began to study the text with mounting excitement. I understood very little of what I considered to be a very boring story and there was not one juicy sex scene, not one detailed description of any sexual act that I recognised, and not one rude word anywhere to be found. After two hours of reading and re-reading the most promising passages, I gave up in my search for titillation with a great sense of disappointment before finally surrendering to the Sandman and drifting off to sleep. Only later did I find out that our nana's copy of *Lady Chatterley's Lover* was published years before the court case had taken place and had been subjected to ferocious censorship.

I returned to school with renewed vigour and a genuine determination to concentrate all my efforts on academia to fulfil the potential that all my teachers agreed I was throwing away. On the first Monday morning, I left for school earlier than was usual or necessary with the vowed intent of using the additional time at school beneficially. I would ensure that I was fully prepared for the day's lessons and cerebrally ready to begin my new scholastic endeavours. My resolve lasted about twenty minutes. I met up again with my old mate Bernie and immediately fell into the same amalgam of indolence and disruption as in previous terms. That said, educational life seemed relaxed and easy and our home life had become almost idyllic, with our dad's change of temperament. This utopia was never going to last of course, but the ferocity of the resumption of hostilities with our dad surprised us all.

In May 1961, just 16 years after the end of World War II, German Panzer tanks rolled through the streets of Carmarthenshire. Around six hundred troops were stationed in South Wales for training and their presence, not unnaturally, was not greeted with too much enthusiasm or joyous celebration by the local populace.

As the small army headed for the village of Castlemartin, protesters lined the streets to vent their anger at the presence of German troops in their community. An equal number came out to cheer them, possibly due to the economic boost the Cold War combat training would bring or possibly, our mum said, because many Welsh were secret Nazi sympathisers in the war and Wales was full of double agents. Our dad reiterated that we should never trust a Welshman anyway as their language sounds like German, so they must be connected.

Swindon's local ITV network was Harlech TV, which covered not only the West Country but South Wales, thus the invasion was covered extensively by the channel. As we sat and watched the protests directed at the young soldiers on the evening news, I innocently remarked that the objections were inappropriate as it was not these particular troops that were involved in the war, but their fathers. Our dad spun round in his fireside armchair shouting, "Bloody little Nazi," and came towards me. I was too quick however, and sensing immediate danger, my survival instinct cut in. I leapt from the settee and ran upstairs, slamming and locking my bedroom door behind me. Our dad was not far behind and shoulder-charged the door, bellowing insults about me being a bloody traitor as the door frame splintered and he crashed into my room. I threw myself onto the bed and curled up waiting for the onslaught. I didn't have to wait long as punches rained down on my head and body. I stayed curled up until the blows stopped and I heard the old man clumping downstairs still bawling about Nazis, traitors and bastards, until I heard the back-door slam. I carefully raised myself, aching from the punches, and peeked out of my bedroom window to see our dad, red-faced and angry, cycling down the road, obviously off to see a man about a dog. I slowly crept downstairs where our mum was still sitting watching television.

"You should've known better," she said with some justification, "make sure you're in bed before your dad gets home."

She was right of course. And our dad went into sulk mode and refused to speak to anyone in the family for the next two months.

As I muddled my way through the school term, I continued to concentrate most of my energy and resolve on the sports field. I again opted to train for athletics rather than being the target of the savagery of Bob Anderson's lethal bowling. Jogging around the running track with the occasional break to practice sprint starts or jump into a sand pit was far more to my liking. I often glanced over to the cricket square as I jogged, watching some uncoordinated fat kid who couldn't run, bravely ducking the speeding missiles from Anderson. I tried all athletic sports that year: sprinting was fine but any further than 220 yards and my legs would tie up so that I was overtaken by the slowcoaches who only selected athletics to hide from Anderson. I couldn't jump over the hurdles as they were far too high. Similarly, high jumping was a no-go, although my long jump was passable, but I could never get the lift needed and my attempts invariably ended with me inelegantly ploughing into the sand a couple of feet from take-off. The hop, step and jump simply confused me and I would mix my hop with my step and my jump with my hop, ending in a tangle before crashing into the sand pit. I could putt the shot well, but the javelin would simply land in the grass about three feet away. The discuss was only allowed under very strict supervision due to due to its obvious dangers, so I never attempted throwing this potentially fatal weapon. My athletics advancement was decided – my training would be restricted to sprinting and, as more and more refugees sought sanctuary from Anderson on the athletics track, this would save me from repatriation to the warzone of the cricket square. Luckily, I was a naturally fast sprinter and worked hard in games lessons, honing my starting technique and sharpening my speed, even returning to the track after school for additional training. My efforts were rewarded when I was selected to represent the school at the Swindon town sports in all three sprint events: the 100 yards, 220 yards and the 4 X 110 yards relay.

The town sports always took place on the large sports field at Ferndale school in Ferndale Road, and each of the dozen or so secondary schools in Swindon was represented. As entries were limited on the sports day, trials were held at the same venue in the preceding week to select those who would take part in the finals. I qualified in all three events and duly turned up on the day having walked the short distance from home, through the allotments and across the brook. All secondary schools were given the day off to attend the event and supporters lined the track, encouraging their schools' participants. The athletes were shepherded to a separate competitors' area where long benches were placed and each school, by accident or design, grouped together around the benches. The best part of the day for me was the sense of belonging to an elite. Dressed in our athletics kit with an official number safety-pinned to the front of our vests, we would carry out ungainly stretching exercises on the benches, replicated by watching the older boys and girls or gleaned from flickering black and white images of Roger Bannister, Chris Chattaway or Gordon Pirie on the television. Of my races, I remember nothing but do know that a few days later I was presented with a certificate presented only for first, second or third places, so I must have been placed in one or more event. Unusually, our dad turned up to watch the sports. The fact that the Southbrook Inn was next door to the athletics track may well have influenced his decision to attend.

My pride was short-lived as I took home my report card at the end of term. I had slumped from twelfth to twenty-ninth in the class and, in a class of twenty-nine pupils, I guessed that my parents would not be deem it a successful and triumphant term. The teachers' comments were again unhelpful, most of them indicating that my efforts were less than satisfactory but so obtuse as to be ineffective. For example, I received an A in English accompanied by the comment that I had achieved *A pleasing exam result. Term work indifferent.*

Every other comment was negative and included, *…could do better…does not do justice to his ability…attention and effort required…could improve…lacks self-control.* Holy Joe wrote that I was *only fair*, but I was sure that the comment was spiteful revenge because I had dared to question the existence of the Almighty. Even the Boss had taken time to scrawl *For a boy of his ability this report is unsatisfactory!* in red ink. I felt that there really was no need for the exclamation mark. Our mum read and signed the report without comment but, as usual, our dad never knew of its existence.

By the time that term had ended and the summer holidays commenced, our dad had started talking to us again and another sea-side holiday arranged to Hayle. Our annual trip did not take place until after our tennis championships had taken place in the street, to run in parallel with a similar event in Wimbledon. Nets were deemed too difficult to set up and would have had to be removed whenever the baker or vegetable lorry were on their rounds, so a piece of string was temporarily stretched across the road in its place, tied between the Paines's fence and ours. This also caused too many issues, not only in its removal for the occasional traffic but because it was sometimes impossible to judge whether the ball had passed over or under the string. A compromise was reached whereby the 'net' was simply a chalk mark joining two drains and the ball was considered in if it crossed the line. The championships could take anything from a couple of hours to a couple of days to complete, so new champions were crowned on a regular basis. Each combatant chose who he or she was to be at the start of each tournament. In the men's draw, the top British player of the day was Roger Taylor who was, quite frankly, rubbish, so most boys elected to be foreign players, perhaps Rod Laver, Neale Fraser or Manuel Santana. In Pound Lane, it was not unusual to find Rod Laver fighting to beat Rod Laver in the final.

The girls were luckier in their selection as Britain had three world class players in the tournament that year in Ann Haydon, Angela Mortimer and Christine Truman. Of course, I was disappointed that Christine spelt her name incorrectly, but she was still my personal favourite. Angela Mortimer was the prettier of the two English players and became a firm favourite amongst the girls, usually winning the tournament by beating herself in semi-final and final.

The championships continued as our family once again left for the long train journey to Hayle, sustained by fish-paste sandwiches and Camp coffee. The previous year had been very wet and, false teeth discovery apart, was a literal and figurative wash out. On our arrival at the same shed we had used the previous year, I was pleased to find that Dan Dan the lavatory man was still on duty and the camp shop still sold Hales's fruit pies and American comics. My fortnight would be bearable no matter what the weather. Our Rae was now fifteen years old and didn't want to be seen with her scruffy young brother in tow, so she disappeared on her own. That was fine by me, as the conversations about which songster was the more handsome, Adam Faith or Cliff Richard (it was definitely Cliff) were beginning to grate somewhat. From nowhere, our Rae reappeared - with a beautiful, gorgeous unknown companion. Her new friend was a girl of about the same age as our Rae and was from Dinas Powys in South Wales. She was delightfully named Bronwen or Blodwen or something similarly, sensuously Welsh. Despite our dad's warnings about the Welsh, I fell instantly and deeply in love but, having been cruelly shunned in the past, was wary of opening my heart to Bronwen. I would follow our Rae at a respectful distance whenever and wherever she went to meet her new Welsh friend, in the hope that she would notice me and perhaps speak. Nothing else mattered on that holiday. Even watching Dan Dan the lavatory man lost its previous appeal, taking a back seat in my daily schedule. I was almost too love-sick to enjoy my Hales's fruit pies and my mind drifted from Buffalo Bill wiping out the Apaches to dreams of holding hands and kissing. Alas, my love was unrequited. I even borrowed some of our dad's Brylcreme and washed every day, but to no avail.

Bronwen apart, I remember nothing of the holiday except that our dad renewed his acquaintance with an old boy in the local pub and they became drinking friends again for the fortnight. I was invited to the old boy's cottage one wet afternoon to see his budgie. I was less than enthralled by the invitation and would far rather have spent the time more productively, watching Bronwen or eating Hales's fruit pies, however I had little choice but to accept the invitation. In fact, the visit was possibly the highlight of the holiday for two reasons. Firstly, the budgie had broken its leg and the old boy had prepared a splint from two matchsticks and cotton thread, which I found fascinating. I spent a happy hour helping the budgie onto its perch to watch it balancing on its one good leg before falling to the floor of the cage in a flutter of feathers, before I helped the avian patient back to its perch again. Secondly, we were treated to a home-made Cornish Pasty which was above delicious, the old man having created the whole thing from scratch. He called the creation what I heard as a *Rudy Baker*, which fascinated me, wondering who Mr. or Mrs. Baker was and how he or she had managed to give her name to the culinary delight. It was some fifty years later, on holiday in America, when I saw that Americans called swede, a main ingredient of Cornish pasties, a rutabaga. Apart from our dad and me, and the old boy of course, I have never heard the pasty called a Rudy Baker or rutabaga since and will never understand how the old boy made this connection.

Chapter 5 – September to December 1961

- Britain applies for membership of the EEC
- Three people die and 35 are injured when a stand collapses during a Glasgow Rangers football match at Ibrox Park
- The first edition of *Private Eye*, the satirical magazine, is published in London
- Birth control pills become available on the National Health Service

It was customary for boys returning to school for the third year to forsake shorts and wear long grey trousers. This had a strange effect on the male population of Headlands Grammar School, in more ways than simply keeping knees warm. Not only did we feel far superior to the young children in the first and second years, but we spoke in a strange croaking, cracking fashion, one minute with a high alto squeak, followed by a deep baritone growl. It was almost as if our hormone rampage was initiated by having warm legs. Some of the bigger lads may have matured a year or so earlier, but this had gone unnoticed. When such a high percentage of the year had reached puberty almost overnight, however, most of us boys in the year became obsessed with our growing maturity. There was a plethora of pimples as our faces began breaking out in a variety of colourful spots, often resembling a volcanic mountain range in miniature, sometimes raising shining yellow peaks before blowing and leaving tender red craters, surrounded by drying lava. Other spots swelled and formed black-headed tors, the geological mix covering cheeks, chins, noses and foreheads. Between the blemishes, longer and thicker hair began to appear, particularly on our upper lips although, in my case, only if I inspected my face very carefully in the mirror. This was a welcome and exciting sign of manhood, and many pleasant hours were spent in front of mirrors, intently searching for the odd rogue hair to justify shaving. I borrowed an old razor that our dad had left rusting on the bathroom windowsill and fitted it with a new Gillette Blue Blade, before beginning my foray into adulthood by shaving the barely visible hair. This activity was impossible without slicing the tops off the spots creating a red, uncomfortable rash, onto which I rubbed a good lump of Germolene. It felt like death by a thousand stings, but our mum always said that stinging pains were caused by good germs fighting bad germs, so the treatment must have been appropriate. More serious cuts were dressed with small pieces of tissue ripped from the toilet roll, a first aid tip gleaned from our dad. This furthered my belief that, in the unlikely event that there was a god, He was not a sympathetic and imaginative creator. Whilst the lads' faces were becoming tarnished by spots, rashes, cuts and toilet paper, we were becoming strangely attracted to, but certainly not attractive to, the previously anonymous girls in our year. For the first time, we wanted to look appealing to the opposite sex, something that had never previously occurred to us, at the very time when we were developing an appearance which would have the reverse effect. I was particularly spotted and blotched, and I often 'accidentally' left the curative toilet paper in place to prove that I had shaved. Conversely the girls looked alluring. Whilst the odd pimple may have been in evidence, our female classmates began to appear decidedly pretty and curvy with previously unnoticed bodily lumps and bumps which were strangely enticing.

As the boys had graduated from shorts to long trousers, so the girls had graduated from gymslips to smart skirts and white blouses. And, if we looked carefully, it was obvious that beneath their uniforms was that peculiar piece of female underwear, the enigmatic brassiere, apparel that was to play a great part in my growing maturity over the following months and years. The girls' hair had lost its dull, simple look and taken on a luxuriant, chic and attractive style. Their faces, while still recognisable as the girls we had left just six weeks before, had transformed to a more adult and attractive shape and texture. They were less the plain and annoying Violet Elizabeth Bott from *Just William* and more the lovely Liz Frazer from *Carry on Regardless*.

We were allocated our new classes and I was not surprised to learn that I had been demoted once more, this time to take my place in the M (mediocre?) stream. I wasn't upset as I was joined by Bernie in the reshuffle. Our mum would have been easy to convince that the M stood for Middle School or Mid-way through or Mostly Good or something similar had she noticed, which she wouldn't and, anyway, she wouldn't find out until the end of term report. One extreme inconvenience, if not a disaster, was the fact that Shirley, my ever-reliable originator of cloned homework, would now be in a separate class. I had to decide whether to cultivate another friendship which would supersede the productive relationship with Shirley, or to resign myself to the fact that I would be responsible for my own homework and destiny. I immediately scanned the array of fresh pink and delicately-spotted girls, tearing my eyes away from their blossoming bosoms, to see if any likely candidate stood out. There was none that I knew well enough at this juncture to begin homework courting. And, with a particularly prominent pimple swelling and threatening to spread across my chin, I decided to postpone my selection for a more opportune occasion. Besides, staring at bosoms and trying to see the outline of a bra was far more satisfying. The form teacher was one A. C. Moon, who I remember mainly because his head was very moonlike. It was very pale, round and smooth, although rumours that he glowed at night were probably untrue. I quite liked Moonie and felt that we could build a satisfactory relationship for the following year.

I was again voted in as form captain and therefore decided not to apply for the arduous responsibility of straws monitor.

Bernie also missed the opportunity of reprising his role as milk monitor as he appeared to be staring at the girls' bosoms when the applications were requested.

Whether because the syllabus in the M stream was deliberately less onerous than the top two streams or whether I had simply matured into a more conscientious student, I know not, but I do know that I was beginning to enjoy the work. All my previous resolutions to improve had fallen by the wayside, but without consciously setting a target of improvement for this term, I seemed to have changed. Perhaps it was the hormones altering my outlook as well as my complexion, or perhaps not having someone to provide ready-made homework had an effect, but whatever the reason, my work improved dramatically. One special teacher can take some solace that years of trying to drum apparently useless information into adolescent brains was met with great success in my case. Merv Comrie was a genial old man with a unique and eccentric teaching style, which I found both interesting and stimulating. He was a bachelor and lived in the Goddards Hotel in Swindon's old town. Whether this was his permanent address or whether he only lodged there for the teaching week and moved to his permanent address at weekends, no-one seemed to know, but it was rumoured that he could be seen sipping a beer in the Hotel lounge most evenings to relax from the strain of imparting knowledge to groups of largely unresponsive teenagers. His forte was extolling joys of the English language and he made even the most banal of its idiosyncrasies appealing, offering rules and insights which live with me, and I guess many others, to this day. Perhaps my English is not faultless, but I still try to ensure that everything I write is grammatically perfect and punctuated correctly. For example, when writing an address, I ensure that it is punctuated in line with Merv's directives.

The Rt. Hon. A. F. Douglas-Home, K.T., Prime Minister,
10, Downing St.,
Westminster,
London.

He had a relaxed and pleasant way of encouraging good manners in the classroom. A pupil yawning – not an unusual occurrence – would be met with a firm, "Please cover the aperture." Hands always covered the aperture thenceforth.

Merv was also a stickler for correct verb usage. Should a pupil wish to go to the lavatory, he or she raised their hand and asked to go, but beware anyone who said, as I did, "Please Sir, can I go to the toilet?"

Merv would look quizzically over his half glasses and reply in his gentle drawl, "I trust that you CAN go to the toilet, Trueman. I think you mean, 'MAY I go to the toilet.'" Which, of course, I did.

Merv also disliked certain ugly or lazy words and encouraged his students to avoid them. He got annoyed at the use of the word *got* for example, recommending that we search for an alternative, so actually Merv *became* annoyed at the word *got*. The incorrect tense in other ugly words were equally irritating to him. The plea that, *I never done it, Sir* would make him more annoyed than the misdemeanour that the student was claiming he never done … or … did … or do. It's probably a blessing that Merv is no longer around to see the ugly, lazy usage of text messaging and e-mailing, so beloved of today's young people.

Merv was also the school careers master and was, therefore, allocated his own office. It was a cluttered room with the untidy appearance of a single gentleman's study, situated on the first floor at the top of one flight of stairs, from where Merv would keep an eye on the world through a fog of cigarette smoke. For some reason known only to Merv, he had a toy hippopotamus which stood guarding his desk. On occasions, he would send pupils to the office to collect marked homework from the previous lesson. "Wirdnam and Widdows," he would command, "Go to my office and collect the exercise books. And mind the hippo; he's not been fed today," before sitting back with his friendly smile to await the homework gatherers' return.

Along with Merv's English lessons, I was still finding Mathematics relatively straightforward. This term we were introduced to a new teacher who would become another of my more memorable tutors. His name was Mister Rackham and, although young, he fitted the standard teacher profile perfectly, with his brown sports jacket adorned with the compulsory leather elbow patches, a badge of office for the teaching profession. He also had an odd haircut (calling it a style would be an over-embellishment) which we knew as a semi-crew cut, and which stood up as if he had just been frightened in a bad horror movie. He also appeared to have difficulty in shaving and always had one sideburn an inch or so longer than the other. He was a decent fellow but was unused to unruly boys and he could not understand why we sometimes found logarithms, quadratic equations and isosceles triangles less than enthralling. Bernie and I were both cruising through his lessons and spent much of the time chatting quietly at the back of the class. Rackham was constantly glaring at us to encourage silence, but discipline, along with shaving, was not one of his strengths. Our discourtesy finally became too much for him and one day he snapped,

"Did you say something Trueman?"

"Not really, Sir," I replied with affected nonchalance.

"Perhaps you'd like to tell the whole class what you were saying."

"Not really, Sir."

"Come on Trueman, let us all here what words of wisdom you are imparting to Wirdnam."

"Well Sir, I was just wondering why you have one sideburn longer that the other," I blurted.

Rackham, was stopped in his tracks. He blushed as his hands involuntarily moved to sides of his face as he felt the offending whiskers.

"Do I?" he asked with a look of surprise and embarrassment, "Oh dear. Do I really?"

I was stunned, and he looked really upset, like vulnerable child. I instantly regretted my remark. "Yes Sir," I replied, "But they look alright. They're fine."

He smiled weakly and simply said, "Please don't talk in class, Trueman," before returning to an explanation of the peculiarities of a polynomial. Oddly, we were much less disruptive for a time after the incident, although I doubt that it was a deliberate disciplinary ploy on his part. Our improved behaviour did not last, however, and our next contretemps taught me a valuable and painful lesson. I was again slightly bored in class and Bernie and I were chatting away again, possibly about Swindon Town's fine run of form or, more likely, girls' bosoms when Rackham snapped again.

"Trueman and Wirdnam, will you stop talking and concentrate. You are disrupting the whole class and I am getting very annoyed," He roared, the first time that he had ever raised his voice. As he bellowed, I opened my desk and took out an old boiled sweet that I had been saving for a special occasion and popped it into my mouth.

An astonished Rackham bellowed, "Get out, get out Trueman."

Doing as instructed I arose and strolled casually out of the door, turned around and superciliously smiled at my classmates as the door closed. I bumped straight into the Boss in the corridor.

The Boss demanded to know why I had been thrown out of class. I could hardly explain that I was being an obnoxious prat, so I shrugged my shoulders and mumbled something about not being sure. I was ordered to remain where I was while the Boss entered the classroom. He reappeared a minute or so later and, with a fierce look, ordered me to follow him to his office. Once inside his inner sanctum, a chamber that few pupils had ever visited, he approached a rack on the wall supporting half a dozen canes. He removed each cane from the rack and tested its flexibility as I looked on with fear and trepidation. Having selected his weapon, he commanded me to bend over his desk. I did as I was instructed and heard the swish a fraction before the cane hit my backside with an agonising whack, making me wince with pain. Five more swishes were followed by five more devastating blows. The Boss had a powerful and practiced right arm but his aim was erratic, and each blow struck a slightly different area of my painful, throbbing rear.

I was released and returned to class by way of the toilets where I wiped away a few tears and dropped my trousers trying to look at the damage. I wasn't tall enough to see in the mirror. After drying my eyes and taking a few deep breaths, the pain began to subside and I felt elated, almost euphoric. I had just had the whacks from the Boss and survived. I was the first boy in our year to get the whacks which, until then, had been a thing of legend and mystery. For a short while, I was a minor celebrity in the school as the story spread although, much as I enjoyed the notoriety, I vowed that I would do everything possible to avoid a repeat occurrence. I never told my parents about the punishment, knowing that our mum's reaction would be that I must have deserved it and our dad would have given me another good hiding.

Now that we had finished with flowers, Biology was also taking an interesting turn and the seeds were being sown for a lifelong interest in natural history. Part of the syllabus was concerned with soil types and a very simple experiment fascinated me and it is one that I have repeated several times since, solely for my own pleasure. The class members were asked to bring into school a small sample of soil from their gardens, a request which we all duly followed without the faintest idea why. In the Biology laboratory, each sample was transferred to a tall glass beaker, and the vessel topped with water. The mix was shaken thoroughly and the beakers, with their muddy brown contents, were carefully labelled and put away until the next lesson. The following week, a miracle was observed. The beakers were retrieved, and the sludgy contents had transformed into striped layers of different hues at the bottom of the beakers. The heavier soil constituents such as sand had descended more quickly that the lighter elements, particularly humus, with fine soils (silt) layered between. This, in itself, was fascinating but a second miracle occurred. The beakers were grouped and the results overlaid on a map of the Swindon area. The map clearly showed similar soil structures mapped onto specific areas of the town, so that some areas had a sandy infertile soil, whilst some had a rich fertile soil, with variations in between. From there, we could analyse the best type of agriculture for any area, which was a real and practical use of an experiment. There was an inevitable fly in the magic ointment when I tried to tell our dad that he shouldn't grow roses in our back garden as the soil was not suitable, even though the colourful blooms were his pride and joy. He said that I should never trust science or scientists as they did not reflect the real world and perhaps the biology teacher should come and look at his William Lobb or Queen of Denmark.

Generally, I didn't like women teachers. In fact, I didn't really like any women especially since, as a young child, I was made to sit on the knees of large and formidable aunts with dead foxes around their necks. Lady teachers smelled of make-up and lavender scent and, it seemed to me, they lacked any sense of humour such that any remark in class to lighten the long dreary days was met with a stony-faced glare. Two women in particular made me feel very uncomfortable and, to be frank, would have put the fear of God into me had I not recently rejected Him. Miss Wildman was aptly named. She was a middle-aged spinster and the senior girls' games mistress, usually to be observed tramping around the school corridors or running around the netball courts in a track suit or short, pleated skirt, which barely covered a set of muscular thighs to rival those of Tottenham Hotspur's Dave Mackay. Brian Mason told us that his brother Bob said that she could crack walnuts between those thighs, but we never witnessed this feat. Miss Wildman also taught History, a subject for which I had little time and no enthusiasm. Any spark of interest I may have had for the incestual lives of mad kings and queens of merry England was soon to be extinguished forever. Her idea of a forty-minute History lesson was to write an essay on the blackboard and have the class copy it verbatim into their exercise books. It was quite possible, without effort, to copy the text word for word, without absorbing one single fact. I did just that. If time was running out towards the end of the period – I was a very neat and tidy but slow writer – I would simply miss out a paragraph here and there. After all, no-one would ever know.

Miss Jacobs was the second woman whom I feared. Although the Boss was obviously Commander-in-Chief of the whole faculty, He was ably assisted by his deputies: Miss Jacobs, who looked after the girls' interests and Mr. Maclean, who was the main disciplinarian to the boys. Miss Jacobs was a small lady who scurried around the school corridors scowling at all pupils but, it seemed to me, principally scowling at noisy pubescent boys. She seemed particularly friendly with Miss Wildman and I often wondered if they shared a home. Whether I was ever taught by the formidable harridan, I cannot remember, but I had recently watched Arsenic and Old Lace on television and had made a mental note never to visit the ladies at home unless it was essential, and then never to take up their offer of elderberry wine. Each morning, there were queues outside each of the Deputies' offices. The boys' queue consisted of those pupils involved in some sort of wrongdoing which could not be managed by the relevant subject or form teacher. The queue awaiting the attention of Miss Jacobs consisted almost exclusively, so we were reliably informed by older boys, of girls who were "on." Quite what being on was, or how girls achieved the state of being on was a mystery, but we gathered that it must be something to do with the mysteries of approaching womanhood, perhaps akin to our need to slice the tops from our spots with a razor. On being told that a girl had been seen queuing for an audience with Miss Jacobs so she must be on, we would nod sagely, adopting a men-of-the world air. We assumed that it was somehow connected to wearing a bra.

I was often sent to see MacLean for minor misdemeanours. My absent mindedness and lack of concentration meant that I often lost things – textbooks, exercise books, pens, sports equipment and, on one occasion, my daps – all of which had to be reported to MacLean. The buff coloured science exercise books were larger than standard and difficult to lose, but I lost mine, so off to MacLean I wandered. After explaining that it wasn't my fault and a big boy must have done it, I was issued with a new book and a bollocking. How it happened I have no idea, but at the next Chemistry lesson, I had two science books. One slightly tattered, containing the results of the term's experiments, the other pristine. Of course, I was forced to abandon the tatty old book and begin using my newly acquired virgin version. This was not a wise decision and one I would regret.

I had built up a reputation amongst my peers of being a good illustrator of the naked female form and, more recently, graphic interpretations of men and women indulging in strange and contorted sexual coupling. The odd positions achieved in this process were not engendered by any warped sexual deviance but simply by a vivid imagination and a complete lack of knowledge of how sexual contact actually took place. The pages remaining in my old science exercise book provided the perfect canvas to practise and show off my erotic art, so page after page was filled with contorted bodies, large male organs and strangely inaccurate, but well drawn, representations of the female genitalia. My art career was short lived as my friends and I soon moved forward with a new fad. I was summonsed to see Maclean one morning and duly trotted along, thinking that I may have been caught carrying out some minor act of delinquency, but was not particularly worried as I felt unusually guilt free. As my turn came to entered Maclean's office, he ordered me to close the door behind me. This sounded ominous. Maclean opened his desk drawer, withdrew my old science exercise book and laid it open on his desk with a picture of large-breasted lady contorted over a bizarrely proportioned man.

"What have you got to say for yourself, Trueman." Maclean growled.

"Er…That's not my book, Sir," I feebly replied.

"It has you name on the front. In your handwriting, Trueman."

"Oh."

"Do you know what it costs to supply this school with exercise books?"

"No, Sir."

"I costs a pretty penny, I can tell you, Trueman, and we cannot afford to have them wasted."

"No, Sir."

"The next time that you request a new exercise because one is lost, you will pay for it. Do you understand, boy?"

"Yes, Sir."

"Get out, Trueman."

And that was it. No mention of the pornographic cartoons. MacLean was only annoyed that I had used the book for something other than the purpose for which it was allocated. He never gave me back the book.

My performance in other lessons continued to be inconsistent, but sport was again my strong point especially as we returned to the rugby season. Although I had not grown to catch most other lads in size, I was gaining strength and my rugby was improving, particularly as I understood more about the tactics of the game. I was selected for the middle school house team, playing against boys a year older than I, but must have given a good account of myself as I was selected for all three games against the other houses. I was selected for the school under fourteens (third year) team, but was again disappointed that I was not elected captain. That prized role went to a big lad called Jack Lindsey who played in the forwards and a new games master, Pete Chinn, decided that the captain should be appointed from the pack. That seemed a weak reason to me, but I was in no position to argue.

Pete Chinn was a very tall, good-looking athlete who reputedly played rugby for the mighty Bath team, although this was never confirmed, and I cannot trace any Chinns ever playing at The Rec. I always had my doubts anyway, not only because he didn't pick me as captain, but because he shaved under his arms. When I told our dad about this, he warned me that I should never trust a man who shaved his arm pits – he must be a fairy. I never reported the comment to Mister Chinn.

Headlands were unbeaten for much of that season with big Jack running his pack with power and discipline under Chinn's coaching strategy and the half-backs and three-quarters generally standing around shivering in the rain. Our success was rudely and dramatically ended when we travelled to Bath to play Oldfield

School. Oldfield was an imposing pile with some brand new and some very old buildings standing in imposing grounds overlooking the River Avon. For reasons that escaped us, it was simply called Oldfield School, with no Grammar or Comprehensive appendage, which added to our sense of awe and reverence. The school also had Fatty Gough.

Fatty was a huge fellow, fourteen years old going on thirty. As we were still growing and in the process of producing spots and shaving off the odd rogue hair, Fatty must have weighed fifteen stone had real bristles on his chin. The two teams shared a changing room and, at first, we had assumed that he was the referee and made a mental note not to cross him. It was only when he donned the blue and yellow hooped shirt that our team realised that he was, in fact, one of our opposition. We also looked at his boots with absolute astonishment and some trepidation as they were at least a size twelve and fitted with steel studs, making my size five co-op football boots look like black ballet pumps. Our unbeaten record was lost, as Fatty trampled through our forwards time and time again with half of the pack hanging on to his shirt, shorts and socks to no avail. The backs simply stood and shivered, watching the mayhem, aware that we had been instructed not get involved in scrums, rucks and mauls. So much for the master plan of making the Jack Lindsey captain. I found it strangely satisfying as I stood and winced while another Headlandian forward was crushed underfoot. Now, if I'd been captain…I had no idea what I would have done, but I wasn't so it didn't matter.

At this time, Bomber continued to supervise the games and gymnastics lessons and decided to introduce the sport of basketball to those interested. This was introduced to replace the weekly gymnastics lesson, a period usually spent balancing on a narrow beam in the gymnasium while Bomber swung heavy ropes at our legs to make us proceed the length of the beam or crash to floor. I was keen to try the new sport as I found Bomber's game of walking the plank decidedly difficult and dangerous. I was, after, selected for the school football and rugby teams so was confident that this would be another string to my sporting bow or ball to my bag. Bomber explained the rudiments of the game before picking sides for basket practice. We lined up in our teams and took turns in trying to score a basket. I watched Wally bounce the ball twice whilst taking a few steps forward to score with ease. I watched Bob Anderson casually but majestically lob the ball into the net from some distance with unerring accuracy. I watched Bernie make a valiant effort to score, hitting the hoop. I watched my effort hit the wall several feet below the backboard. The exercise was repeated and my ball sailed several feet to the left. I carefully adjusted my aim to counter my previous errors in direction – a little higher, aim to the right – throw. I aimed higher, I aimed to the right,

but my attempt was another abject failure as the ball slipped from my grasp and fell a few feet from my feet. I tried to blame my lack of inches but being short was no excuse. I had seen the Harlem Globetrotters on television and they had a player who not much more than a dwarf and was a magnificent player. I tried again and again without success until Bomber ran out of patience and ordered me back on the death beam.

Whether my lack of prowess at basketball had annoyed Bomber more than was obvious, whether my reputation as a bit of a troublemaker had reached him or whether he just didn't like me, I don't know. Whatever the reason, I always found myself on the opposite side to Bomber in rugby games lessons and he seemed to target me as his personal nemesis. He usually split his time during the match in whichever part of the team he felt needed bolstering, such that he was rucking with the forwards one minute, feeding the scrum next like a stocky Dickie Jeeps the next and picking up the ball and running as a back on more rare occasions. I knew that he would head my way on his forays with the ball in hand, but always stood my ground and was usually aided by the fact that other brave lads were hanging on to him by the time that he reached me. One warm and pleasant Wednesday morning, we took our places and the weekly game began. Bomber was, as usual, playing on the opposition but had unusually taken up a position as centre from the beginning. At the first opportunity, he had to run with the ball, he ran at full sprint with his galloping style, knees high and the ball gripped tightly to his huge chest. Our players parted like the Sea of Galilee until it was just Bomber and me. As thundered towards me, the world seemed to slow down and he came forward in apparent slow motion. I moved to the right as came forward, a feint that forced him to his right, and as he came nearer, I took a couple of paces forward and launched my skinny frame at his legs, just managing to thump my shoulder into his big hairy thigh. For a moment, I felt that he may drag me behind him on his attack on our goal line, but then he was falling and down we went. The ground undeniably shook this time as we crashed to earth. We unwound ourselves from the tangle of arms and legs, and possibly from a non-sporting brainy kid who did not understand the implications of being crushed beneath a charging games master. The game was still going on around us as we scrambled to our feet and Bomber patted me on the back. "Well done, Trueman," he gasped before returning to his more favoured role of trampling fat kids in the scrum. I felt that I had earned his respect at last, but he still tried to knock me off the beam with a rope the next time that we were in the gym.

Both basketball and beam balancing were suspended as usual in December as we took our partners for dancing practice in readiness for the school soiree. Although the resentment and embarrassment about wasting valuable time as a Gay Gordon remained, there was something of an unspoken air of excitement amongst the lads as we formed and orderly line along one wall of the gymnasium. Following a brief demonstration of the dance by the Physical Education teaching team, just to remind us of how silly we were about to look, the boys were commanded to *Take your partners.*

I was a little nonplussed as Shirley had been my regular dancing partner for two years and she was not present. I was being commanded not only to speak to another girl I barely knew, but to hold her and dance with her. I had secretly always found Dawn Matthews very attractive. She was dark-haired and dark-eyed and very pretty and appeared to be growing a very shapely bosom. Along with my cohorts, I trudged across the gym – it didn't pay to look too keen – and I approached Dawn.

"Please may I have the pleasure of this dance?" I requested in the demanded manner but in a rather unenthusiastic tone, which I hoped sounded smooth, casual and cool. Dawn looked genuinely pleased and stood graciously as I took her hand and led her onto the dance floor. As we formally coupled, my left hand gently holding Dawn's right arm in the air and her left hand resting gently on my shoulder, I slipped my right hand lightly around her waist. I was immediately overwhelmed with a strange, warm and exceedingly pleasant glow which seemed to start somewhere near my groin area and spread outwards until my whole body was tingling with an all-encompassing feeling of bliss. I'm not sure that I heard the music start but suddenly we were floating across the dancefloor as one, our bodies intertwined and moving rhythmically in unison to the sounds of the Blue Danube. I was transformed into Gene Kelly and Dawn became my Debbie Reynolds, not an easy conversion in school uniform and white daps. In retrospect, I probably sweated, stumbled, shuffled and clumped around the improvised ballroom with Dawn gamely trying to follow my uncoordinated lead, whilst trying to avoid being trampled by my clumsy feet. But it felt so good that I didn't care.

The music finished, we stopped and thanked each other and returned to our respective sides of the hall.

I was still floating when Bomber and Miss Wildman demonstrated the Valeta before asking us to take our partners. In my euphoric state, I was slow to cross the room and, as I made a beeline for Dawn, I was usurped by Pete Griffin. One of my closest mates whom I had known since I was five: someone I cycled to school with daily: a fellow football fan with whom I had often played down the brook, a boy whose dad was a mate of my dad. And he'd stolen my girl. To make it worse, Dawn seemed extremely happy about the situation, smiling almost gleefully as she and Pete gripped each other with much more purpose than she and I had managed minutes before. I looked around to see if there was another Debbie or Doris or Ginger available, but in my desperation, could only head for the small group of girls who tended to be the wallflowers and asked one if I could have the pleasure. She was a short, stocky lass called Ruth and sported wild black hair and a black moustache, somewhat thicker than the one I was trying to cultivate. Yet she was friendly and, to my surprise, I quite liked her company as we twirled our ungainly way around the floor.

On returning to the boys' side of the hall, Tony Duggan was explaining that, if we held our hands just a little higher than the prescribed waist position, it was just possible to feel the girl's bra. This erotic discovery was confirmed by Pete Griffin which I found most distasteful but thought that I would certainly try the tactic during the next dance, a ladies' excuse-me. As the girls rushed across the hall towards their target, I was somewhat miffed to find that Dawn headed for Pete, but I consoled myself with the fact that I could begin my brassiere treasure hunt with Ruth. Tony and Pete were correct. I started with my hand on Ruth's waist as prescribed, then moved it surreptitiously upwards, over a large roll of fat and there, almost but not quite concealed by a deep crease, I felt the edge of the mysterious garment. As Ruth was shorter than I, it was easy to leave my hand there without being obvious, so I did. Again, the flush of pleasure began to spread over me, perhaps not as intense as the first instance but, nevertheless, a warm and pleasant sensation. Perhaps, I thought, there was more to this cissy dancing lark than I had at first imagined.

It's probably overstating the point to say that the 1961 Christmas soiree was to change my life forever, but it certainly had an impact that I shall not forget. As we shuffled into the assembly hall there was very little interaction between the sexes, except when required to dance. One girl in particular I had always found attractive and, on rare the opportunities that we had spoken, I found her pleasant and friendly. This changed to one of absolute adoration, verging on worship and a feeling that would continue until we left school some two and a half years later. I have been in love just twice in my seventy-odd years. The strongest and deepest is with my wife of over forty years, but the first was with Jane Parr.

Jane was best friends with Julie Wheeler with whom Tony Duggan had formed an unlikely relationship. He was tall, gangly, uncoordinated and ill-disciplined: she was small, well-behaved and matronly, but they became the best of friends. It was not unnatural therefore that Jane and I were matched. We had other similarities in that we were both from council house backgrounds and were keen sportspersons. She was the best athlete amongst the girls in our year and played both hockey and netball for the school. We were both relatively small but athletic, bright but belligerent and both had a self-destructive, rebellious streak. But that night we were Bill and Bobbie Irvine as we tripped the light fantastic on our way to the World Ball room championship. We even went as far as eating sandwiches and drinking our squash together at half time. I enjoyed the contact so much that I forgot all about feeling for the presence of a bra. I felt guilty about ignoring Ruth, especially as she appeared to have shaved for the evening, but obviously not guilty enough to leave Jane.

When the soiree ended, we were heading back through the school to the changing rooms to replace our daps with outdoor shoes, when Tony noticed the Boss's trademark homburg hat on a stand outside of his office. He quickly snatched the hat and threw it to me, whereupon I thumped it heavily, turning it inside out and left it looking a little worse for wear. I returned it to Tony who hung it back on its peg. Nothing was ever said anything about the incident.

Tony informed me that we would be walking home together with Julie and Jane, which was a little surprising as the girls lived in Stratton, the opposite direction to Pinehurst, but nevertheless the opportunity to cling on to more magic moments with my new love was not to be missed. As we strolled towards Jane's house, I was aware that this was my first real venture into romance, and I was unsure how to play it. We were both in school uniform which didn't help the romantic ambiance of the stroll and I wondered whether or not I should risk holding her hand, but Tony wasn't holding Julie's hand, so I guessed that this was inappropriate. The fact that I was pushing my bicycle would also have made the exercise difficult. When we reached Jane's house, we chatted for a minute or two, said goodnight and she went in whilst I rode back to meet Tony. Not the romantic end to an evening that I had imagined but taking her gently into my arms and delivering a long and lingering kiss in the moonlight would have been difficult whilst supporting my bike.

My school report that year was the best that I had ever received. I finished fourth overall in the class, with top three finishes in English, Biology and Physics and a slightly disappointing but satisfactory sixth place in Maths. The comments from teachers were, on the whole, positive with comments including *Good work, Good result* and Good progress. Mr Moon's summary stated that I should gain *Good G.C.E. results.* For grammar school schoolteachers, there seemed a distinct lack of an imaginative use of adjectives. I'm sure that Merv Comrie didn't approve of this lazy English, however *good* was good enough for me and I felt that perhaps I had now found my level and turned the corner towards academic success.

Our mum was up at the crack of a dismal, dreary dawn on Christmas day to begin boiling the vegetables to a soggy death. The capon was placed in the oven with the Paxo stuffing and homemade mince pies. A Christmas pudding was boiling on top of the stove, adding to the smog engulfing not just the kitchen but the whole house. And still our mum was working, making more pastry for sausage rolls. Our nana was sitting in the dining room, smoking her third fag of the morning with her third cup of tea. The dining room had been upgraded from the year before as our mum had purchased a new dining set in the sale at Normans's furniture store. We were now the proud owners of a matching dining table, six chairs and sideboard. Our mum had taken her new sideboard very seriously and decided that we should enhance the look with a tray of beverages for the season. She had acquired not only the usual bottles of Sauterne and our nana's sherry, but a bottle of cheap port, half a bottle of Bells whiskey, half a bottle of Gordons gin, half a dozen bottles of Babycham, a bottle of Warninks advocaat, six half-pint bottles of Usher's light ale and two large bottles of Corona lemonade. The bottles were arranged haphazardly alongside a mixture of odd glasses and festooned with paper chains. Our mum kept wandering into the dining room and admiring her creation with a satisfied smile.

It was eleven o'clock and dinner was scheduled for two o'clock. I stumbled downstairs, yawning and asked, "What's our dad on this year?"

"Earlies," our mum replied, "Be home at two."

"Where's our Rae?"

"Gone out. Be home at two."

"I'm going out. See you later"

"Be home at two."

Our dad arrived home from the pub at half past two having completed his early shift at twelve and visited two pubs or clubs on the way home. He was soaked as the early morning cloud had developed into a constant drizzle. As he took off his overcoat and shook off the rain in the kitchen, our mum asked, "What's it like out?"

Our dad looked at her with a mixture of incredulity and pity. "Wet enough for walking stick," he replied. "Where's that dinner?"

After Christmas dinner, our mum, our nana and our Rae cleared away and washed up and I sat in the dining room with our dad hoping for another war story. But our dad was too busy attacking the drinks on the sideboard after his lunchtime beers and bottle of Sauterne. He took a half-pint bottle of light ale and poured the contents carefully into a pint glass, previously borrowed from Ferndale Working Mens' Club. After studying the glass carefully, he added a little port, some whiskey and a dash of gin, leaving perhaps half an inch in the glass. He eyed the concoction carefully. "Looks a bit lethal," he said and filled the half inch with lemonade before taking a decent swig. "Medicine," he announced and took his creation into the sitting room. There was to be no war story that day.

I didn't have to wait long. On Boxing day after another early shift another trip to see a man about a dog and another glass of medicine, our dad sat quietly for a while, his mind transported back twenty years.

"We was in a farm'ouse in Italy," He began. "Winter of 1944. Lots of our tanks 'ad broken down and we run out of replacements, so some of us was told to join an infantry regiment. Run out of tanks? What a way to run a war! And me. In the infantry. I'd spent the last five years sat in a tank operating a radio, and they puts me in the blessed infantry. Anyway, we was just wandering about wherever we was told to go and for some reason we crossed a river. We 'ad to wade across and it so cold our trousers was stiff with ice when we got out. Jerry was only a couple of hundred yards away, so we bunkered down in this little Eyetie farm 'ouse. We set up our one machine gun and radio and just sat waitin' for orders. Then someone went for look round the house and shouts out, Jack, look what I found in the cellar, so I goes down the stairs and it was full of barrels of wine. Eyetie vino. Well, we naturally thinks we can't waste it and sets about drinkin' it. Now…," he paused and took a long swig from his glass, "It might be because we wasn't used to Eyetie vino, or it might be because it wasn't ripe, but we all got bad bellies. Real bad runs. And the only latrines was across the yard, so that's where we had to go. If we was Jerry or Eyetie we'd have gone in the corner of the 'ouse, but we was British, and we knew what was right." Another long swig. "As we sprinted across the yard, Jerry was shooting at us, but never 'it one of us. Not one. That is, til old Blackie went across and 'e was a bit cocky with the vino, so 'e stood in the yard and give them Jerries two fingers." our dad paused, and looked me in the eye, "And do you know what them bloody Jerries did?" I shook my head. "They shot one of 'is bloody fingers clean off. The only thing they 'it all day, Clean off."

Our dad chuckled as he rose unsteadily and tottered across the room towards the stairs and bed.

Chapter 6 – January - August 1962

- James Hanratty is hanged at Bedford Prison for the A6 murder
- The last trolleybuses run in London
- Brazil beats Czechoslovakia 3–1 to win the 1962 FIFA World Cup.
- Death of Marilyn Monroe

For some unknown reason, Mr. Moon did not appear as our form master at the start of the new term and was replaced by someone called P. J. Smith. This master or mistress did not take us for any lessons and I have no idea who he or she was or what he or she looked like. Another nondescript, faceless teacher who, as far as I remember, had no impact on my education of future, unlike Mister Perkins.

Perkins had taken over from the man in the brown coat as our handicrafts master, which essentially meant that he taught boys the finer points of woodwork and metalwork. His previous role was as a tutor at Swindon Technical College, where he taught craft apprentices, mainly from the British Rail factory but also from other engineering firms in the town, a fact that he was never reticent in reminding us. My disaster of the kitchen stool was way behind me at this point, as was my attempt at creating a less ambitious pencil box. The box would have been fine had I been able to measure accurately and master the intricacies of dovetail joints and been able to use a saw and a chisel accurately. Suffice it to say, that a whole term's effort to make a small wooden container for writing implements, using the skills passed on to me by a man in a brown coat and honed as near to perfection as was possible, ended up as kindling for the fire at home.

In the woodwork classroom were two lathes. I had seen older boys creating magnificent *objets d'art* from a simple lump of wood and felt that, with my artistic flair, this would be my route to carpentry success. I chose an ashtray stand as my project for the term and studied the plans, which showed a shapely and elegant pedestal secured on a neatly turned, circular base and topped with another neatly turned wooden plate into which an ashtray could be fitted. I knew that our mum would be thrilled as it was thought very *de rigueur* in better class households to display a special stand to hold the overflowing, stinking ash and butts from discarded cigarettes. Our mum who sat in the corner of the sitting room permanently engulfed in a tobacco smog from her Tipped Woodbines, used a large rectangular ash tray emblazoned with *Ind-Coop Superdraught* that our dad considered very stylish and had managed to smuggle out of North Swindon Club under his coat as a Christmas present for our mum. This receptacle was always balanced on the mantle shelf above the fire and I reasoned that an elegant stand with a real glass ash tray would make a sophisticated and stylish addition to our home.

Operating the lathe was not as simple as it had appeared in the hands of more skilled operators, but under very strict supervision from Mister Perkins, I made a passable job of turning a three-foot length of two by two into a shaped stand. It's resemblance to that shown on the plans was more by coincidence than design, but nevertheless the final object just about passed Perkins critical examination. The floor stand and the top were also turned, again under close supervision, but were so similar that I confused the two and was unsure which was which but, not to be deterred by mere details, the three component parts were rubbed down, stained and assembled to make a recognisable, if slightly unsteady piece of furniture. I spotted a glass ashtray in the hardware shop opposite the school, on sale for the princely sum of one and sixpence, so I saved some weeks' sweet money and bought the final accompaniment to my chic work of contemporary furniture. I proudly took my masterpiece home and presented it with glowing pride to our mum. She seemed less than enthralled but brightened up when she realised that it was our dad's birthday in June and the stand would make an ideal present for him. Our dad seemed very pleased when he was presented with the present and I imagined that the stand would become a loved and treasured family heirloom, returned to me in the future to pass down to my children and my children's children. It was several weeks later that I was somewhat miffed to see the one and sixpenny glass ashtray in his shed holding a dozen or so large, rusty nails, undoubtedly purloined from British Rail, and the elegant pedestal planted in the back garden propping up a rose bush. The base and top were never seen again, possibly adding to our meagre store of winter fuel.

The more academic lessons were becoming something of a chore but, confident in my new-found ability, I was able to relax somewhat and returned to my cavalier attitude towards learning facts and completing homework. English and Maths were again my strengths. These subjects were relatively straightforward and needed little effort in terms of actual study, but History, Geography, French and the sciences began to become an even greater intrusion into my valuable time. I again represented the school at football and had an enjoyable season, building on my reputation as a vigorous and enthusiastic, if not over-skilful, full back. I was picked to represent Rockley house middle school in football, one of only a handful of players from the third year selected. I was somewhat irked when my Rockley team played Barbury House and Wally, was not only selected to play for the opposition but was the best player by some degree on the pitch, and scored a goal whilst playing at half-back.

I was also becoming a little worried that my bodily hair growth had stalled and many of the other boys were now sporting thin tufts of pubic and underarm hair whilst showing distinct signs of genuine shaving rashes. Tony Duggan even claimed that he needed to shave every single week. To prevent embarrassment, I hatched a simple plan to increase my own bodily hair growth. It was a well-known fact amongst us that if hair was shaved, it grew back thicker, longer and stronger, so I began to shave regularly: not just my spotty chin but under my arms and around the pubic area. I soon became aware that my skills with a Gillette Blue bladed safety razor needed honing as I regularly had minor cuts to my pubis and armpits, which I struggled to conceal from my peers when changing for games lessons. I was, however, encouraged to see similar nicks appearing on several of my classmates. I found it particularly galling during a Maths lesson with Rackham when he commented that Wally appeared to need a shave, unless he was growing sideburns. And Rackham knew a thing or two about sideburns.

We looked forward to a break from academia when it was announced that the whole of the third and fourth years were to attend a music concert in the school hall. We were warned that we must be on our best behaviour and set an exemplary example of good behaviour as pupils from nearby secondary modern schools had been invited to attend the recital. On the day, we were seated in the hall awaiting the other school pupils to arrive, when Green Gilbert reminded us that we were to sit up straight, be silent and attentive to show our guests how well-behaved and well-mannered we were. The visitors arrived and began filing into the hall and I was excited to see that Pinehurst Secondary Modern pupils were on the guest list and were seated across the aisle from me. I turned and nodded at familiar faces, including Johnny Paines who lived opposite in Pound Lane, Mick Kell, Les Hedges and Spuddy Taylor, all of whom also played in the league-winning Pinehurst Junior football team and with whom I had maintained contact. For the first time since passing the eleven plus and attending grammar school, I felt proud of my achievements. The Headlands Grammar School pupils sat resplendent in smart, matching uniforms in the school's impressive main hall and I could imagine the feelings of awe that the secondary modern kids were feeling as they trooped into the arena. At this time, there was no uniform for Pinehurst and the boys were in mufti, most of them clean and smart but not a proper uniform with matching blazers and ties. And there were those kids from the poorer areas of Pinehurst who looked dirty, scruffy ragamuffins. All was still and quiet as we sat upright with backs straight, proudly trying to give the impression of a casual coolness as the guests stared at the imposing surroundings, I hoped in admiration, but the following proceedings suggested otherwise.

The musicians entered from the back of the hall to make their way to the stage. There was a faint titter which, as the musicians advanced became louder until it was a cacophony of giggles and belly laughs from our guests. The leading musician marched down the aisle with his violin tucked nonchalantly under his arm. He had long hair which, although not exactly flowing behind him, certainly swayed somewhat as he moved. He was not just needing a haircut but had what we considered to be long, girls' hair. This was 1962 when short back and sides were compulsory for all males, where no man's hair was ever over his ears or reached his collar, years before the Beatles were criticised because their tidy mop-head styles were considered a danger to national identity and security. And this man's hair reached his shoulders. As the violinist approached the stage and the laughing grew infectiously louder, he stopped, turned around to face his future audience and bellowed, "I am not a comedian. I am a musician," before continuing on his way to the stage. When I told our dad about the incident later he said, "Never trust a man 'oo don't keep 'is 'air cut. 'E's probably a foreigner or a nancy-boy."

The recital screeched on with the long-haired violinist affecting alien poses, his eyes closed as if in a transcendental trance and his right arm scraping at the strings as it pumped up and down like, well, like a fiddler's elbow. The sound was not that disagreeable but very, very boring. To a generation weaned on Anne Shelton, raised on Ruby Murray and pubescent with Helen Shapiro, scraping a bow across strings with no singing was a monotonous dirge, no matter how good the tune. My colleagues and I sat patiently waiting for it to end, whilst the Pinehurst contingent twitched, fiddled and scratched in boredom. Towards the scheduled end of the recital, there was a further distraction behind us and we naturally turned to see what was causing the disturbance. There was a distinct tinkling sound and we noticed a trickle of liquid running between the seats. The trickle became a small stream as it ran with more purpose towards the front of the hall and it was apparent that someone was peeing from his seat. A red-faced Pinehurst teacher rushed forwards and grabbed one particularly scruffy individual by the arm and dragged him out of the hall, pee now flowing freely down his leg. The music was forced to a premature end and we filed out of the hall, carefully avoiding wet patches, as Tarz and his crew rushed in with buckets of sand and a mop. We were ecstatic. From an inauspicious beginning, it had developed into a truly noteworthy morning. We had avoided real lessons, laughed at a weird man with long hair and a violin whilst someone from my previous school had pissed themselves in the assembly hall. A day to remember indeed.

Lessons were now becoming more and more complex and my interest was becoming less and less intense. I simply could not be bothered. If I had discovered an interesting new hobby or was preoccupied with a girlfriend or, indeed preoccupied with anything else, it would have been understandable, but I simply did not want to do anything. I began staying in bed later, couldn't be bothered to go out with mates, abandoned Saturday morning swimming at the baths and generally slumped into a period of malaise. Even though our mum gave me a plentiful ration of Phensic, my malady persisted.

Micky Millmore's mum had a medical book which was a great source of delight at the time. It contained diagrams and descriptions of both female and male internal organs and offered advice on how to overcome any illness known to man at that time, although I was surprised that Phensic did not appear as a cure anywhere in the book. There was a chapter about masturbation which stated that any boy guilty of the heinous sin of *self-pollution* could expect any number of illnesses:

Disturbances of the stomach and digestion, loss of appetite or ravenous hunger, vomiting, nausea, weakening of the organs of breathing, coughing, hoarseness, paralysis, weakening of the organ of generation to the point of impotence, lack of libido, back pain, disorders of the eye and ear, total diminution of bodily powers, paleness, thinness, pimples on the face, decline of intellectual powers, loss of memory, attacks of rage, madness, idiocy, epilepsy, fever and finally suicide.

Although we laughed at the description, I became seriously worried. I had just discovered the pleasures of the flesh, albeit a solitary pleasure, and was genuinely worried that this was the cause of my disorder. I could not claim all the illnesses described, but certainly was experiencing a decline in intellectual powers, and I was pale and thin with an abundance of pimples. I felt weak, had occasional digestive problems and did get angry at times. After careful consideration, however, I decided that I need not give up my carnal inclinations altogether, but I would just reduce the regularity until the latter stages of *madness, idiocy, epilepsy, fever* became obvious, when I would review the situation, before contemplating suicide.

My lethargy continued with only occasional flashes of stimulation to spark my interest. One such incident was in Biology where we were to study the digestive and sexual organs of the rabbit. I was already something of a specialist in this area, having watched our own rabbits mate and give birth, so was confident that I need not concentrate too hard in class. Presumably, the objective was to understand the internal workings of all mammals but, if this was explained, I never understood it and assumed that the rabbit was unique in its physical make up. I was most surprised when we were presented with diagrams of the insides of male and female rabbits and realised that they were similar, if not almost identical, to the diagrams of male and female humans in Micky Millmore's mum's book. The men rabbit had testicles and a penis: the lady rabbit had a vagina and a vulva and even a clitoris, although quite what the latter was, and what purpose it served, was never fully explained. I was truly worried that my intent to reduce my sessions of masturbation would be difficult, if not impossible, while we were encouraged to study such sexually explicit and stimulating pictures at school.

I was beginning to form closer friendships based around school colleagues rather than those from Pound Lane. Micky Millmore was my best Pound Lane mate for years and he, too, had passed the eleven plus and went to Headlands Grammar School, but he was in the year above me and our friendship became more distant. Our dad was always suspicious of Micky Millmore's dad. After all, Mister Millmore had not fought in the war and, despite his sons' protestations that he was needed to build spitfires at Swindon's Vickers Armstrong works, our dad remained unconvinced. The Millmores were also the only family in the street to own a car and had recently purchased a Volkswagen Beetle, a German car. Our dad never trusted Mister Millmore at all after that betrayal of everything that he had fought for. War record and appeasement apart, the main weakness in Mister Millmore's character, according to our dad, was that he did not drink. Our dad had never seen him in any club or pub that he frequented, and that included every drinking establishment within a three-mile radius of the street. As our dad always said, "Never trust a man what don't drink. E's frightened of giving 'imself away."

I was becoming friendlier with Tony Duggan. He had lived in the next street but one to me in Tintown all his life, but I had never met him before we attended Headlands together. Tony was of Irish Roman Catholic stock and therefore attended Saint Joseph's Catholic junior school, somewhere so far away that he had to travel back and forth by bus. Now, however, we found that we had much in common, most of our shared interests being undesirable traits such as rebelliousness, disruptiveness, laziness and an apparent penchant for masturbation. The one thing that intrigued me about Tony and his Roman Candle friends was what happened during morning assemblies. The Catholics were not allowed into assembly as either their religion would not allow it or ours would not accept them for some mysterious motive. Tony and I talked about possible reasons for the severance and, through our understanding of History and Religious Instruction lessons, augmented by information gleaned from our parents, decided that it was because Henry the Eighth wanted six wives and the Pope and his Catholics were against polygamy, so he was disqualified from the Catholics and built his own churches, establishing the Church of England. But then carried on believing in the same God and religious practices in precisely the same way as the Catholics, except that he had multiple wives and services were not carried out in Latin, all of which seemed a bit of a waste of time and effort. We reasoned that if you were king, why not just stop conversing in foreign, have one wife and as many mistresses as you required without telling anyone and continue your life as before. From what our dad told me, that's what the royal family have always done and still do today and that's just one of the reasons they should never be trusted.

During assembly, Tony and his fellow Catholics were banished to a first-floor classroom which overlooked the main hall. This secret sanctum had a hatch, which allowed the papists to watch the general proceedings once the religious service was finished. When I questioned Tony about what took place in the little room with the hatch, he would always say that nothing much happened there, that the attendees just waited until they could open the hatch to hear general school minutiae like sports results, special events and disciplinary issues. I was intrigued as to why people who believed in the same god and generally worshipped in the same way with basically the same prayers and hymns should be separated...and I wasn't wearing the *nothing much happening* explanation. I guessed that there was a mysterious and secretive ritual carried out each morning, including candles, Latin incantations, incense and, perhaps, voodoo dolls secreted there for the occasion: or perhaps they worshipped a false idol concealed in a locked cupboard. After all, why was the room locked at all times, other than assembly? Despite my pestering, Tony was giving away no information and we finally agreed that my curiosity would not be satisfied unless I could go inside and see for myself. We hatched a plan that the following morning, I would slip away from my classmates as we filed to the main hall, creep up the stairs to the exclusive sanctuary and Tony would surreptitiously sneak me in. I trusted Tony when he assured me that human sacrifice was not one of the Roman Catholic practices.

The plan worked to perfection as I managed to evade everyone and arrived at the door to the special room at the same time as Tony. He opened the door and I slipped inside. It looked just like any other classroom, smaller perhaps, but just a classroom with a few desks and chairs. Two or three students were working at desks, rushing through the previous night's homework at a guess, and a few more were sitting around looking bored. Tony signalled for me to sit behind an empty desk and he sat on the desk hiding me from general view, but no-one seemed interested or worried that an infidel had been cleverly smuggled into the inner sanctum. There was not a candle or false idol in sight. After a few minutes, I could hear the muffled sounds of other bored pupils in the main hall singing *Morning Has Broken* or some such dreary mantra, before the stifled sound of *The Lord's Prayer* and other unidentifiable mumblings. The tedious drone of the school song filtered into the room from below, signalling the imminent cessation of the service:

> *Home of our youth, our future's mould,*
> *Our Guide when young, our love when old.*
> *Give us the strength to face the fight,*
> *To shun the wrong, uphold the right.*
> *Floreat semper schola.*

…and so on for another three or verses. The Catholic students ignored the racket and continued with their belated homework or chatted quietly. I wondered why they were allowed to ignore the school song, even though it was somewhat pretentious and rather boring.

On cue, the small hatch was opened and we could hear the Boss updating the assembly with the usual list of do's and don'ts in front of his captive, though certainly not captivated, audience. As the main hall attendees filed back to their classrooms, we too were released into the outside world. "I told you nothing much happened," Tony said as we made our way back to our respective classrooms. I wondered why Henry the Eighth had bothered with all the hassle, just to stop a minority listening to tedious prayers and singing monotonous hymns.

The winter term came and went and, after Easter, blurred into the Summer term with a dreary round of lessons where I worked harder at avoiding work than working at work. The only bright spots were games and Saturday morning football representing the school, as the year dragged slowly on. Tony, Bernie, Pete Griffin and I unconsciously became aligned with a small but troublesome group of disillusioned and rebellious mutineers, undermining authority both in and out of school. We often found ourselves wandering away from our home turf to spend time with Julie, Jane and their girlfriends. The relationships remained friendly and platonic as we visited each other's homes and spent time doing as little as possible but grumble about lessons, teachers, uniforms, parents, siblings, rules and regulations, evening curfews, pocket money, the weather, television and a variety of other subjects. We could not understand why no-one listened to us and why life was so unjust and unsatisfactory. The girls seemed to find the platonic nature of our relationships acceptable and agreeable, whilst the lads (I assume that the others felt as I did) found it irritating, awkward and frustrating. The underlying reason that I, and presumably the other boys, spent so much time with the opposite sex was really the vain hope that, one day in the not too distant future, the girls would allow us to become much closer and hopefully accept a French kiss or even feel them up.

After Easter, the switch came from football to cricket and athletics, which split up our small gang of mutineers. Pete and Bernie were keen cricketers with Pete being a fast, wild and lethal bowler and, although not a patch on Bob Anderson, was equally as feared as he took great delight in thundering the ball directly and dangerously at the batsman. Bernie was a competent if awkward and unorthodox batsmen and Tony, as one of the most unsporting and physically uncoordinated boys in this or any other school, kept himself busy standing on the boundary watching the athletics girls in training, fairly certain that he would never have cause to become an active participant in the game.

Once again, I selected to join the athletics squad and the athletes were often left to their own devices, the games teachers safe in the knowledge that we could come to little harm running around a track. As the sexes were mixed for athletics, I was taking a healthy interest in training with some of the girls, although concentration was not easy. Both Dawn and Jane, the two girls who had been the objects of my desire for the last year or so since the pains of puberty had ignited my hormones, were also excellent athletes and we would often train together.

As sprinters, we practised acceleration-oriented drills of ten yards or so. The routines included perfecting the *Take your marks* and *Get set* positions, before reacting to the starter's *Go!* and accelerating through to maximum velocity before slowing gradually and returning to the start line looking intense and earnest. Three or four times in each session we would race over 100 yards. The full races were handicapped, with the boys starting a pace or two behind the girls, the handicaps designed to achieve a blanket finish. What was not taken into consideration is that we boys were positioned a couple of yards behind nubile young females. At the *Take your marks* command their bottoms would sway provocatively as they settled into position. At *Get set*, the buttocks would raise suggestively, the blue serge knickers stretched across the perfect, rounded cheeks, the muscles on the back of their calves and thighs taut and quivering with anticipation, awaiting the command to start. The position was held for a few seconds before the shout of *Go!* would urge us into explosive action. The mesmerising sight of the firmly strained rumps was often too much for some boys and it was not unusual to miss the *Go!* altogether or to sprint uncomfortably with the predictable physical reaction to the eroticism before us. It made the exercise very hard. I volunteered for extra sprint training after school when I discovered that Dawn and Jane were regularly staying to perfect their technique.

The training did some good and, again, I was selected for the school athletics team, but I have no recollection of what happened or how I or the team performed. I guess that the sight of all those baggy, navy-blue knickers with my imagination of what lay beneath had somehow affected my memory.

I expected a poor result at the end of the term and, indeed, the end of my third year. I was not disappointed or was very disappointed depending on one's viewpoint. I did little or no revision for the examinations, preferring to moon around following the girls like a dog sensing a bitch on heat, or simply avoiding work for no specific reason. I wasn't particularly worried about this as I had been relegated twice before and had survived, so had nothing to worry about. Nothing that is, until we were given a letter from the anonymous Form Master Mister Smith informing our parents that there was to be an open evening where progress, or lack of it, could be discussed with a whole range of our teachers. There was no way to avoid what I thought was the inevitable by failing to deliver the message. Our mum could not avoid meeting Derek Windslow's mum or Brian Mason's mum in the street or at the Co-op, and they were bound to mention it. The letter also had a tear-off slip which was to be countersigned by parent and returned to school to verify that it had reached its intended recipient. I was stuffed, so bowed to the inevitable and passed the letter to our mum. She signed and the slip it was duly returned as I waited in dread for the expected parental visit and subsequent bollocking. When the evening came, I was optimistic that all would be well when Z-Cars was on the television and, true to form, our mum decided to stay home as she didn't want to miss an episode of her favourite programme. She considered it more important than checking on my progress at school. "Besides," she explained, "your dad's on ten til six and I've got to get his tea and his sandwiches ready. And besides it's the teachers' job to teach you so we can't do anything about it."

Our dad added that we should, "Never trust a teacher anyway. They're only in it for the long 'olidays."

As expected, my report was disappointing, with the usual comments about making little effort and making more effort with the inevitable *Could do better*. I was saved from complete humiliation by Merv Comrie who wrote that *Very good effort and progress have been made*, and by the Boss who had appended the comment, *On the whole a good report* in red ink, which it clearly was not. I am sure that the Boss had confused my report with a more conscientious pupil. I imagine some hardworking but disillusioned student received a report with the Boss's comments meant for me and saying something like, *A lazy, mouthy little sod who needs a rocket up his arse*.

I was satisfied that the comments were generally fair except in games where Pete Chinn said that my work was satisfactory but could be very good, even though I had represented the school at both football and athletics and attended additional training sessions. Perhaps he meant that I would be better in training if I tried sprinting without an erection. The other negative comment which I considered unfair was in Biology. I stated that I had produced *A disappointing result*, where I fear that my diagram of the reproductive organs of a female rabbit may well have been confused with those of a human female in Micky Millmore's mum's medical book.

I studied the report with a mix of shame and embarrassment but a small glow of optimism and vowed that my days as class clown and rebel were over. Next term I would become a hard-working, model student.

This was about the time that I began smoking. Encouraged by Tony Duggan, I felt that holding a cigarette in my mouth and occasionally blowing out a plume of foul-smelling smoke made me look cool and mature and would add to my reputation as a rebel. Our mum also said that a smoke would help me concentrate on my schoolwork, so gave me the odd cigarette to improve my academic performance. She was convinced that smoking was an aid to good health and often related the story that, when pregnant with our Rae, her doctor had encouraged her to smoke help her general wellbeing. Our Rae was now sixteen and had left school. She was working in a local factory, Plessey Semiconductors, making something electrical or electronic on the assembly line and earning good money. As recommended by our mum, she had also taken up smoking as an aid to her general health and happiness and became my back-up when cigarettes were hard to come by. Tobacco was an important part of our family lives. If I couldn't pinch a fag from our mum's packet of Tipped Woodbines or some tobacco from our dad's Old Holborne tin, then I would sit sad-faced looking at our Rae when she lit up, knowing that anyone who would face the wrath of our dad over a lost puppy would cave in to a pathetic sigh and give me a smoke.

We were sharing a cigarette one evening, our Rae to relax after a hard day on the production line and me to relax before abandoning an attempt at homework, when there was a knock at the front door. No family in Pound Lane ever used the front door. The back doors were left permanently unlocked and led directly into the kitchen where most family interaction took place. Our Rae looked casually out of the sitting room window, almost leapt backwards and cried, "Oh no. He's here," before running upstairs and telling me to "Open the door, then." It must have been serious for our Rae to run.

I didn't understand what was going on but answered the door anyway. As the door opened, I was faced by an extraordinary, if not extra-terrestrial vision. Standing in the doorway was a Dan Dare figure with a shining black crash helmet, a black leather jacket and big black boots. I was taken aback and wondered whether I should slam the door and notify the authorities (whatever that meant), but then noticed a big black and chrome motorbike standing in the road, where there should have been a spaceship.

"Hello," Dan Dare said pleasantly, "Is Rae in?"
I thought that a strange question, but answered honestly, "Yes."

There was an embarrassing hiatus. "Can I see her then?" the spaceman asked, breaking the silence. Before I could answer, "Not at the moment, she's run away," our Rae came tripping down the stairs and pushed me out of the way. In double quick time, she had changed into her best top, best slacks and managed to apply make-up.

Our Rae had gone all girly, flitting around and smiling or giggling. The alien creature removed his helmet and took off his jacket to reveal a human being, a young man with a dark Tony Curtis quiff who introduced himself as "Mac", although to me, he morphed from Dan Dare to Ricky Nelson. Our Rae led him into the front room where they sat on the settee together, which I thought strange as there was a spare chair, and I was disappointed to find that my cigarette had burnt out in the large Devenish Ales ash tray. Mac must have sensed my upset and pulled out a pack of cigarettes and offered me one. A Rothmans King Size. I liked Mac.

Having got the bug for travel, our mum and dad had surprisingly selected that year's summer holiday destination as Great Yarmouth in Norfolk, way across the country on the east coast. We were joined by our dad's brother, Uncle George and his new wife, Auntie Annie. East Anglia was Annie's old stamping ground and she had sold it to George who sold it to our dad and as the jewel of the east. The trip again involved an epic train journey broken by a hurried commute on the underground from Paddington to Liverpool Street to catch the train north-east. There was a further change at Norwich before arriving at our destination. Apart from the train journey, just a few incidents of that holiday are crystal clear in my mind most of the fortnight has been banished to the black hole somewhere in the back of my mind. I don't remember where we stayed, where we ate or what we did. I do remember that our Rae's sole topic of conversation was Mac.

"Mac doesn't have cereal for breakfast: he just has toast."

"Mac's not having a holiday this year. He's saving up for a car."

"Mac's an electrician. Almost qualified"

"Mac's passed his driving test on a motorbike *and* in a car."

"Mac's favourite tv programmes are The Avengers and Ghost Squad."

"Mac's mum and dad own their own house in Upper Stratton."

"Mac only smokes king size."

To be fair, I was now getting fed up with Mac and I'd only met him once.

On the second Wednesday of the holiday, our dad, Uncle George and I went by train to Norwich to see the Canaries play at home to Cardiff City. It was a tedious scoreless draw, but I enjoyed the fact that I was watching second division football and our dad had bought seats, which was a new and exciting departure from standing in the rain on the County Ground's Stratton Bank. Of the game, apart from being pretty dour, I remember nothing.

I do remember that I was becoming more aware of clothes and fashion and was unhappy that I had to wear an old but serviceable pair of bumpers. My discontent was increased when the rubber sole began to fall away from the main shoe and our mum stuck the two parts together with an Elastoplast, which detracted somewhat from my developing image as a cool and trendy fashionista.

For reasons unknown, I was walking with our mum on the sea front day and we had a photograph taken by a beach photographer. I held a small woolly monkey in a small woolly outfit, provided by the photographer. When the picture was developed and we showed it to our dad he said, "What an ugly little animal...and so's that monkey he's holding." Building self-confidence in others was not one of our dad's strong points.

We were returning to wherever we were staying from an outing to a pub one evening, when Uncle George stopped and stared out across the grey briny. He called me over to his side, put his hand on my shoulder and said, "Over 'ere, we're English and proud of it. Over there," he pointed out to sea, "all wogs, wops and dagos. Never trust any of 'em."

Our dad nodded in agreement and tapped the side of his nose, so I knew that it must be true.

Chapter 7 – September - December 1962

- Ford launches the Cortina, a family saloon costing £573
- First broadcast of *University Challenge*, with Bamber Gascoigne as quizmaster
- Severe smog in London causes numerous deaths
- Golden Wonder introduce flavoured crisps (cheese & onion) to the UK market

A couple of weeks before the start of the new term, our dad was mending yet another puncture on my new second-hand bike which I had been using for the last three years. It was somewhat different from the shining blue and chrome vehicle of 1959 as three hard years of use had taken their toll. I had repainted the frame a few months earlier in camouflage pattern of green and brown and added RAF roundels, the target shaped markings seen on warplanes and saved from a failed attempt to construct an Airfix Lancaster bomber. The mudguards were long since disposed of, as was the tattered saddle bag. The Sturmey-Archer 3 speed was decidedly dodgy, needing expert nursing to change gear while the wheels were showing signs of rusting despite my efforts with silver paint. The brakes had offered only token resistance for months and the chain was slack and rusty. The saddle and handlebars had been raised to maximum height and had taken on a strange twist whereby the handlebars pointed to the left and the saddle to the right. Apart from that, the bike was fine.

Our dad stepped back from his labours, his hands covered in rust and dirty oil, his face red from vigorous but futile use of the hand-pump. He looked at me and nodded. "You needs a new bike," he stated as if he had just discovered some long-lost secret of the universe. "We'll go to town on Saturday." With that, he dropped the bike and picked his own from the shed, checking his watch in panic: he was on two til ten and had to get to the club to see a man about a dog by midday.

On Saturday morning, our dad and I started the walk to buy my new bicycle with our mum's warning words ringing in our ears. "Don't go getting anything fancy. Just a solid bike that's going to last."

There were several bicycle retailers in town, but we made a detour via Gorse Hill and the County Ground to Mitchell's Cycles, a family-run firm that looked as if it would concentrate on dandy-horses or penny-farthings. I was a little disappointed as Halfords always had a display of sleek and shining racing machines in the shop window, whereas Mr. Mitchell had a display of old second-hand boneshakers in front of his rather untidy-looking shop. "I knows old Mitchell," our dad explained, " 'E'll do us a good deal."

"Bugger!" I thought, "Here comes another second-hand wreck."

As we walked into the shop, I was struck dumb with amazement as I gazed at a row of beautiful shining cycles, any one of which was beyond my dreams. A cornucopia of colours, chrome and cables shining like a hoard of the most glorious of treasures. I stood, mouth open and stared in rapt silence at the magnificent machines.

A man in a brown overall looked up from fiddling with a bicycle. "Hello Jack. 'Ow is it?" he asked.

"Poor but 'appy, Mitch," came the inevitable reply, "Poor but 'appy."

Within minutes my new bike was selected and a deal done. "Special price for you Jack. I'm not making any money on this one," Mitch explained. Our dad smiled and quietly mumbled, "Bollocks Mitch," so that I wouldn't hear him, but I did.

The bicycle was beautiful. A shining black racing bike with thin, white-walled racing tyres, drop handlebars and a five speed Derailleur gear shift. Now I understood what love really was. I also understood that, at £19/19/11, this was more than two week's housekeeping for our mum and probably a month's beer and fags for our dad. I thought deeply about the sacrifice they had made, but quickly decided that I should not involve myself with their financial matters. I had a shining, brand-new racing bike. With drop handlebars. And Derailleur gears.

I cycled slowly alongside our dad as we made our way home, wishing that I could just be alone and free to pedal off as fast as possible, but I felt that that would be a little insensitive, so stayed by our dad's side. Until, that is, we reached Gorse Hill club, where our dad turned in sharply saying that he had to see a man about a dog and left me alone. The bike moved sweetly and quickly with little effort as I pedalled easily home. After rapidly showing my acquisition to a clearly unimpressed mother, I was soon out again to present my new bike to Derek Windslow, Geoff Peaple and Pete Griffin. They had been riding similar machines for the last couple of years, but seemed reasonably impressed, even though they laughed at my malapropism when I pointed out that it had Disraeli gears, the cycle met with their approval: it is impossible to explain just how important their approval was.

I was looking forward to returning to school. I had lost touch with some of my friends over the holiday, especially Bernie and Julie and Jane, and was happily anticipating renewing our relationships: and showing off my new racing bike with drop handlebars and Derailleur gears.

On the first day at school, the whole of the fourth year were told to remain in the hall after assembly, where we were to be addressed by the Boss. As he stood centre stage with his thumbs hooked into his gown, he reviewed the gathered throng sitting before him, as we wondered just what misdemeanours we were to be admonished over. But the Boss seemed in light-hearted mood, almost genial. He explained that we were about to start a great adventure in education as our two-year syllabus was carefully designed to enable us to pass our General Certificate of Education Ordinary Level examinations to take place in the summer of 1964. The two years, he stressed, may seem like a long time now, but it would pass quickly and every minute must be used constructively with the aim of passing the examinations. All that had passed in junior school and the previous three years at grammar school, whilst not irrelevant, were merely a basis for the intense study to come. Previous achievements would count for nothing and the whole of our future lives, our success and happiness, would depend on the next two years. As he finished his rousing speech, I couldn't help thinking that all the worry and stress I had suffered for the previous three years were unnecessary. I thought that, had I had understood that only the next two years were essential to my education, I could have ignored completely what went on in the classroom, asked Shirley to complete all my homework and saved myself a great deal of trauma.

Two new pupils arrived in the M class and were absorbed into my circle of mates. Neither were exactly conscientious or particularly hardworking and fitted in well with the largely rebellious crew. The first was a lad new to the school and the area, whose parents had recently moved to Swindon from somewhere primitive, cold and mysterious called Yorkshire, in the frozen north of the country. Richard Clewlow was to become a close friend over the next two years and, indeed, for several years afterwards. Alan Widdows had been asked to repeat the fourth year after missing most of the previous term through illness and was, anyway, only a little older than the rest of the year, the youngest in his previous year. Alan owned a cat and affectionately spoke of *our moggie*. He was therefore known throughout the school as Moggie Widdows. He was also adored by the girls in the fourth year. He was slightly older than his contemporaries, was quiet and moody like James Dean according to Dawn, was very smart, making even school uniform look cool, had a prominent Tony Curtis quiff but, above all, was said to look like Cliff Richard. I failed to see how a combination of James Dean, Tony Curtis and Cliff Richard could possibly be an advantage, but then, I wasn't a fourteen-year-old, besotted schoolgirl. Pete Griffin took an instant dislike to Moggie, his antipathy not unconnected Dawn's obvious infatuation with him.

We waited in our new classroom for the new form teacher to arrive, creating the usual hubbub and generally being noisy for noise' sake, when the door opened and in walked Mr. A J Rackham. My nemesis was to be our form master and, more to the point, was still sporting ill-matched sideboards. I groaned audibly, much to the amusement of my peers and confident that Rackham would take no action. We gradually quietened down and faced our new leader. But this seemed a new Rackham. It was almost as if he had resolved to be tougher and more disciplinarian than in previous years as he addressed the class.

"You will be seated in alphabetical order of surnames," he announced. "Girls to my right, boys to my left, beginning at the front of the class and filling the first row, then the next row beginning again from the front." For a while confusion reigned but we eventually managed to seat ourselves in the required positions and to Rackham's satisfaction. Except that at the back of the class, furthest away from the teacher's desk were Trueman, Widdows and Wirdnam. As we were settling into our ideal new positions, the new boy Clewlow was shown in and, rather than go through the whole disruptive alphabetic process again, was directed by Rackham to sit in the next available desk. That was at the back of the class in the empty seat in front of to Wirdnam.

Clewlow, or Clewey fitted in almost immediately, whether because he was "easily led" and unfortunate enough to be seated amongst the naughty boys or because he was naturally gifted at causing disruption, I cannot say. What I can say is that he spent more time passing crude notes, flicking elastic bands and making animal noises with us than he did concentrating on learning the rules of trigonometry. Rackham's whining voice delivering the order, "Widdows, Wirdnam, Clewlow and Trueman, come and see me at the end of the lesson," became a regular feature of maths lessons during that term.

Smoking was an important part of our social life and was aided and abetted by the fact that I was soon to be richer than I imagined possible. Tony Duggan had started work on Saturday mornings delivering groceries and as general help in a small, old-fashioned grocer's shop in Fleet Street in Swindon's Town centre. He approached me one day and said that the butcher in the shop next door was looking for a new delivery boy and, if I was interested in the position, he would introduce me on the following Saturday. I was enthusiastic about the opportunity to earn money and duly met Tony early on the Saturday morning. Off we cycled into town for my introduction to the butcher and I was I told that I could start immediately. My role was simple. I was to clean the large walk-in refrigerator, clean the mincer, sort the eggs, run errands and deliver orders. I began with the fridge and scraped congealed blood from the floor before scrubbing and wiping down the walls, all with a rather mucky cloth and a bucket of warm, soapy water. I couldn't help thinking that I was spreading more germs and potential infections than I was preventing but apart from the cold, the job was easy. I was then shown how to dismantle the meat mincer and clean the individual parts in the sink before re-assembly. The machinery stank. Saturday morning was its only clean of the week, so that any scraps of meat stuck in the blades from Saturday afternoon onwards were not removed until the following week. The customers must have had strong stomachs in those days of austerity, as we never heard any reports of

Page 162

digestion problems or food poisoning as a result of consuming rotting meat from our butcher's mincer.

Sorting the eggs was a light relief from cleaning. Several dozen eggs were delivered on Friday mornings and put to one side awaiting my sorting skills. The butcher explained that all eggs were priced at half a crown a dozen, but many customers were willing to pay more for brown eggs in the mistaken belief that they were somehow healthier. I was to separate the brown eggs which were then displayed at two and nine a dozen, thus securing an extra threepence a dozen straight into the butcher's pocket. As he told me with a wink, "Eggs? They're all the same. They all comes out of a chicken's ass."

My final role was to make deliveries. I began by using the old delivery cycle owned by the shop. This pre-war machine was the type with a large basket on the front and a metal advertising sign attached to the main body, proclaiming "Hargreaves Butchers, purveyors of fine meats". It never mentioned rotten mince or over-priced eggs. The bike was barely usable with a rusty chain, tyres with little air or tread and a fixed wheel with no gears. Not only was it leg-numbing hard work to ride but, having finished my deliveries, I was to return the vehicle to the shop before picking up my own racing bike, with drop handlebars and Derailleur gears. I soon came to an agreement with the butcher that I could deliver the meat using my own bike, after which there was no need to return to the shop. A decision which would later cause me possibly the greatest embarrassment of my butchery career.

My deliveries were very few, usually just three or four each week, and all could be accommodated on my ride home from work. The final delivery was to a short, stocky and elderly lady in Harcourt Road, a terrace of small two up, two down houses behind Ferndale Road, near the rail works. I had been warned by Brian Mason's older brother Mick that it was not uncommon for lonely housewives to answer the door to virile young delivery workers, whilst wearing sexy lingerie, in an attempt at seduction. Despite the warning, I was not prepared for the first time that the short, stocky and elderly lady answered her door in large knee-length flannel bloomers and a woolly vest. If this was a seduction attempt, the sight of me turning and jumping her gate before cycling rapidly up Harcourt Road would have been a disappointment, although I am more inclined to believe that she was just an absent-minded old girl who had simply forgotten to get properly dressed. I really hoped.

I left work on that first morning feeling rich beyond compare with Frank Sinatra playing loudly inside my head, *Who wants to be a millionaire, I do*. I had a ten bob note and two huge shining half crowns in my pocket and, for someone who was used to scraping by with perhaps a shilling pocket money plus whatever I could beg, steal or extort, fifteen bob was a fortune. The fortune would enable me to become independent of my parents for football and speedway admission, snacks and, most importantly, cigarettes.

I was to regret the abandonment of the delivery bike some months later when I was asked to cycle to another branch of Hargreaves butchers near the County Ground to collect a bag of pigs' hearts. The delivery bike was by now almost completely seized having been left outside for months and the tyres were completely flat. There was nothing for it but to use my racer. I duly rode to the sister store and collected the plastic bag of hearts, preparing for my return to town, more than somewhat disappointed that my saddlebag was too small to accommodate the precious cargo. But this was no problem to an experienced cyclist and delivery boy, so I simply held the bag on the handlebars with my right hand and set off on my hazardous journey, steering and braking with my left. After all, it was only about a ten-minute ride along Manchester Road. I was unable to change gear but was still able to cycle slowly and steadily in third gear, somewhat unsteadily but reasonably safely. All was well until I became a little over-confident and increased speed as I approached town and the junction with Corporation Street. I was following a double-decker which, inconsiderately in my opinion, stopped suddenly at a bus stop. Panic took over as I realised that did not have time to brake. I could not overtake in the busy road, so swerved onto the pavement, hitting the kerb with shuddering bump. The plastic bag had been sitting awkwardly on the bolt which secured the handlebars and the impact caused it to split at that point. Quite what happened next, I do not fully recall but I ended up sitting on the pavement, one leg cocked awkwardly over the bike with blood splashed over me and the cycle, with animal offal rolling over the pavement through dark red, congealing blood. I do vividly recall several screams and one woman almost fainting before I gingerly pulled myself to feet, rounded up the escaping hearts and carried on my journey by foot pushing my bike, with many hearts stuffed in my saddle bag and the rest carefully secured in what was left of the plastic bag. Back at the shop I quickly unloaded my cargo and swilled the hearts under the tap before laying them on the tray provided for display in the shop window.

Tony and I cycled home together after work, detouring to stop at the scene of my accident and more than somewhat pleased and amused to see shoppers staring at the apparent carnage, doubting that the victim had survived the accident, "…What with all that blood and with his heart lying in the gutter," declared one mourning onlooker.

Very much to my chagrin, back at school all pupils were to decide between games and art for the new term. This was a difficult choice as I loved sport but had decided that I would pursue a career as a commercial artist, even though I had little idea what a commercial artist did. It infuriated me that I was forced to choose between the only two subjects in which I really excelled, but my love of sport won the day and my career as the English

Norman Rockwell was abandoned before it began. Bomber Brown had disappeared from the school by this time and been replaced by an equally tough new games master called Mister Stephenson, with whom I seemed to get on very well…initially. He was another rugby-loving master, built like a brick shithouse, who seemed to enjoy trampling small boys in mud during games lessons. As newly elected Middle School Representative for Rockley House and mainstay of the school rugby team, he and I looked to be on the same wavelength and enjoyed a friendly but respectful relationship. My new career as a butcher's assistant was somewhat compromised by sport. I was again selected for the school rugby team which played many of its games on Saturday mornings. When there was a clash between work and rugby, I would drag myself out of bed at the unearthly hour of seven thirty and cycle madly to the shop by eight in order to complete my cleaning and egg-sorting by nine-thirty, before cycling furiously to school for the match. Tony was co-opted into making my deliveries for a small contribution to his cigarette fund. We never spoke about the old lady's vest and pants, so I assume that he was equally as traumatised by the experience.

Early in the term, I was called in to see Stephenson along with Wally, Ian Melrose and Bob Anderson. We were informed that, on the following Wednesday evening, trials were being held at Pinehurst School for the Swindon Boys football team and we had been selected to attend. When we arrived, there were about forty lads present from different schools in Swindon and we changed into an assortment of football shirts before taking our positions for the trial match. I renewed acquaintances with my old teammates from Pinehurst Junior School, all of whom had been selected for the trial. Each lad was given one half of around thirty minutes to stake his claim, so I had just half an hour or so to display my skills. I felt confident that I would pass the trial and soon be proudly wearing the red of my beloved Swindon Town at the County

Ground. The game started and I stood poised and ready to demonstrate tough and uncompromising tackling, followed by immaculate passing of the ball to initiate an attack. The ball never came near the winger I was marking or, indeed, within fifty yards of me. Much as I ran, took up good defensive positions, covered other defenders, broke forward and called for the ball, only once did I get within ten yards of the ball. As the opposition attacked, I took up a defensive position to check any run by the left winger: for the first time, the ball was hammered in our direction and I moved in stylishly to intercept the pass, like a young Terry Wollen. I moved towards the ball with the intention of calmly bringing it under control before executing a glorious delivery to my own right winger. The ball hit my knee and bounced over my head allowing the winger to run on and score. I worried what would Terry Wollen would have thought.

At the end of the session, the teacher pointed at various players with the instruction to return the following week. I was not called. As no names were recorded, I was tempted to turn up the following week anyway, but never had the courage to carry out the subterfuge. Of course, Wally was selected and played the season as captain of Swindon Boys alongside Spuddy Taylor, Dave Corbett, Les Hedges and his cousin Leroy, all of whom were my teammates at Junior school. Much to my shame, I explained to friends and family that I had been selected, but the matches always took place on Saturday mornings, which would clash with my new-found work as butcher's boy and playing rugby for the school which, I lied, were more important to me.

In the meantime, I consoled myself with the fact that rugby was really my forte in sport anyway and I continued to represent the school team with the oval ball. I have vague flashes of games but clearly remember the annual trampling by Fatty Gough at Oldfield School. I was embarrassed during one game when the referee, a games master from the opposing school, stopped the game after I had made a tackle, called both teams together and said that everyone should take note of my ability and try to copy what I did. I swelled with pride until I spent the remaining half hour dropping the ball, tripping over, miskicking and generally looking like an incompetent novice. It was fair justice for my arrogance.

Headlands school ran a film society where, six time each year, the main hall became a cinema and films were shown, projected from the Catholics' clandestine room. The films shown tended to be classics from the early 1950's and generally emphasised good over evil with a moral message such that our young minds were improved and not corrupted. We watched *The Ten Commandments, The Bridge on the River Kwai* and *Around the World in Eighty Days* but *From Here to Eternity* and *Peyton Pla*ce were considered too risqué for our corruptible young minds and never shown. As with all extra-curricular activities, the rules of entry stated that we were to wear school uniform and change into daps before entering the school hall.

One very cold Saturday evening in December, the Film Society was showing *High Noon*, where the handsome Gary Cooper bravely faced a ruthless gang of killers alone, the townspeople turning their backs on him. It was a controversial film with political overtones caused by Carl Foreman, who wrote the screenplay, being accused of *Communist propaganda and influence* in the Hollywood motion picture industry. The controversy passed us by completely: to us, it was just an exciting cowboy film with the unbelievably beautiful Grace Kelly, the unbelievably evil Lee Van Cleef, lots of guns and shooting and killing baddies. It was made more exciting for me by the fact that Jane Parr had agreed to come with me. Of course, I never had the courage to ask her out but, as Tony was going with her friend Julie, they had arranged the foursome. I stopped short of offering to pay Jane's sixpence entrance fee. Tony was with Julie as usual and, after a detour for a quick fag, we took our seats as a foursome in the back row, as was traditional for couples. It crossed my mind as we sat in the dark that perhaps I should put my arm around her and even try to kiss her, but I was sure that any close physical contact would result in being thrown out by an over-zealous prefect.

The four of us left the school gates after the show and immediately lit up another of Tony's Senior Service each, especially purchased with my meat delivery money, to impress the ladies. We walked home together as far as Julie's house where we left Tony, and Jane and I carried on alone. Near Jane's House in Meadowcroft was a small, dark lane between gardens and we strolled nonchalantly into the lane before stopping for a good night kiss. It was not easy as Jane stood with her back to the hedge bordering the lane, which was on a slight rise, making her several inches taller than me. After some adjustment to our position, we managed to assume a position where we were pretty well level and started to kiss. This was my first real snog and I knew that I should do something with my tongue, but was uncertain what, and was surprised when Jane's tongue found its way into my mouth. I thought the experience a little odd but strangely pleasant before deciding to go for broke and moving my hand over her school mac in the general area of her left breast. Jane did not object as we kissed and I held her bosom, although she was quite a small, slim girl without too much bosom to hold. We finally broke the embrace as she was under curfew to be home by ten o'clock and, after seeing her to the door, I trotted back to meet Tony for the walk home. I was ecstatic that, despite the fact she had been wearing a bra, school blouse, cardigan, blazer and a gabardine mac, I was pretty sure that I had felt her up. I'm not sure that Jane had even noticed.

My new girlfriend became something of an obsession, and I spent as much time as possible with her. It wasn't perhaps the most romantic of romances. There were no candlelit dinners, no starry-eyed liaisons gazing over moonlit lakes and no dreamy smooches to Ray Charles singing, *I can't stop loving you*, but we did meet regularly and hold hands as we wandered around the local council estates. We would also find quiet corners where we smoked our Dominos cigarettes and exchanged saliva. We did attend that year's Christmas Soiree as a couple and were partners in every clumsy dance, before sneaking out for a cigarette and walking home together. I was just happy to have a girlfriend and to casually tell everyone that I was going out with Jane Parr. At around the same time Pete Griffin and Dawn Matthews had started going out with each other, although their romance appeared a much more intense relationship and they cut themselves off from the rest of the group, preferring their own company. We were soon to find out why.

With rugby and courting and my butchery work taking precedence, something had to suffer and, inevitably, schoolwork was way down the list of my priorities. As I struggled with the work, I became more and more disruptive which meant that my learning was adversely affected and became more and more difficult, which made me more disruptive. I was spending most of my spare time doing anything to avoid the homework which I did not understand. As in previous terms, English and Maths were relatively straightforward, but I was struggling with most other subjects. This was not helped by my lack of application in the classroom, typified by Chemistry with Bill Still. Bill was a gentle old boy of indeterminate age who was genuinely enthused by mixing chemicals together and heating them in a test tube over a Bunsen burner, something for which I could see no practical use and found boring to the extreme. To carry out experiments, we worked in pairs and my regular partner was Bernie Wirdnam, who remained a leading light in the smoking set and a close ally in subversion. One experiment was to mix black powder with water in a test tube and heat the mixture over the Bunsen burner before allowing it to cool and thus produce beautiful blue crystals. This was based on copper sulphate but whether that was the black powder, the crystals or both I have no idea. As far as I remember, Bernie mixed our powder with water and heated it as instructed, but, on cooling, whilst the other students' mixtures began to create brilliant blue crystals, ours sat in their dish looking like wet coal dust. Bernie had the idea that we should assist the process by using a catalyst, in this case blue ink from his fountain pen. It seemed a good idea to me and so, when Bill was preoccupied dreamily explaining something in the periodic table, we emptied Bernie's pen into our mixture and reheated the test tube. The next Chemistry lesson, Bernie and I were taken to one side and Bill angrily stated that he could only guess why our crystals had taken on the hue of blue/black Quink. We were ordered to return to the lab at the end of the day for punishment.

I was late getting to Bill's lab and Bernie was waiting in a queue with two or three other miscreants. "Is the old fool here yet, Bernie?" I asked as I joined the queue. Before Bernie could reply, another master stepped out from an adjoining lab and ordered me into his room.

"I heard what you said, boy," the master growled, "For your disrespect, you will be punished. You have the choice of accepting your punishment from me or seeing the headmaster."

I still had vivid memories of the whacks received at the hands and cane of the Boss, so opted for the immediate punishment at the master's hands. It was a grave mistake. I was made to bend over a chair as a huge plimsoll was brought down on my behind with vicious power causing pain far beyond the Boss's cane. I received six of the best, each blow accurately hitting the same spot and more painful the previous wallop. I was dismissed and returned to my fellow wrongdoers desperately trying not to let my agony and resulting tears show. What made the whole painful process worse, was that Bill Still never turned up to see us anyway.

My relationship with Rackham, meanwhile, began to grow from its previous antagonistic association, to take on a much more deferential attitude. Although the boys in the naughty corner were still a long way from ideal pupils, our diversions became more respectful and were restricted to making the odd silly joke, which Rackham was prepared to ignore for the sake of peace in the classroom. The relationship was strengthened by the fact that lessons were not held in the school but, due to lack of classroom space in the school, we had decamped to the Women's Institute building some ten minutes' walk from the school. On our thrice-weekly march, we debated how the school could have run out of classrooms. There were the same number of classes and pupils that there had always been and, unlike a Secondary Modern school whose intake was governed by the level of procreation of the families in its catchment area, the intake to Headlands was restricted to specific numbers each year. Rackham insisted that there was no shortage of space within the school, but the teaching staff simply wanted to banish our class from the school grounds to offer the remaining tutelage short but welcome periods of peace. He further claimed that he had literally drawn the short straw to look after the class on its temporary release. He kept a straight face throughout the explanation and even the most sceptical of us wondered if there was an element of truth in his assertion. Towards the end of term, I even found myself walking with Rackham and chatting amiably, rather than hanging about at the back of the line, trying to light up a fag without being seen.

That year's examination results and subsequent school report followed the usual pattern. Despite my pledge to improve and concentrate on work this term, December sneakily arrived before I was ready for it and I simply ran out of time to knuckle down. It wasn't that I didn't want to work, there simply wasn't time in my busy life for History, Geography or French. I was, by now, quite used to the negative and unhelpful comments on my report, typified by Turd Stewart's enlightening declaration that *He must work really hard*. The only good comment was from Rackham who said that I was beginning to make full use of my ability. As form master, Rackham's comments were firm but fair and stressed that my attitude left much to be desired, but did say that I was the only pupil in the class to have *Had a school detention or similar punishment*, so our mum was pleased that I had, at least, achieved something positive.

Britain's *Big Freeze* began in December, just as preparations for Christmas began. There was already a heavy covering of ice and snow when a particularly heavy snow storm arrived late on Boxing Day and continued into the following day.

On 29 and 30 December 1962 a blizzard swept across South West England and Wales. There were 20 feet deep snow drifts in places, driven by gale force easterly winds and blocking roads and railways. Villages were cut off. Trees and powerlines were brought down. There were reports of people unable to get out to buy food and coal stocks were running low. It was deemed a national emergency. We thought that it was great fun. Even as fifteen-year-olds with fledgling interest in pop music, fashion and the opposite sex, nothing was as exciting as snowball fights, making ice slides and hurtling down Montgomery Avenue on home-made sledges. It seemed that when we awoke every morning we had been treated to another deep downfall and the whole area was alive with the sound of kids risking life and limb in the winter wonderland. Our dad brought home some wooden planks and two metal strips, borrowed from the British Railways, and promised to help me make a super two-man sledge. Our dad was never one for delicate woodwork and we hammered metal runners to the underside of four planks of wood, held together with four-by-two struts. He hammered two large screws to the front, and attached a length of rope to hang on to and the sledge was ready. It didn't look much like an Olympic bobsled, and it took two strong boys to pull it to the top of the hill, but it was fast. It was much stronger and heavier than the other more skillfully manufactured toboggans and, once started on its downhill journey with two reckless but courageous passengers on board, could only be stopped by crashing into the icy snow drift down the brook. It is fortunate that no cars were on the road at the same time as our Cresta runs, or our survival chances would have been minimal. The sledge had the additional bonus of making excellent firewood after the snows melted and the runners were used to support our dad's roses for years afterwards.

After Christmas dinner, our dad, mellowed by beer and Sauterne and replete with chicken, roast potatoes, murdered sprouts and Christmas pudding, stood up as if to make an earth-shattering announcement. As a matter of fact, it was an earth-shattering announcement. "You ladies, go and sit down in the sitting room," he announced with due gravity, "Me and our John's washing up."

I don't know who was the more surprised, our mum or me. The ladies moved somewhat sheepishly into the sitting room, leaving a kitchen and dining table full of dirty crockery and cutlery. I had no idea how to start clearing up the mucky clutter, let alone how we would attack the actual washing up. Or dad took control. "Just bung everything in the sink. You wash and I'll wipe," he commanded.

Somehow, we managed to shift all the crockery into the kitchen and dump it into a sink of hot water, where I began the onerous task of washing up and balancing the clean plates and dishes on the draining board. Our dad was wiping the sparkling crockery dry and beginning a new pile of spotless dishes on the worktop. Our dad stopped wiping for a moment and said, "Always remember son, a 'appy wife is a 'appy life," and tapped the side of his nose. I thought the statement a touch ironic, from a man who had never lifted a finger to help in the house before and was now washing up for the first time in almost twenty years of marriage.

A few more minutes went by and our dad stopped wiping again. "Broken the back of it now," he announced, "I need to go for a widdle," and left to go upstairs. He never came down again, retiring to bed and leaving me to finish washing, wiping and putting away. But our mum was a happy wife.

Our dad had been at the club on Boxing day seeing a man about a dog and struggled to negotiate a heavy snowfall by pushing his bike home, which meant a delayed dinner. "What's it like out?" our mum asked staring through the kitchen window at the deep covering of snow.

"Cold enough for a walking stick and still black over our mother's," our dad replied blowing onto his hands.

After dinner, I waited expectantly for one of our dad's now annual war stories and wasn't disappointed. He moved unsteadily into the sitting room, carrying his glass of beer, gin and sherry cocktail and slumped into an armchair, all thoughts of an 'appy wife evaporated with the alcohol. He gazed at nothing in particular on the floor and said, "Cold enough for a walking stick alright. Not like in the desert. That was 'ot. Summer 1941. We was trundling around North Africa, following directions from some office boy in Cairo. Never seen Jerry for months. That was 'ot, so 'ot you could fry eggs on the tanks. If you could get any eggs. Seen blokes do it. Put some engine oil on the tank, leave it a minute or two then break an egg in it. Fried up lovely. Best eggs ever. Now, that was 'ot. We had a gunner from Devizes. Called 'im Flanker, 'cos 'e was always trying to work a flanker. One day, 'e says 'e'd 'ad enough and was going to get sick leave 'ome. So 'e put 'is 'and on the tank and left it there 'til it blistered. Right mess it was. Must 'ave 'urt like I dunno what. Off 'e goes to the M.O. and says 'e can't use a gun with 'is 'and like this and 'e should be given sick leave. Course, the M.O. 'ad seen it all before. Trooper, 'e says, I got two choices. Either I can put a bandage on that 'and, and you get back to your tank or I can amputate it from the elbow down. Never seen old Flanker move so quick back to 'is tank."

Our dad chuckled and refueled his glass with whisky and advocaat.

Chapter 8 – January – August 1963

- The Big Freeze – the UK has the worst winter in the 20th century
- Aldermarston to London march demonstrates against nuclear weapons
- National Service ends in the UK
- Great Train Robbery takes place in Buckinghamshire

The year started as the previous year had ended. The *Big Freeze* was the most severe weather of the 20th century in the UK, with snow and ice covering much of the country for many months. As we reluctantly prepared for our return to school, the ex-Pinehurst contingent of grammar school boys were unconcerned about the fact that there were twenty feet snowdrifts in some parts of the country, or that the sea had frozen over in Kent, or even that Swindon Town would be able to play just one game in the whole of January: our main worry was that we would have to negotiate our precarious way through the hordes of brutal thugs from Pinehurst Secondary Modern, armed with an inexhaustible supply of lethal weapons. We met outside Derek Windslow's house on the first morning, dressed in our warmest clothes including duffel coats and thick gloves with scarves wrapped around our faces. We discussed the options. We could either risk ambush by taking our normal route to school, via Beech Avenue and passing Pinehurst Secondary Modern, hoping that the inmates would show mercy, or take the longer route via the allotments and Pinehurst Road, thus evading their potential attacks. To a man, we agreed that the former option was courting almost certain death and that cowardice was still the better part of valour, so we would take the long way round. We maneuvered our bikes through the snow and ice of the allotments and cycled briskly up Pinehurst Road, speeding through the circle to school. The odd guerrilla attack came but was ineffectually carried out by young and inexperienced troops, allowing us to reach our destination with only superficial damage. Our homeward return journey home for lunch took the same route, as did our afternoon return to school and evening homecoming. We arrived home in buoyant mood, feeling like Wagon Train pioneers who had evaded an Indian attack on their hazardous journey across the Mid-Western plains. I even adopted a Ward Bond drawl on the journey.

The following day, we met again outside the Windslow's, confident that our secret wagon-train route through the untamed territory would again see us safely to our destination. We had underestimated our native foe. The traverse of the allotments went smoothly, as did the hard ride up Pinehurst Road but, as we entered The Circle, the enemy struck, and struck with vicious accuracy. The Apaches had grouped outside Mecon's chip shop, setting lookouts at all approaches and, as we entered hostile lands, a loud "Whoop" signaled our presence and the feral braves attacked. It was pointless trying to fight back as the ferocious warriors were well armed with piles of deadly snowballs primed and ready, so all we could do was put our heads down and speed onwards, vainly hoping for John Wayne's US Cavalry to arrive in time to save us. As snowballs rained down, some weapons had turned to hard ice and some contained stones, but we managed to escape with our lives. We continued our journey, sustaining few physical injuries but with badly injured pride, as our attackers jeered and laughed at our distress. Even Pete Griffin didn't want to stop and fight. The return journeys that day were quieter as the Apache war parties rested on their laurels, possibly celebrating with war-dances around Pinehurst campfires, releasing younger braves to execute sporadic lone-wolf attacks.

On the third day, with the snow still blanketing the ground, we agreed that we would revert to the usual journey, which we hoped may confuse our adversaries or, at worst, shorten the attack. We set off cautiously, eyes peeled and ready to take evasive action. Surprisingly, no assaults came. Our previous attackers glared at us ferociously but allowed us to pass in peace.

It was only on talking to some of the Pinehurst lads over the following weekend that we learned that there had been a formal complaint from Headlands about the assaults, and the Pinehurst headmaster had threatened his students with death or worse, homework, if the attacks continued. But, as Mick Kell and Spuddy Taylor explained, they had won the war and accepted our surrender anyway and so another victorious battle was unnecessary.

The first games lesson of the term was a disappointment. I was keenly anticipating the new football season. Although my skills were far more suited to the rough and tumble of rugby than the adroit proficiencies of the soccer field, the beautiful game was still my first love - this despite my disillusionment at the rejection by the Swindon Boys selectors. Terry Wollen remained my hero and I continued to try to emulate his skills as a right full back although, I must admit, with little success. We turned up at the school changing rooms on the appointed games morning, boots and kit stuffed into duffel bags and looking forward to the game. By this stage in our careers, there was no coaching in games lessons as we were simply split into teams and played games of football without supervision. Stevenson announced that football was cancelled that day. The pitches remained covered in snow and ice, and outdoor games were considered far too dangerous. Stevenson had obviously never been hacked knee-high by Micky Mason on the tarmac in Pound Lane and hammered headfirst into Church's lamp post. That was dangerous.

The anticlimax for many boys, but relief for the fat ones, were abated by Stevenson's announcement that we were to take part in a cross country run instead. As we changed, a cunning plan was devised between Tony, Bernie, another smoker called Gareth

Davies and me. We could conceal cigarettes about us and take the opportunity to have a smoke *en route*. Gareth was a tall good-looking lad whose Welsh father was a teacher at another Swindon school and who lived in the somewhat upmarket area of Old Walcott, a private estate of detached and semi-detached houses with tidy gardens, net curtains and cars on the drive. I never really liked the lad. Whilst the Pinehurst crew tended to be unruly and ill-disciplined, his waywardness tended towards underhandedness and maliciousness. He took great pleasure in bullying weaker or younger boys without motive, but he always had money and money meant cigarettes. We knew that Stevenson would be on the lookout for the secretion of contraband, so we each carefully tucked two cigarettes into a sock. The other sock contained a few matches and a some *strikey*, the ignition strip at the side of a matchbox. The route of our run was a figure of eight, taking us through the Seven Fields football pitches between the school and Penhill estate, towards Haydon Wick and back via the cemetery. Tony, Bernie, Gareth and I began the run by maintaining a steady jog in the middle of the pack until we reached the crossover point where we diverted and hid behind a bush, gleefully waiting for the last runner to pass before each lighting up a contraband Bristol cigarette. We managed to stay hidden, smoking two fags each before the first of the runners, an old Pinehurst mate, Bob Francome, had reached the crossover point and made the final lung-busting uphill lap back to school. Bob was a very keen sportsman whose lack of skill in ball games was more than counteracted by fitness and enthusiasm. We knew that Bob would be amongst the leaders, fired by his strength and determination. We had decided that we would allay any suspicions about our whereabouts by following Bob at a respectable distance and labour home in the middle of the field but, as we set out on our lazy jog homewards, Tony Duggan decided to rejoin the race, much to Gareth's annoyance.

Tony was no sportsman but as he had run less than half the distance of the other competitors, he managed to hang on in the sprint for home, coming eighth overall. As we three remaining nicotine addicts struggled home, panting unnecessarily deeply, Tony was being congratulated by Stevenson and quizzed over whether he had considered entering the long-distance races at the school sports to be held later that year. Tony looked really pleased with himself and said that he would be pleased enter. The fact that he run a middle-distance race against the other boys' long distance, seemed to have slipped his mind.

As I lumbered in, Stevenson put an arm out and stopped me. "Disappointed in you, Trueman," he said, and my thoughts were that we had been rumbled. Had my face not already been red from the exertions of the run and the cold, I may well have blushed.

"Sir?" I questioned, putting on the best air of innocence I could manage.

"Thought you would do better. Finish in the top three or four." He said.

"Never had much stamina," I explained truthfully, "More of a sprinter really."

"Mmm. Come to my room when you're changed." Stevenson commanded.

I did as commanded, to find Bob Francome also waiting. Neither of us had any idea why we had been singled out for the audience, but incorrectly guessed that it was something to do with the run. Stevenson called us into his office, a small, cluttered changing room next to the gym, housing a desk in a corner, almost hidden amongst sporting paraphernalia. He explained that Swindon Education Authority were setting up an initial trial of the Duke of Edinburgh's Award scheme and schools had been asked to recommend candidates. Bob and I had been selected from Headlands and were to go to Drove Road School the following

Tuesday evening at seven o'clock for the initial introductions and instructions. With a curt, "Good luck," that was the end of our briefing to what would become an important part of our existence for the next year and a major influence for life. The news spread round the school and we learnt that Dawn, my ex-nearly-girlfriend and Pete Griffin's current girlfriend had also been selected, although the jungle telegraph suggested that our selection was for various assignments, from joining the Duke of Edinburgh's Regiment as boy soldiers to attending a royal garden party at Buckingham Palace.

On the Tuesday evening, I mounted my racing bike and set off across town to Drove Road School as instructed, arriving in good time. I was very nervous on arrival. In fact, I was bloody scared as I waited alone on a cold dark evening outside a school I had never been to before, just longing for a friendly face. Instead of the cocky fifteen-year-old Jack-the-lad persona I usually presented, I felt like an abandoned five-year-old refugee. Other young boys and girls began to arrive, many being dropped off in cars and some being escorted into the school by parents. I was on the verge of turning around and cycling home, excuses running wildly around my mind, when Pete Griffin arrived with his by now, long-term girlfriend Dawn.

"What you doin' here?" I asked, "I thought only me and Bob been picked."

"Just come with Dawn." Pete answered, which I though a very odd reason for giving up a night off, when he could have been hanging about doing nothing. Why choose to go back to school?

Bob then turned up and my confidence grew a little as we followed other youngsters into the school. We learnt that we were a select few, nominated by various schools and youth groups in the borough for the first ever Duke of Edinburgh's Award Scheme managed by the local education authority. It was explained that we were being offered the chance of a lifetime in trailblazing the scheme in town and, although participation was voluntary, a very dim view would be taken of any invitee rejecting the opportunity. Under such pressure, no-one even fleetingly thought of bailing out. The presenters continued that we were to take part in four disciplines to attain the award: plan and undertake a hiking and camping expedition, follow and record a worthwhile hobby, achieve specified sporting standards and take part in a community-based activity. Further, we were informed that the community-based activity would be to study for a first aid certificate under the tutelage of the St. John's Ambulance Brigade on following Tuesday nights at the same venue. At the same time, we would be taught the intricacies of map reading and overnight camping in preparation for the expedition. The hobbies and sports achievements were up to the participants to sort out but would need to be ratified at the end of the process. The most exciting announcement was that, later in the year, we were to attend a week's course in North Wales, where the qualifying expedition would take place. We were offered entry into either the bronze or silver award scheme which would lead to the highly respected and venerated gold award. I selected the bronze award as a reasonably achievable target. Bob, never one to lack confidence, decided to plunge straight in and go for silver. We also asked to select a suitable hobby as an integral part of the scheme. I selected cycling, for no other reason than I had a new racing bike, with drop handlebars and Derailleur gears, and imagined that I would spend the following year pedaling merrily around the highways and byways of the west country. Finally, each invitee was given a personal interview where a number of forms were completed and signed on the dotted line, confirming that we would turn up at the same venue each Tuesday evening for lessons in first aid, map-reading and tent erection. I was more than a little piqued when Pete Griffin asked if he could also take part. The administrators looked embarrassed, explained that he had not been nominated and shook their heads before they relented and sanctioned his request. To me, it devalued the event. Bob and I, along with all other candidates had been nominated by our schools or employers which, in my eyes, made us somehow special. Pete had been accepted because his girlfriend was special.

Although Bob was an old Pinehurst friend and we had maintained a loose friendship since junior school, we were like chalk and cheese. In his academic work, he was hard-working, conscientious and well-behaved. At sport, although not naturally gifted, he was fit, enthusiastic and determined. He did not smoke, swear, lie or cheat. He was humble, polite and affable. He was everything I was not. This difference was reflected in our attitude to girls. Whilst I was determined to take any opportunity to indulge in physical contact with young damsels, Bob treated them with courtesy and respect. Over the following days, we talked excitedly about the prospect of our trip and my focus was on the opportunity of carnal intimacy with the girls, an intention that Bob argued was improper. His father was a lay-preacher and had instilled into him a strong sense of right and wrong. Bob really believed that pre-marital relationships were sinful and to be avoided. At the time, this did not auger well for the future, but never has any leopard changed its spots to such a degree as Bob Francome.

Whether the Duke of Edinburgh Award Scheme had had an effect, whether I was growing up at last or whether courting Jane had changed my outlook I know not, but that term I buckled down and began to work harder than ever before. My relationship with Rackham may also have had a beneficial effect as we developed a mutual respect and understanding. I was still trying to be a bit of a lad but showing more respect and, as form master, Rackham offered great encouragement. His enthusiasm over Mathematics stimulated my interest even more than before and I enjoyed every lesson. I even began to look forward to homework. I enjoyed the challenge of quadratic equations, Isosceles triangles, logarithms, coefficients of variation, BODMAS and SOHCAHTOA. Had I realised that almost the whole syllabus would be about as much use in future life as an ashtray on a motorbike, I may not have been so keen on spending so much of my valuable time in this odd pleasure pursuit.

Other subjects also began to spark interest. Although those lessons requiring the gathering and storing of facts, my haphazard mental filing system remained my Achilles heel. I was capable of reading whole chapters of textbooks on Glaciated Uplands or the main causes of discontent in the reign of Edward VI, whilst my mind was wandering somewhere else altogether. I could read and understand every word but not one iota would stay in my brain, losing the space reserved for it to thoughts of football, rugby, Jane and cigarettes.

This lack of knowledge of basic facts almost caused a serious accident one fine Sunday morning when I had arranged to cycle with Tony to see Jane and Julie. He arrived at our house on his bike but carrying an electrical contraption, explaining that it had been given to his brother Paul by Tony Edgington's dad, having been put out for the dustmen the previous week. Tony had temporary borrowed it for experimentation. It was, he said, a doorbell or, more accurately, the chime; a pair of cream tubes with gaudy, golden musical notes stuck onto them. At the back was a plate containing electrical bits and bobs including wires. Coincidentally, we had been learning about electricity during Physics lessons, including the way that an electric bell functions, so saw this as an ideal opportunity to carry out a practical test. Of course, Tony couldn't do this at home as his brother didn't know that he had borrowed the equipment. We teased out the wires and decided that there was no need to affix an electric plug as we could simply stick the wires into a socket causing the electricity to enter the machine and produce a melodious chime. Our mum was in the kitchen making a cup of tea when the sparks flew from the chimes and a loud bang cracked from the fuse box. Her kettle sighed sadly and refused to work. I guess that our lack of grasp of the difference between direct current by battery and domestic alternating current needed some polishing. Fortunately, no-one was hurt and Mr. Moody from next door heard the bang and soon had the blown fuse replaced. Our mum, unreasonably I thought, never let Tony and I experiment in the house again: after all, nothing was allowed to come between her and a cup of tea.

Experiments did continue however, taking place in Tony Duggan's dad's shed. Tony's elder brother Paul was a science boffin at Headlands and had converted the shed into a science laboratory. He was trusted by the science masters to the extent that he was encouraged to bring school equipment home to carry out his own experiments. He was also helped by Tony Edgington's dad's job as a driver on the dust carts, a position which gave him first choice of any refuse that may be deemed useful. One day, he brought home an interesting-looking wooden box, about four inches cubed, with mysterious wires and grips attached. A calibrated sat neatly on the box lid. Tony and I studied the box in great detail trying to work out its use. We came up with several theories: a small radio or prototype television perhaps, or a rustic table lamp or torch: we even discussed the possibility that it may be a time machine, but without too much confidence. When Paul saw the contraption, he immediately cracked the mystery. He said that, with the addition of a battery and by holding on to the grips, the machine would send an electric current from the grips through the user's body. The power of the charge would be controlled by the plunger. He rooted around in his shed cabinet and proudly produce a large six-volt battery, inserted it into the box, raised the plunger and flicked a switch, challenging anyone to hold the grips. Tony and I, still ignorant of the difference between AC and DC, refused the opportunity aware of what had happened to our mum's fuse box and the door chimes. Paul confidently agreed to test the machine first. He lived through the experiment, so we then spent many hours holding on to the machine whilst Paul adjusted the plunger. A strange, but not unpleasant tingling feeling of electricity pulsed through our bodies, and we even formed a circle and held hands to pass the charge through four bodies. Paul further hypothesized that the machine was to aid the relief of pain from rheumatism, but as none of us suffered from the condition, this could not be proven. Sending electricity through our bodies became addictive as we returned to the shed many times to get connected, increasing the charge to its maximum, the until the sensation was barely bearable. Eventually the battery went flat and we moved on to other experiments.

One of Paul's specialties was in constructing torpedoes. With the clever use of aluminium cigar tubes that his dad obtained from the American air base, and various chemicals that he was sworn never to divulge but included baking powder, he built small torpedoes which, when placed in water, should shoot forward several feet before exploding. We often followed him down the brook, where he would launch his missile, but he never quite managed to control its direction and the trial usually ended with the torpedo travelling just a foot or so before spinning madly around several times and exploding. This frustrated Paul but pleased his followers as contaminated brook water splashed anyone naive enough to stand too close.

As the year progressed, I settled into a routine which included schoolwork, football, and courting the lovely Jane. It wasn't the intense sexual love affair I yearned, but at least I could boast that I was going out with a girl. If we were both free, I would walk her home from school, grab a quick snog on the footpath near her house before an uncomfortable cycle ride home. On

Saturday nights, Jane's parents were in the habit of attending the Wheatsheaf Inn for an evening's alcoholic recreation, so I would journey to Meadowcroft where we could take advantage of the empty house and be alone for a couple of hours. I always dressed up for the occasion – after all, it was a date – which included taking a bath and changing my underwear a day before I need. We would spend the evening involved in somewhat different experiments to those in Tony's dad's shed, as any pair of fifteen-year-olds should and would do when left alone for the evening.

I usually rode my bike to Jane's but, for reasons unknown, I was on foot one Saturday and had to cross The Circle and walk past the Moonrakers and the shops at Clive Parade, a dangerous place to be if I was recognised as a grammar school boy out alone on a Saturday night. I successfully negotiated The Circle and the Moonrakers, but in front of the shops I was confronted by half a dozen rowdy girls from the Penhill council estate.

One shouted, "'Ello 'andsome. Give us a kiss," which I took as a compliment, but continued to walk past whilst the girls threw out a few lewd comments and even attempted wolf whistles. I was feeling pretty pleased with myself and unconsciously adopted a slight swagger as I walked away. Pleased that is, until one of the girls shouted, "Ooh look. He's got ducks' disease," to great laughter, adding, "Mind you don't bang yer ass on the kerb when you step down." The happy, flamboyant swagger changed to a miserable, slouching trudge.

The long, cold winter hung on, warmed by my continuing romance, although Jane had hinted that staying in every Saturday night wrestling on the settee was not really her idea of courting. We agreed that one cold Saturday in March that the following week we should go to the pictures and were quite excited to see that *What a Crazy World* was playing at the Savoy cinema in town. The film was packed with pop stars including Marty Wilde, Susan Maugham and the great Joe Brown, in addition to recognised thespians like Harry H Corbett and Bill Fraser. It also starred Freddie and the Dreamers as themselves: an ideal film to impress my girl and show that I was a man of refined artistic taste. For reasons lost in time, we arranged to meet at our house and catch the bus from the nearby stop into town. We had also invited Tony and Julie and one or two other friends, including Gareth Davies. Why he was invited I do not know, except that he always had cigarettes, although why he thought it reasonable to cycle half way across town to meet at my place, then catch a bus to town nearer to his home, I didn't understand, but the decision was made.

I was a little concerned when getting ready for the outing that I did not have any clothes suitable for my first ever real going-out date. I only owned my school uniform and scruffy casual clothes that were not suitable for a cool fifteen-year-old guy taking his sweetheart to the flicks. I donned a new pair of grey trousers which were too long, but our mum had bought them in a sale some months previously, saying that I would grow into them, and a reasonably new sweater knitted by our nana. I had the choice of a pair of school shoes or bumpers and decided that school shoes were more apt after our dad polished them to an army-style shine. It was a cold night but the only piece of apparel that I owned which would keep out the cold was my school mac, so I had no choice but to wear it. To set off the ensemble, our mum insisted that I wear a short yellow small scarf tucked inside the lapels of my mac, which she maintained was very much the style of the day. We had no full-length mirror in the house in which to review my livery, which was probably just as well.

My friends arrived at the appointed time and I was happy to see that Tony also looked somewhat less than stylish, although he was wearing a pair of fashionable if slightly too large, blue jeans purloined, I assumed, from his brother Paul. The girls looked gorgeous. Although I have no memory of their outfits, I did notice that they were both decorated with heavy make-up. As we waited, Gareth arrived and parked his ten-speed racing bicycle in our shed before strutting forward to join us. I felt physically sick. His hair was slicked with Brylcreme creating a superb Tony Curtis quiff: he was wearing new, tight, blue denim jeans with a three inch turn up, a new grey bomber jacket and magnificent winkle pickers with a point that seemingly appeared from the shed long before he did. If I had been that way inclined, I'd have fallen for himself. As it was, Jane seemed unnaturally soppy and girly, worryingly I had seen our Rae adopt similar behaviour when Mac was around. We set off for the bus stop, a ten-minute walk away. I tried to walk alongside Jane with thoughts of holding her hand to cement the relationship and signify my ownership, but she scurried alongside the long-striding Gareth chatting like a star-struck groupie. I scampered behind like their pet dog seeking attention. The girls sat together on the bus, probably saving me further heartache but, once in the pictures, Jane sat between Gareth and me, paying far more attention to my erstwhile friend. Two or three times I tried to slip my arm around her shoulders, but she just moved closer to my now sworn enemy.

The film ended, and I had barely watched Marty Wilde or Joe Brown and even the stunning Susan Maugham had failed to capture my attention. I'm not even sure if Freddie or any of his Dreamers appeared at all. We made our way by bus back to my house and the evening ended in disastrous fashion as Jane, Julie, Tony and Gareth left together, Jane explaining that there was no need for me to see her home and leaving me to lick my aching wounds. I reasoned that just because he was bigger than me, trendily better dressed than me, more mature than me and better-looking than me, there was no reason for Jane to switch her attentions to Gareth bloody Davies. I reasoned that it must be the ready supply of cigarettes that turned her head.

I had secretly sworn vengeance as my romance with Jane fizzled out although she insisted that we remained friends, which did nothing to repair the gaping void in my life. Vengeance took its time coming but come it did. A few weeks later we were playing football in the school playground at morning break and I was on the opposing side to the turncoat, treacherous Gareth Davies. We clashed in a tackle and I immediately lashed out kicking him hard across the shin. He responded by raising his fists. "Got you now, you Welsh bastard," I thought and moved forward, my own fists raised. At, last, I would have retribution. As I moved towards the traitor, I barely saw the blurred fist as it crashed into my mouth, immediately knocking me backwards. I was somewhat surprised as these schoolboy bouts usually took the form of aggressive wrestling matches, but real violence was rare. I moved forward again and felt several more punches thud into my face, which caused great pain, but not as great as the surprise I felt. For the third time, I went on the attack, taking several more punches before managing to get close enough to grab my opponent and drag him to the floor. We lay there for a moment, Gareth looking for a way to extricate himself in order to punch me again whilst I just held on grimly hoping that someone, anyone would arrive to separate us. Belatedly, a prefect arrived and we were separated. I had a badly split lip dribbling blood and saliva, two loose teeth, a swollen cheekbone, a broken nose bleeding copiously and both eyes bruised, beginning to turn dark blue. Gareth had grazed knuckles. I called it a draw.

My injuries healed and the athletics season returned for my most successful season. The school sports day was not only a competition between the houses but acted as the trials for the team to represent Headlands Grammar School at the town sports. I had spent every games lesson and a few evenings practicing and training with Jane and Dawn, again occupying much of the time staring longingly at young buttocks moving gracefully and alluringly in their navy-blue knickers. I used the knickers much as I guess the greyhound uses the hare – something to chase and try to catch. And much like the greyhound, I wouldn't really have known what to do with my prey if I had managed to catch it. Although my intentions were less than honorable, the additional training was successful, and I was placed in both the 100 and 220 yard sprints and led Rockley House to victory in the four by 100 yards relay. I also managed a respectable third place in the shot-putt, largely because the event was unpopular and the other entries tended to be the fat, unathletic kids who were press-ganged into taking part. The sports day results were augmented by additional training sessions as I was selected to represent the school in all three sprint events.

I successfully negotiated the trials and, come the day, the Headlands team assembled at Ferndale School sports field. I proudly joined my team-mates in the competitors' enclosure. After changing, I assumed posing positions, stretching, warming up, pressing up and generally acting in the way that I imagined a real athlete would act in preparation for competition. After weeks of my begging, whining and cajoling, our mum had bought me my first pair of running spikes as an early birthday present, so I made a point of changing into the spikes several times and testing the new footwear by carrying out short sprints in front of my team members. I positioned myself as close to Jane and Dawn as possible but was disappointed to find that Jane, whilst friendly, was a little remote. I realised that the romance was completely dead and would probably never be re-kindled. I was even more disappointed to see that Dawn was once more chaperoned by Pete Griffin, who spent the whole afternoon fussing over her in the competitors' enclosure like an attentive chaperone, even though he was not taking part in any of the events. I took this as a guide to courting technique and began to fuss over Jane, offering to fetch her a bottle of water which she accepted and to massage her thighs, which she rejected. The more I fussed, the more attention she seemed to pay to the older team members, so I sat and sighed and sulked. This stratagem also failed to elicit a reaction, so I went with Richard Clewlow behind the bike sheds for a smoke and felt much better.

One of the early events on the programme was the boys under 15 javelin competition. All Headlands teammates were certain than Bob Anderson would win, so we trooped over to the throwing arena to watch his progress. As he took his javelin and flexed his muscles, he a pointed out to the line judge that he was likely to kill someone if the spectators on the far side of the track were not moved out of his line of fire. The judge called another judge and a long debate took place before they decided that Bob was overestimating his ability and should continue with his throw. Bob refused and asked someone to fetch out sports master. Stevenson arrived and, after protracted discussions, the spectators were gently removed and Bob took his throw. The javelin landed almost exactly in the spot where people were previously gathered and, indeed, he probably would have killed someone. Later that year, Bob was selected to represent Wiltshire in the English Schools Championships in Chelmsford, winning the title with an impressive throw of over 55 yards. A few years later he was selected to represent Great Britain in the Olympics Games of 1968 in Mexico, but a broken arm put paid to his international career and he resorted to the next best thing, becoming world darts champion twenty years later.

I managed to qualify for the individual finals but was outside the first three in each, perhaps retarded by the lack of a pair of pulsating navy-blue knickers to chase, or perhaps by the weight of a broken heart. It was almost certainly because the other finalists were simply faster runners, but that was something I did not want to contemplate. There was compensation when the Headlands team won the 4 X 110 yards relay and we waited until the end of the events to proudly celebrate our success with other

Headlands winners. Our mum didn't seem too impressed with my victory as the delay meant that I arrived home late for my tea.

A couple of weeks later, my teammates and I received a note to say that the relay team had been selected to represent Swindon in an athletics match against Marlborough and Dauntsey, to be held at Marlborough College the following Saturday. We were told to meet at the Swindon Corporation Civic Offices in town to catch the coach to Marlborough. I was delighted and very proud to have been selected for my first representative appearance and trained hard in the week preceding event, specifically in perfecting the relay changeovers. On the Saturday, I caught the bus to town and proudly carried my kit in my duffel bag through the town centre to the meeting point. My new spikes were tied together by the laces and hung around my neck, making it clear that I was real athlete on my way to a real competition. Unfortunately, I never saw anyone in town that I knew, but felt that I looked professional enough to elicit admiring glances from several shoppers *en-route*.

On arrival at Marlborough College, we were directed into the most luxurious of changing rooms where we donned our athletics kit. We were issued with numbered labels and a safety pin with which to attach the label to our vests. The team manager, a sports teacher from another Swindon school, explained that rather than teams selected from the historic market towns of Marlborough and Dauntsey, we were competing against Marlborough College and Dauntsey's School, both private, fee-paying boarding institutions. This did nothing to diminish my pride, which was further boosted by the team announcement where I was somewhat surprised and elated to find that I had been selected not just for the relay, but for both the 100 and 220 yards sprints. Whether this selection was based on economics to reduce the number of athletes to transport from Swindon, or whether to even out the team strength against a far smaller population, I know not, but gave it little thought. I was representing my beloved Swindon town in athletics, which didn't quite compensate for my failure to play for Swindon Boys' football team, but was a decent enough consolation prize.

It was a fine, sunny afternoon and the Swindon team sat together on a grassy bank overlooking the athletics track. The Marlborough team were encouraged by their supporters with shouts of, "Marlborough, Marlborough," with an emphasis in the last syllable. With the refined accents of the pupils the chant sounded to our ears like, "Maw-bra, Maw-bra." We thought it jolly amusing to reply with our own chant of, "More-knickers, More-knickers," until being severely reprimanded by the team manager.

The racing proceeded and the strong Swindon team were well ahead in the points accrual. I had grabbed a fine second in the one hundred yards and Bob Anderson had easily won the javelin, possibly killing several future Prime Ministers in the process. I was confident as I lined up for the 220 yards. The gun blasted and off I tore, rounding the left-hand bend and coming into the straight at top speed, I was aware that I was leading and gritted my teeth as I forced my legs to stride faster and faster towards the line. I was leading, I was going to win I thought…except, that is, for a big lad from Marlborough who had just breasted the tape and casually turned around to watch the rest of the sprinters finish. I was shattered, both physically and mentally. Not that I had been beaten – I was used to that – but by being beaten by such a distance. Another commendable second place was no compensation for such a humiliating defeat. The winner's name was Martin Winbolt-Lewis. It was a few years' later that he won a bronze medal in the 1966 Commonwealth Games and ran in the 400 metres and 4 X 400 metres relay at the Mexico Olympics. And I found out that he was nearly a year older than me anyway, so felt much better and overcame my shame, albeit many years later.

In May 1954, Doctor Roger Bannister was the first man to run a mile in under four minutes, possibly the most iconic moment in British athletics History and certainly one of the most famous sporting occasions of the twentieth century. The feat was realised during an athletics meeting between British AAA and Oxford University at small athletics track in Oxford called Iffley Road. In July 1963, I was again selected to represent Swindon Schools in the 4 X 110 yards relay at an athletics meeting at the same Iffley Road track. Many times, I had watched the film of Bannister straining every muscle, every sinew with the veins in his neck bulging to breaking point and his teeth gritted as he forced his body onwards, almost tying up in the home straight before throwing himself across the finishing line to collapse into the arms of waiting officials. To be able to run on the same track was an awe-inspiring moment. The stadium, if indeed it could be called a stadium, was not much more impressive than that at Marlborough, except that the track was cinders-based and there was a ramshackle stand overlooking the home straight. I have no idea of the outcome of the race in which I competed, but the excitement of simply being able to run on that track was immense and was a fitting climax to what turned out to be the end of my athletics career.

Throughout the football season, the whole of Wiltshire had been captivated by the spectacular rise of Swindon Town in the Football League Division Three. I rarely missed a game on Saturday afternoons, cycling along County Road to join the excited and noisy throng of supporters to watch our heroes play. This was a remarkable season for the Town, building on the previous season's promise and producing excellent results to challenge for promotion. The team was managed by the experienced Bert Head and included many local youngsters, including Ernie Hunt, John Trollope, Mike Summerbee and my personal hero Terry Wollen.

This season also heralded the emergence of the finest player ever to pull on the red jersey of the Robins, Don Rogers, who replaced the veteran Arnold Darcy at outside-left. Bert's babes went on to secure promotion to the Second Division for the first time in their History. The tragedy of the season was that Terry Wollen broke his leg in a game against Notts County in December 1962 and was never able to fulfill his tremendous potential as the best right back I had ever seen.

Things could not have gone better in most areas of my life, matters of the heart excluded. My final report that year was the best that I had received at Headlands, with almost all teachers stating that I had improved. Naturally, there were the grumpy ones who wrote *Can do better*, but Mr. Rackham summed up the results with a positive, *Definite Improvement*, although he let himself down somewhat by pointing out that I had S*till managed to acquire a school detention*, as if it was some kind of special achievement. Luckily, that's exactly what our mum thought it was.

I never missed a Tuesday evening preparing for the Duke of Edinburgh's award and enjoyed the first aid to such an extent that I can still name every bone in the human body and apply a sling to a broken arm or leg. I enjoyed the theory behind the mysterious hieroglyphics of Ordnance Survey maps and looked forward to putting what we had learnt into practice, particularly when we were given details of our trip to North Wales. Throughout the Tuesday training sessions, I had become very fond of one of the girls taking part in the scheme. Her name was Trish and her father had something to do with army or navy recruitment in Milton Road. I was gradually falling for her. She was very pleasant, very pretty and very soft spoken and was the owner of very big breasts. Of course, I never had the courage to tell her about this attraction but was sure that, once we were together in the wilds of Anglesey and away from parental control, the exotic location would offer the opportunity for us to know each better. Then, using my sophisticated charm and experience, sweep her off her feet like Clark Gable to Vivien Leigh, without his big ears of course. Mixed with the eager anticipation of my first holiday away from my parents (I discounted the week at our nana's with our Rae) and getting to know Trish, was an deep apprehension about living with other people. What if I didn't like the food? Would they make me eat vegetables? Would I be able to sleep in a strange bed? When would bath night take place? Would there be a ready supply of Phensic? Would someone hear me on the lavatory?

I was pleased that Bob Francome confirmed his attendance but less than happy that Pete Griffin would also be there, fretting and fussing about his beloved Dawn and potentially irritating the whole group.

We stayed in a school in Holyhead, sleeping in dormitories and sharing tasks that previously were a mystery to me. Making beds, sweeping and dusting and preparing food were jobs which happened magically at home, although I strongly suspected that our mum was somehow involved. In addition to the teachers and education people who were concerned with our Tuesday evening training sessions, we were accompanied by two trainee sports masters, fresh from university and there to gain valuable work experience in dealing with hormonal teenagers, and a chap about eighteen or nineteen called Simon, who was a church youth group and had somehow wheedled himself onto the trip as Team Leader. On the first night as we were preparing for bed, Simon suggested that we should raid the girls' dormitory. Quite why was never explained, although Simon insisted that, in such circumstances, it was expected of us. We sat on our beds and waited a respectable amount of time until all lights had been extinguished, before sneaking out of the dormitory, creeping quietly down the stairs and into the school playground. Simon was becoming more and more excited and found it difficult to contain his eagerness, his whispering voice rising an octave or two as he asked, "OK team. To the girls' dorm. Er…anyone know where it is?"

We stood around and looked at each other, shrugging and shaking our heads. Simon the Team Leader had obviously failed in his first task and failed to identify the location of our target. We continued shrugging and looking form one to the other until Simon showed his true worth to the mission. "It must be this way," he giggled like an over-excited schoolgirl and led us through an open door into a hallway. As we stood in a group, in complete darkness wondering what to do next, one lad exclaimed, "This is bloody stupid. What would we do even if we reached the girls' room?"

The best that Simon could suggest is that we would have a great pillow fight. The rebel firmly stated, "Bollocks," and guided everyone back to our own dormitory. Simon was not to put off easily and suggested that we find out where the girls were sleeping and repeat the surprise attack the next night, but the enthusiasm was drained and the assault was never mentioned again, although the nocturnal sounds coming from Simon's bed suggested that he had secretly been anticipating more than just a pillow fight. We never bothered much with team leader Simon again. Even when he leapt out of bed each morning shouting, "Hands off cocks, on socks. Time to get up," he was largely ignored.

Apart from peeling potatoes and messing about with brooms, the week consisted of exciting days out, including a hike on the first Sunday to the top of Mynydd Bodafon or Holyhead Mountain, the highest point on the island and, in mid-week, clambering to the summit of Snowdon, the highest in England and Wales. It was on the trek up Snowdon that I made my move with Trish. Halfway up the long slog to the summit, she almost fainted, with a severe case of altitude sickness being diagnosed by the student teachers. It was agreed that the group should split and that she should continue to the peak, but at a slower pace and I volunteered to join the slower group. As we walked, I stayed with her, chatting easily about the scenery, weather and other incidentals whilst giving her encouragement. I must have come across as a caring and helpful aide because Trisha finally noticed me and held my hand as we reached the summit, even offering a gentle squeeze and thanking me. We were both disappointed when, after all the effort in reaching our goal, we found that a train ran to the top from Llanberis and there was a cafe full of elderly Mancunians drinking tea and eating Eccles cakes.

One of the major reasons for the trip was to enable participants of the Duke of Edinburgh's Award to complete the expedition section of the scheme. Pete and I joined two other lads and were attired in suitable, socks, boots and anoraks and loaded up with a tent, sleeping bags and provisions before being abandoned in the wilds of Anglesey to walk back to the school via an overnight stop, which we were to organise once on the expedition. We were dropped somewhere near Beaumaris on the east of the island, to walk the twenty-five miles back to Holyhead, using our recently gained knowledge of pathfinding and Ordnance Survey maps. The first day went well and we covered two thirds of the distance before stopping for the night. We had arrived in a small village which I cannot remember but had an unpronounceable name, which doesn't narrow the specific area down much in North Wales. The village pub had a large garden which backed on to a small river and seemed an ideal camping spot, so we politely explained our situation to the pub landlord who was happy to let us camp next to the river. Exhausted we settled down for the night after a meal of sausages, fried black on a small gas stove, but not before washing up our utensils and plates in the cold water of the river and securing our remaining provisions by hanging them outside the tent as instructed on our Tuesday nights at Drove Road. We slept well but were awoken in the early morning by strange cackling and scratching sounds outside the tent. In the half light, we plucked up courage to leave our shelter and investigate the noise. Several chickens had ransacked our eatables and were happily pecking away at the remaining bread and bacon, leaving us with nothing but two eggs which they had relinquished. Our eagerly awaited breakfast of egg and bacon sandwiches was diminished, and we had little appetite for the remaining two eggs which were ceremoniously tossed into the river. We pooled our cash and feasted on Mars bars from the village shop, before setting off for base unscarred by our experience. We had been walking for perhaps half an hour when Pete said that we should hurry up. As we were on schedule to make it back in good time and were loaded with our chattels, the other three of us disagreed and settled for a steady pace. Pete sulked then set off on his own, almost running even though we reminded that one of the rules of any expedition was to travel at the pace of the slowest. We knew that he was rushing to get back to his beloved Dawn and thought him a soppy fool, and we carried on at our own pace. We were happy on our eventual debriefing when we were congratulated for staying together and it was hinted that Pete had received a well-deserved bollocking.

Pony trekking and visiting castles filled other days, with Trish and I spending as much time as possible together. On the final full day, we had a relaxing trip to a nearby beach where we sunbathed, swam and generally did seaside-type things. Almost immediately Pete and Dawn went for a walk, disappearing behind rocks at the foot of the cliffs at the back of the beach. They did not return for some time. Whilst I sat quietly chatting to Trish, Simon was in his element trying to organise games of rounders or sandcastle competitions, splashing any girls who dared venture into the sea and largely being a pain in the ass. At one stage, he was getting very excited about taking a PE lesson which all boys ignored, but some girls were reluctantly coerced into taking part.

He encouraged the nubile young ladies to touch their toes, bend their hips, spread their legs and generally arrange their flexible bodies into as many unnatural but revealing positions as possible. All the while his voice became more and more trill until he eventually flopped on to his stomach and called time on the activity. He almost immediately jumped up and ran towards the cliffs at the beach edge, with a prominent erection trying hard to escape his swimming trunks. A few minutes later he sheepishly returned, somewhat red-faced and sweating but with the bulge somewhat reduced. Those cliffs certainly saw some interesting activity that day.

On the final evening, we were treated to a visit to the Hippodrome Cinema in Holyhead. Everyone sought out their best clothes for the occasion – not an easy job as clothes had been left unpacked, crammed into the suitcases we travelled with or sloppily stuffed into drawers with scant regard for their appearance. On reaching the cinema and conducting a roll call, the Swindon staff found out that Bob Francome was missing. He had gone missing two or three times during the trip, but no-one seemed concerned, assuming that he just needed some time alone during what was, after all, a disquieting time for teenagers during their first time away from parents. This feeling of sympathy and compassion for Bob was shattered as he appeared from around the corner with two very attractive, if overdressed and over-made up, young ladies. Bob introduced his new companions and explained that they were friends that he had made over the week when going AWOL from our billet.

The cinema was the first that we had ever seen boasting double seats in the back row. Trish and I took advantage of this romantic novelty and noticed that Bob and his two companions were also in the same row. Quite how the seating was arranged between Bob and his two girlfriends I could not see. As I wondered whether or not I should put my arm round Trish, the slurping, sucking and smacking sounds from Bob's direction indicated that his previous declaration that intimacy should be reserved for marriage was well and truly abandoned. I believe this incident to be Bob's start of a long and distinguished career as a lothario.

We travelled home on the Saturday and I sat next to Trish for the whole journey holding hands. This surely was the start of a magical and, hopefully, sexual romance. I was too shy to make a further date with my new-found love and, anyway, our mum and dad had arranged our annual seaside holiday to follow immediately after the North Wales expedition. I decided that I would rekindle the affair on our resumption of our Tuesday nights' training.

This year, Hastings had been chosen as the lucky hosts of the Trueman family, and our Rae wanted to invite Mac, but our dad thought it immoral, so she had been allowed to invite her friend Wendy as a substitute. My protestations that I was old enough to stay home alone her were rejected, so I was to spend a long and lonely fortnight in sunny Sussex.

As usual, my memories of this trip are generally vague, but some incidents remain crystal clear. I know that we would have travelled by train, using one of our dad's free passes, but I don't remember the journey, whether we were sustained with fish-paste sandwiches and Camp coffee or if and where we changed trains. I do remember the arrival at Hastings station. As we left the main building, our dad lugging two heavy suitcases and our mum laden with an assortment of bags, we were met by a dozen or so lads of my age with sleds, calling, "Take your cases Mister?"

Our dad loaded the cases and bags onto the sled of one lad and showed him a slip of paper with the address of our bed, breakfast and evening meal accommodation. The lad set off up the hill and we hurried along in his wake until we reached a large Victorian terraced house, our home for next two weeks. I felt jealous and embarrassed. He was my age and running his own business, a fledgling transport service, delivering tourists and their luggage to the numerous lodgings in the town at a bob a time. I was holiday with my mum and dad. For a while, I contemplated emulating this entrepreneurship at Swindon before acknowledging that few tourists would come to savour the delights of the town and, anyway, our dad had burnt my sled. The odd, and perhaps unique, agreement with the digs included the clause that our mum would purchase the ingredients for the evening meal, but the repast would be cooked by the landlady.

Towards the middle of the holiday, our mum and dad had a row. What it was over, I didn't know at the time and have never found out, but it resulted in our dad abandoning the family and returning to Swindon in one of his sulks. This would not have been so bad except that he held all tickets and money and so we were abandoned, destitute without even the consolation of meals being provided. Our mum obtained a temporary job as a washer-up in a local hotel which paid little, just sufficient to prevent us all from a slow and painful death by starvation. Our Rae, Wendy and I were deposited on the beach each morning while our mum went off washing up and we were collected each evening to return to our billet. After three or four days had passed, we were gathering up our things on the beach one evening and our dad turned up. He was loaded up with bags of vegetables from his allotment and assured us all that his return to Swindon was essential to gather provisions for the remainder of the holiday. From then on, the holiday carried on as if nothing had happened.

Displayed around the town were notices advertising a jazz night in a cave during our stay and I thought that this would be just the thing for me to attend: it seemed the type of groovy scene that a cool dude could hang loose and dig some sounds and maybe pick up a chick. I decided to go and I warned our mum that I may not be home until the early hours so don't wait up. I arrived at St.

Clement's Cave at seven thirty and paid my five-bob entrance fee, strolling casually into the cave. I was alone. Apart from a chap behind the bar casually polishing glasses there was no-one – not one soul – in the place. I sat on a wooden bench and waited. After the longest half hour of my life, the band arrived, half a dozen young men dressed as old sailors or pirates and carrying a sign which proclaimed *Prince McBride's Smugglers' Band.* I spent the next half an hour watching the motley crew dragging instruments into the cave and setting up before the warmup. Each band member blew or banged or strummed or picked his instrument independently. I couldn't help but think what a bloody awful row it was. Finally, and much to my relief, other punters began to arrive, but I was a little disconcerted to find that the average customer seemed to be approaching old age, which to me meant the mid-twenties. Many men were long-haired and bearded, the girls were wearing long skirts and, unless I was very much mistaken, some had cast aside their bras. I appeared to be in the midst of a beatnik party. I self-consciously ambled to the bar and ordered a Coco Cola, returned to my seat and concentrated on the band. I wasn't sure if the performers were still warming up or not, as they all appeared to be playing different tunes at the same time. I soon realised that this was the norm as the beatniks applauded each haphazard and random number, saying, "Far out, Man," and "Bring it home, daddio." I thought that, as bad as it was, the band sounded better when they were warming up.

The cave began to fill with cigarette smoke which drifted towards the cave ceiling creating an atmospheric and foggy B-movie ambiance. There was a rather sweet smell pervading the atmosphere, which I didn't recognise but guessed was pot or grass or hash or marijuana or weed or joints. Whichever one, I was sure that it was an illegal drug. I had rarely felt so out of place and the patrons formed into happy beatnik cliques, leaving me sitting with my empty coke bottle in the corner. I tried to look casual as I got up and strolled towards the door, nonchalantly leaving my coke bottle on the bar, and climbed the steps to the cool outside. The sun was beginning to set and the whole town was cloaked in a grey, misty light which gave it a very sad and forlorn air. The atmosphere fitted my mood exactly. I wandered around the town, to the beach and the amusements before making my way back to our digs. Our mum and dad were out at the pub but the landlady answered my knocks and let me in. I went straight to bed. It was nine o'clock.

Chapter 9 – August to December 1963

- John F Kennedy assassinated in Dallas, Texas
- Secretary of State for War, John Profumo's affair with Christine Keeler causes a scandal
- Martin Luther King's "I have a dream" speech delivered in freedom march in Washington DC
- Beatlemania hits the world

Our first day back at school after the summer holidays began disastrously. Clewey, Bernie, Moggie, Tony and I met for a pre-school smoke in the public toilets, behind the shops in Clive Parade, opposite the school, and swapped stories of our summer exploits. I, of course, exaggerated slightly, enhancing my brief, hand-holding affair with Trish into a full-blooded sexual encounter. Although my imagination went wild with tales of erotic, but possibly impossible or illegal carnal activities. My mates were equally unsullied by personal experience and knew no more than I, so my wild tales went unchallenged.

Swaggering raucously into our new form room, we noisily joked and pushed and generally acted like self-important teenagers, with bodies on the verge of manhood and the brains of children. As with every new summer term, changes had occurred over the six weeks since we last met as schoolfriends. Short trousers, squeaking voices and first attempt shaving cuts were well behind us, although colourful spots and pimples remained but were under control with the application of Clearasil to augment prolific squeezing. The main difference this year was that, over the holidays, the boys' hair had been allowed to grow and most had started to comb the hair forward in the fashion initiated by the new popular music quartet from Liverpool, The Beatles. I had retained my traditional quiff and was confident that the untidy, silly

Liverpudlian group would be a short-lived phenomenon. Due to the almost instant success of the foursome, other similar groups were making hit records: Billy J Kramer and the Dakotas, Gerry and the Pacemakers, The Searchers and Brian Poole and the Tremeloes were carried along in the wake of the Beatles' success. I was still listening to Radio Luxembourg regularly, so was aware of the presence of the new music movement but was equally aware that the music greats like Johnny Kidd, Frank Ifield and Mike Sarne would be making hits long after these mop-haired northerners were but a distant memory.

We continued our noisy class reunion. Then Mr Holroyd walked in. My excitement drained faster than our dad could drain a pint - and that was fast. Our new form master was to be Mister Holy Joe bloody Holroyd, a teacher I had spent the previous year annoying with my challenges to his sincerely held belief that the Bible was a true and literal historical record, proving that an old man with a beard sits on a cloud micro-managing everything and everybody on Earth. God help me, I thought. I was sure that Holy Joe stared at me, and me alone, as he entered the classroom and made his way to his desk, before commanding, "Sit!"

He began a homily about this, our fifth year, being the most important year of our lives and, as we were such disgusting sinners, our redemption could only be achieved by intense suffering, self-flagellation, purity in body and mind and belief in the infinite power of the Lord. The opposite path of idleness, ungodliness and masturbation could only result in immediate casting into the pit of Hell and eternal damnation. So just bloody well watch it, all of you. He never actually said any of that but, by his tone, I knew what he meant. After the initial shock, I calmed down and relaxed in the hope that all would be well in the coming term.

At the annual house meeting, I was elected to carry out the onerous task of house secretary. The new Senior House

Captain explained that my role consisted solely of writing minutes for all the house meetings that term, meetings that totalled only one, and that I should keep my nose out of all other house business. Just my sort of job, I thought. But I was disappointed that the position did not warrant a badge.

I had, according to my last report, finally turned the corner leaving my wild and rebellious days behind, enjoying schoolwork and becoming a mature and conscientious student. I had a new girlfriend with whom I was looking forward to rekindling our torrid and lusty affair, depending only on her accepting that she was my new girlfriend. I was well on the way to receiving a Duke of Edinburgh's bronze award, with just a few ends to be tidied up before a successful conclusion. I was excelling at sport with new rugby and athletics seasons ahead. I was House Secretary, with nothing much to do. A happy and successful future was irresistibly mapped out for me, so I looked forward to the new term with excitement and high expectations.

Soon after the start of the term, the school held trials for the first and second rugby fifteens. As this level included sixth-form pupils, up to eighteen years old, sixteen-year-old players from the fifth year were unlikely to be selected for the first team, but one or two of us thought that we may scrape into the seconds and turned up for the trial. I was positioned as inside centre for the trial match and can vividly remember the game. I was flying. The ball was hitting me perfectly from the fly half as I moved forward at full speed, feinting, swerving and passing opponents with comparative ease before either releasing the ball to my outside centre or crossing the line myself for a try. I have had other games where I played well amongst many average or poor performances, but nothing like this. I never wanted the game to end and felt that I could have played on all night and the next day. I wasn't surprised when I was selected for the first fifteen for the first game of the season, away to local rivals Commonweal Grammar School.

I left my job in the butchers at half past nine on the Saturday morning, rushing the cleaning of the smelly mincer, and cycled up the long hill to Commonweal. Again, I felt as if I could do no wrong repeating the feeling of supreme invincibility, scoring a try which I remember clearly today against what was, to be an honest, weak opposition. I was called to one side at the end of the game by another of my old foes, Stevenson, coach to the first fifteen.

"If you want to play the rest of the season," he grimly stated, "You will be at the school at the appointed time and travel with the rest of the team. Not turn up late on your bicycle smelling of rotten meat."

"Thanks for the encouragement Stevenson, you shit-faced bastard," I wanted to say, but meekly managed a feeble, "Yes, Sir."

This gave me a predicament. My career as a butcher's boy was bringing me a better standard of living. I could now afford the important luxuries of life – cigarettes, speedway, sweets and chips. Yet, my rugby career meant that I had to be at the school every Saturday morning by ten o'clock latest for home games and nine o'clock for away games. There was also squad training on Thursday nights when I should have been delivering packs of sausages to an old lady in her vest and knickers. The decision was straightforward and it was with regret that my promising career in the meat distribution industry would have to be abandoned.

My decision was made easier when our dad came home from the club one Sunday afternoon and told me that he had arranged a job for me. A mate of his ran a cleaning business and had the contract to clean the outside of the shops in the town centre and needed extra help on Sunday mornings. The cleaning shift had no specific deadlines as shops were not allowed to open on Sundays in those far off devout and pious days. The target was to start around eight thirty and finish well before pub opening time. The money was an improvement on my butcher's salary at a heady one pound per shift. I jumped at the chance and soon began my second career, this time as a doorway hygiene operative. It soon became obvious why the extra help was needed. Most of the shop doorways had been used as lavatories on the Saturday nights, the traditional night out in Swindon's exhilarating town center. My job was to wander up and down Regent Street with a bucket of water and a mop and swill out the urine and vomit left by Saturday night revellers. Not a profession that I intended to pursue in earnest for the long term but, at a pound a week, would certainly fill a temporary need. I enjoyed the early Sunday morning start although the constant stink of piss and sick somewhat blemished my euphoria.

The rugby season went well and I never missed a first fifteen game in a season that saw Headlands Firsts unbeaten, a feat, we were informed, that had never before achieved in the school's History. I enjoyed being the youngest and smallest on the team and was treated as something of a mascot by the older players. It was a proud feeling when passing other, older team members in the school and they would acknowledge me a nod or an occasional, "All right, John," whilst ignoring my classmates. Big Dougie Watkins was the exception and would not acknowledge me in school hours but became my hero and mate on our rugby trips. Dougie was a strapping, sandy-haired sixth former, held in awe by the junior scholars and generally acknowledged as the hardest boy in the school. He played wing forward and woe betide any opposing scrum-half brave or stupid enough to hold onto the ball too long, or he was likely to be battered or crushed by the advancing Big Dougie. We were a strange partnership: the big, tough, strong forward and the skinny little quarter back, yet we became the best of mates on match days, although the friendship stopped short of sitting together on the coach to away matches. During the week in school, the relationship reverted and we resumed our roles as the tough prefect scaring younger pupils and the belligerent youngster antagonising prefects.

My memories of specific games after the season's opener at Commonweal are unclear, but certain instances are lucid, my recall unclouded by time. We were playing an under eighteen side affiliated to Gloucester, one of the top club sides in the country. Their team seemed to be made up of huge young farmers, strong and fearless but oddly lacking in technique, skill and speed. We were struggling to hold on to a narrow lead when the ball broke to the three-quarters for one of the few times in the game and off I set, jinking past the cumbersome opposition: until being stopped in my tracks by a ruddy faced farm labourer who, rather than tackle properly, decided to grab me lift me into the air in a painful bear hug. The ball was tucked under my left arm and trapped by the tree trunk-like arms of my opponent. My right arm was free, so brought my elbow down with as much power as I could muster into the farmer's face, catching him over his right eye. He dropped me with an angry roar, and I set off again, only to be recalled by the piercing whistle from the referee. A small fracas had ensued with Big Dougie in the middle of it all, as the farm boys pushed and shoved, pointing at their stricken team-mate who stood in blood-spattered bemusement. Strangely and thankfully, everyone left me alone. The referee called me over and delivered a stern lecture as I responded with a courteous apology, explaining that it was accident, a theme in which I was well-versed. The farmer's boy was treated by the application of an Elastoplast and I kept out of his way for the rest of the game.

Another Gloucester trip took us to play Sir Thomas Rich's Grammar School. Unlike our own grammar school which was built as a result of the Butler Act after the Second World War, Sir

Thomas Rich's was a fee-paying school opened almost 300 years earlier in 1668 and its extensive grounds contained such luxuries as a swimming pool and, strangely to me, a bowls green. The school specialised in sports, especially Rugby, and we were told, boasted many future internationals as alumni. It reminded me of my visit to Marlborough in the summer where the students were all terribly well-mannered and polite, speaking with an intonation that I had previously heard only on the wireless. Of the game I remember little, except one major incident. I was pushed out to the left wing for the match and quietly patrolled the touchline watching the play take place on the opposite side of the field, when the ball was booted forward by an opposing player and was heading dangerously for our try line. I started to move across to cover the break when I noticed that our usually reliable full-back, Dobbin Reece, was not there. I scampered across the pitch and, as the ball crossed our line with a hoard of roaring attackers chasing it down, I launched myself from some distance and managed to get my hands on the ball just before the opposition arrived. I remember the feeling of flying the air, previously only experienced in dreams, and the congratulations of my teammates, but little more of that game.

One other abiding memory of that year was of being crushed by opposition forwards after catching speculative kick-ahead and being winded so badly that could not catch my breath at all and was sure that I would die. The referee rushed over and picked me up before bending my body forward and instructing me take deep breaths. I wanted to say, "I'm trying to breathe but can't, you hopeless bugger," but just managed, "Uuuuggghhh." When I finally managed to suck in some oxygen, I was aching, shaking and dizzy, but the game carried on and I was immediately back in the fray. Health and Safety considerations had not yet been invented. I had previously been very excited about playing as this game was in Chippenham, where out mum and our nana came from, although my trip to my maternal ancestral homeland was a distinctly painful experience which I hoped never to repeat.

My greatest season in sport therefore remains in my memory as scoring a try in the local derby, cracking open a farm boy's eyebrow, making the first ever human non-powered flight and being close to death.

A game that I do recall clearly was not connected to the glories of the first fifteen. There were no under sixteen or fifth form sports teams. Students in this year were classed as seniors and competed with sixth formers. One exception was a game arranged against our old foes, Oldfield School in Bath at under-16 level. There was no first fifteen fixture on the Saturday of the game, so I duly took my place as a member of the squad, miffed that I was not selected as captain. On the coach to Bath, thoughts returned to Fatty Gough and his attempted genocide of our forwards in previous years, so we hatched a plan. Pete Griffin, Gareth Davies and I agreed that the most effective way to stop Fatty would be tripartite attack. If he started one of his rampaging runs, in the best traditions of a rugby tackle I was to take his legs, Gareth would grasp and hold on to his middle and Pete was to deliver as hard a punch as he could manage to his head. The plan never quite worked as planned, but Fatty's growth had stalled over the last year while many of our players had grown rapidly, such that Fatty was smothered with bodies whenever he attempted his previously unstoppable runs. Pete managed to dispense two or three vicious blows on the referee's blindside anyway, which stopped Fatty in his tracks such that he became a dormant threat, the fearful spell of invincibility finally broken.

Despite playing rugby, I maintained stronger interest in my first love of association football, spending every Saturday at the County Ground watching my beloved Swindon Town. They made a wonderful start to life in the upper echelons of the game with their young team scorching to the top of the second division table by the end of September, and regularly pulling in crowds of over 20,000 spectators, including a record 28,173 to see them thrash Manchester City by three goals to nil. With the huge crowds and my new-found wealth, I abandoned my bicycle as transport to and from matches, travelling by bus. This meant rushing out at the end of the game and sprinting to the bus stop to ensure that I caught the overcrowded vehicle and, even then, it required courage and strength to push one's way onto the bus or, like me, to sneak to the front of the queue and pretend to be with an adult about to board.

I was also excited about continuing Tuesday evenings with the Duke of Edinburgh Award squad, especially resuming my relationship with the lovely Trish. In my imagination, we would sit together, studying a range of geographical features, landmarks, field boundaries, valley contours, summit heights, rivers, roads, railways, villages and towns. We would practice bandaging each other in case of imaginary broken bones and apply poultices to imaginary bee stings and dog bites. I would walk her home afterwards, summing up the courage to kiss her passionately good night and maybe, just maybe, I would manage to hold one of those ample breasts. As it was, she ignored me. She wasn't rude or hostile, she just acted as if we had never experienced that summer of love and seemed bemused when I tried to sit by her or make intimate conversation. I guessed that the breast-holding plan was out of the question. I was getting used to rejection. First Dawn, now firmly joined at the hip to Pete, then Jane who had a brief fling with Gareth and now ignored me, and now I had lost Trish.

It was soon after this traumatic rejection that my problems with alcohol began. To have a drink problem at sixteen takes some courage to admit to, but my problem became serious. The problem was that no licensed premises would serve me.

As taller boys with a definite need to shave, Tony Duggan had been served beer in the Moonrakers and Bernie was able to buy bottles of cider from the Rodbourne Arms off-license. Gareth also claimed to be drinking regularly in the Plough Inn in Old Town with his older brother. Even our Rae proudly confessed that Mac had taken her out in his dad's car to a country pub where she had a whiskey mac (although I was temporarily confused why her drink was named after her boyfriend or vice versa). In fact, everyone I knew could buy beer or cider or whiskey except me. I had occasionally tried to buy alcohol in various outdoor beer houses attached to the Southbrook Inn, the Moonrakers, the Rodbourne Arms, the Kingsdown Inn and the Wheatsheaf, but had been thwarted on each occasion by observant and over-officious vendors. The Wheatsheaf, near Headlands school, was a newly built estate pub which had somehow managed to look run-down from the start and which was notorious for allegedly serving under-age drinkers. One Friday evening in late autumn, Tony Duggan and I decided that we would use some of our hard-earned cash on a lads' night out at the pub. We dressed in our best non-school uniform clothes, which I had also worn playing football down the brook but had nothing else. I shaved and applied liberal amounts of aftershave and toilet paper which, I hoped, would disguise the fact that I didn't need to shave. We made our way through Pinehurst past the Circle, past the Moonrakers and into Stratton before arriving confidently at the door of the pub. Had we known what loins were, we would have girded them before casually strolling into the public bar. Tony, looking several years older than I, strode to the counter and ordered two beers. The barman studied us closely, smiled nicely and said, "I can serve you, but not your little mate. Sorry." The shame I felt was indescribable as everyone in the pub turned to stare at the two youngsters trying to be grown up, until one grizzled regular at the bar said, "Go on. Give the boys a drink: Won't do no 'arm," advice which was seconded by other drinkers. The barman ceded and poured two pints of Ushers bitter, telling us to, "Go and sit in the corner, out the way."

Tony seemed to enjoy his pint and I pretended to enjoy mine as we sat in the corner as instructed, quietly drinking and smoking but saying almost nothing in fear of being unmasked as imposters and asked to leave. I did see Jane's mum and dad sitting at a nearby table with another couple, and coolly acknowledged their presence with a nonchalant wave whilst wondering who was wrestling her on their sofa. They waved back before leaning forward and saying something to their friends: something which made them all laugh heartily and which, I guessed, was something to do with my juvenile looks. We decided that another pint was in order, followed by a third. Having barely started the third drink, I was aware that the room and everything in it had started to move slightly out of focus and speech became difficult. I also needed a pee and pulled myself to my feet and headed for the gents. As I stood in front of the urinal, I experienced a strange sensation of swaying and was unable to stand straight. Each time that I swayed to the left I tried to straighten up but over-compensated and leaned right before swaying left again. I managed to complete my pee with a minimum of spillage over my hand and trousers, but as I headed back to the bar, I was overcome with a feeling of extreme nausea – much like the travel sickness I was used to, but somehow with less control. I stumbled into the car park and immediately projectile vomited several feet against the pub wall before stumbling into the hedge which surrounded the pub car park. My legs refused to hold my weight and I sunk to my knees groaning between further cascades of beery orange puke.

Several minutes later Tony came to my rescue and lifted me up, disentangling me from the hedge. "Where you been?" he asked somewhat rhetorically, "We was all worried about you. In the end Jane's mum said I should come and find you." The shame I felt for spewing was nothing compared to the shame I would feel if Jane's mum and dad told her what had happened. But, of course, they did.

Tony and I staggered home and I was pleased to see that he, too, appeared to find the simple task of moving at a regular pace by lifting and setting down each foot in turn a difficult procedure. He explained that he would have been fine if he had not been forced to drink most of my third pint as well as his own to retain credibility in the pub. I mumbled something about being grateful for that before heaving the last of my drink onto the pavement.

It was still relatively early and we decided to return to Tony's house allowing me to recover before going home, knowing that his parents would be out drinking at the American officers' club at Fairford or Brize Norton, whilst making a deal to do with contraband cigarettes or Bourbon whiskey. We flopped into armchairs and Tony switched on the television hoping that *Doctor Finlay's Casebook* would be finished and we could watch the *Dick van Dyke Show* and fall in love with Mary Tyler Moore all over again. But all that was on was the interlude card. Tony turned to ITV and there was just flickering film of something in America which made little sense. In our nebulous state, we gathered that something had happened in Dallas, Texas to do with President Kennedy, but we didn't understand what.

"Best president that America's ever had," Tony proclaimed proudly, "And he's Irish just like me."

The back door crashed open and Tony's mum and dad burst in, His mum was crying hysterically and his dad was saying something about bloody communists shooting President Kennedy, but his rich Irish brogue became almost unintelligible through emotion and, I suspect, an abundance of whiskey. We finally gathered that the president of the USA, John Fitzgerald Kennedy had been shot in in the head in Dallas Texas by a crazed gunman and was in hospital, apparently not feeling very well. Mrs. Duggan continued to cry, Mr. Duggan continued to repeat whatever was stated on the television, translated from English or American English to Irish English and Tony looked embarrassed. I decided to go home. It is a well-known maxim that everyone remembers where they were when Kennedy was shot. I certainly do. I was hanging in a bush, outside The Wheatsheaf in Stratton, vomiting violently.

During the following days, I spent hours in self-reflection. I finally put my failure to pass as old enough to buy booze to the simple fact that I owned no appropriate mufti: I had only clothes that I either wore to school, had worn to school or would wear to school, or scruffy old apparel more suited to playing football down the brook. It was difficult to stride into a pub and order beer when dressed in grey trousers and a blazer or old Tesco Tearaway jeans with muddied knees. And perhaps the fact that I could barely see over the bar counter may have contributed to the issue. I decided after this embarrassment that I would immediately stop wasting my money and would save to buy clothes which would enhance my stature and give gravitas to my aspirations to look like an adult. Naturally, wasting money did not include giving up cigarettes which were an integral part of my proposed grown up look. I even broached the subject with our mum and dad, explaining that I really needed some better clothes for going out and, as Christmas was a matter of just a few weeks away, please could I have some clothes for my presents this year.

Tony was still very friendly with Julie who was still very friendly with Jane and had heard that Jane's mum had related the sorry tale to my beloved ex-girlfriend. Although we had barely spoken since she packed me up, I still adored her, mainly, I guess, because no other girl had ever shown me even a glimpse of carnal opportunity and I remembered our Saturday nights on her settee as the climax of my erotic career, even if not reaching a climax. After my disgrace at her parents favourite watering hole, I worried that Jane would have thought me a complete dick.

I need not have worried what Jane thought. One of the highlights of playing rugby for the firsts was that we travelled to far and distant towns to play our games, including trips to Bath, Gloucester, Stroud and Salisbury. These outings had shown me towns that I had previously only glimpsed from a train window as we hurtled past towards our holiday destinations. The greatest expedition undertaken was one Thursday when six of the team were selected to travel to Taunton for trials for the West of England schools' team. Along with Big Dougie, Dobbin, and three others we boarded a mini-bus to begin the long journey into the depths of far-away Devon. I sat alone in a double seat with the older lads cramming into the back seats. They were in a predictably boisterous mood, singing rude songs and telling rude jokes, banter which I never joined in but enjoyed listening to. Ozzie Wheeler was the ringleader of this group. A bespeckled but good-looking young man with a reputation as a lothario, he had recently began courting Alice, a stunning sixth form blond who was, without doubt, the school beauty queen. As the rugby songs began and the coarse jokes were told and re-told, Ozzie twisted his glasses over his nose and declared, "Broke these glasses last night. I was kissing Alice goodnight and she closed he legs," which resulted in great guffaws from all present and a gasp of astonishment from me. As the ribald repartee continued, someone asked Dougie how he was getting on with his new girlfriend Jane. My ears pricked up immediately. "Careful there Dougie, she's underage – jail bait," called one lad. I was stunned. From what was being said there was only one Jane that it could be, and that was my Jane. I looked at Dougie with a forced smile and he, at least, had the good grace to look embarrassed.

The trial came and went in an instant and I was not selected for the West of England *te*am. But I didn't care. The news received on the way down was much more important and upsetting. Rejection was becoming a way of life.

Towards the end of December, the time came to complete my Duke of Edinburgh's Award Scheme qualification. The trek across Anglesey was deemed satisfactory despite the chicken attack and desertion by Pete. We had all passed our Saint John's Ambulance test, theory and practical exams, through our detailed knowledge of bones, breaks and bandages. The remaining modules involved us proving that we had maintained a worthwhile hobby for the year and could reach certain standards of athletic achievement. I had almost forgotten that I had selected cycling as a hobby, but I still felt that the other activities in which I spent most time; smoking, daydreaming and trying to buy alcohol, may not have been deemed acceptable. Stupidly, I had never thought of opting for football or rugby which would have been a more straightforward and easier option. At the outset, I was instructed to keep a detailed log of my cycling activities, which would be assessed at the end of the qualifying year to judge whether my cycling activities were, indeed, acceptable as a worthwhile hobby. The scheme organisers had arranged for me to present my detailed log to the owner of Mitchells Cycles for ratification, coincidentally the retailer from whom my new bike was purchased a year or so earlier. The return to one of our dad's mates should have given me confidence that all would be well. What did not give me confidence was that my plans to travel by bike across the west country had slowly faded and cycling was limited to journeys to school or to the County Ground, which was hardly a hobby. And I had abandoned my bike for the bus for the recent games. In addition, as I had not cycled anywhere of note, I had not quite started the log, let alone maintained it. Undeterred, a couple of weeks before the arranged meeting with Mr. Mitchell, I sat down, invented and documented several exciting expeditions to a variety of interesting places within a fifty-mile radius of Swindon, a distance I thought achievable in one day, and some expeditions included an imaginary overnight camp. I fantasy travelled to many of the places visited on rugby days and, according to my log, had visited the Roman baths in Bath, camping on Oldfield Park, the cathedral where Henry the eighth was crowned in Gloucester camping at Sir Thomas Rich's and, perhaps less excitingly, visited Stroud Town Clock and camped alongside the Stroudwater Canal. I devised several day trips with a circular route and, again, with a maximum cycling distance of fifty miles and restricting the visits to Wiltshire. The visits included Savernake Forest, Avebury Stone Circle, Lacock and Castle Combe. I drew maps and explained the route taken, estimating times based on an average of ten miles an hour. Never had I visited so many exciting places and seen so many interesting sights, albeit imaginary – and all in a fortnight. To endorse my trips, I recorded regular maintenance including cleaning and oiling, I invented punctures and replaced brake pads, until I had created an impressive diary of my fantasy year.

I called in to see Mr. Mitchell one Friday on my way home from school, introduced myself and presented my immaculately cleaned and oiled bicycle with the impressive tome and accompanying authorisation form. Mr. Mitchell looked at me, looked at the bike and said, "Jack's boy, aren't you?"

I nodded and he said, "Where do I sign?"

That was it. Two weeks' hard graft for nothing, I could have presented him with a copy of the Beano and he would have signed it. I had mixed feelings as I left the shop. I was annoyed that I had wasted the time and effort, but somehow relieved that my duplicity had not deceived anyone. Now I had just the athletics targets to achieve and the award was mine.

As it was not athletics season, I contacted Mr. Stephenson and explained that I needed someone to sign an authorization that I had achieved certain athletic standards, hoping that he would react like Mr. Mitchell. He didn't. Instead he took me out one lunchtime where we reviewed the qualifying events and set out to confirm that I could achieve the standards. Stephenson was assisted by a small, spotty, junior lad, commandeered out of the blue at the last minute. The problem was that there were no athletics track markings on the school field, which made measurement impossible. Some trials were easy: press-ups, shot putt and similar tests could easily be counted or measured by Spotty, until we came to time the 100 yards. I had constantly been running around 11.5 seconds that summer with a personal best time of 11.2, so the 12.5 seconds time to match as the award target was of no concern. Stephenson stood on the dead ball line of one of the rugby pitches and pointed up to the posts at the far end of the pitch. "Go up there and take your marks," he commanded, "That's about a hundred yards," and sent Spotty to verify my position.

I took my marks and got set but due to the distance between us, Stephenson waved a flag to signify *Go!*. I tore down the rugby pitch at top speed, even dipping into the imaginary tape. I turned and Stephenson held out his watch. "Twelve point eight," he announced. "You'll have to do it again."

"You sure, Sir?" I asked.

"Are you suggesting my stopwatch is wrong, Trueman? You'll have to do it again."

I did it again. "Twelve point nine," Stephenson stated and I had the feeling that he was enjoying himself.

My protests were limited to a feeble, "But, Sir," before I made way back for a third effort. This time, I glared at Spotty. "Move forward," I ordered, I and if you ever tell anyone, I'll kill you."

Spotty moved as directed and I took up my starting position about five or ten yards closer to Stephenson's finish line. For the third the flag dropped and off I set. Legs and lungs burning as I crossed the line again. Stephenson held out his watch. "Twelve dead." I'd now passed all the tests and captured Stephenson's signature to prove it – but I was sure that I'd run the longest one hundred yards ever. Three times.

My problems with Stephenson did not end there. Big Dougie approached me at morning break one day during the last week of term and asked if I had been told that there would be photographs taken of the first and second fifteens that lunch hour outside the gymnasium. I was delighted that my season of playing rugby would be recorded for posterity and could barely wait for the lunch bell. I rushed over to the gym and joined my team-mates, grabbing a first fifteen shirt before realising that I had no more kit. No shorts, no socks and no boots. I approached Stephenson who was positioning the players of each team. I explained that I had no kit. "Then you can't be in the photo, Trueman," he asserted casually, "The notice has been in the sixth form common room for a week now."

"But I'm not in the sixth form, Sir."

"So you're not, lad."

"But, Sir, I can stand at the back and no-one will see that I haven't got kit on."

"No, Trueman. If you stand at the back, no-one will see you."

"I can go home and get my kit, Sir. It'll only take about twenty minutes…"

"No, Trueman."

"I can…I can…"

"No, Trueman."

I watched as my teammates formed two lines and stood proudly, arms folded, looking tough and grim-faced and threatening, as all good rugby teams should look. I turned and rode my bike home, holding back tears of anger and frustration.

Back in the classroom, I was reminded that this end of terms' examinations would take the form of mock GCE 'O' Levels. The papers would be in the same format as the final examination and held under strict exam conditions. I had done little revision or, indeed, little work that year. Written homework was rushed or copied, and homework which included any kind of studying was ignored. Three months had passed and my valuable time had been spent clearing up human detritus from shop doorways, playing rugby and football, preparing for the Duke of Edinburgh, smoking, daydreaming and generally trying to avoid schoolwork. I was, however, confident that my natural ability would carry me through and anyway and, by the time I realised that the exams were upon us, it was too late to do anything about my lethargic and unproductive term. When the examinations took place, I remember particularly staring at the French paper and understanding little, inventing French words and phrases in the vain hope that the interpretation may magically translate correctly. They did not. I remember a question about in the History paper about how the Romans coped with the cold northern English weather. I had no idea, particularly as we couldn't cope two thousand year later in our house, which was always freezing in winter.

Following my best report from the previous term, this term's report, just five months later, was possibly the worst. Every remark indicated that I had put in little or no effort. The observations ranged from the customary, *Could do more* to *Little work done* to *Not satisfactory*. Holy Joe's summary was that I had an

Indifferent attitude to work, which was a fair comment. Fair that is, except for games where I had excelled, playing as the youngest and smallest member of the first fifteen and almost dying for the cause, to be given a B+ and told *A little more effort would bring out his best*. I would have expected this from Stephenson, but it was written by his honcho, Pete Chinn. I thought bollocks to all of them.

Our dad had the whole of Christmas off, from Christmas Eve through to the 27th December. He went off to the club or pub or both with Les Wiltshire on Christmas Eve, having decided some years ago that he was better off without the rest of the family as we had caused a fight with his family the last time we were invited out. Our Rae and Mac had also gone out, waving goodbye from Mac's dad's Vauxhall Cresta, leaving me with the less than enthralling prospect of a night in with our mum and our nana, watching *Maigret* or *Emergency Ward 10*. It was freezing outside with a bitter wind from the north. I wrapped myself up in my warmest clothes and wandered the streets, calling at the Duggan's but their house was in darkness. The Windslow's were at home but Derek said that he was staying in with his family for the evening. The Masons were having a family party to which I was invited but did not feel sufficiently confident to join and the Millmores were away for Christmas. I eventually meandered through the dark streets towards Bernie Wirdnam's house in Whitworth Road, passing the cosy council houses of Tintown, each protected from the glacial outside world, a dull glow of the lights barely penetrating their winter curtains. I imagined large families sitting together, drinking beer and smoking cigarettes, laughing and joking. Perhaps *Rockin' around the Christmas* tree to Brenda Lee or *Feeling glad all over* with the Dave Clark Five. I struck a match to light a cigarette but the wind blew it out. And when I arrived in Whitworth Road, Bernie was out. "'E is at ze club wiz 'is fadder," his French mum explained. I pulled up the collar on my coat and wandered home. I passed the

Rodbourne Arms and could see the merrymakers inside supping pints of beer, their ladies sipping port and lemons, as they sang along to the juke box. I could hear the muffled tones of Gerry and the Pacemakers singing *You'll Never Walk Alone*. I walked home. Alone.

I was miserable on Christmas Day. We had to wait to open presents at our Rae's insistence as Mac was coming around for the morning's gift exchange and was staying for dinner. I mooched around waiting for his arrival and brightened up just a little at ten o'clock when the Cresta arrived outside. Presents were opened and I was now the proud owner of eleven pairs of socks. I was looking forward to my usual box of fudge from our nana but this year she gave me twenty Woodbines, explaining, "Sixteen's too old for fudge and, besides, all them sweets aren't good for you."

There was some compensation when our nana produced a large bag of clothes. She had recently moved from her bungalow to a warden-controlled flat in Chippenham and the warden had a son, reputed to once have had a trial for Swindon Town. He had passed a selection of his cast-off clothes to his mother who had passed them on to our nana to pass on to me. I was over the moon with the clothes and had never before owned such a rich collection of non-school garments, namely t-shirts, shirts, sweaters and a donkey jacket. Not that trendy, but better than anything else I owned.

Our nana then helped our mum boil sprouts to a sloppy death in the kitchen for the rest of the morning. Our Rae and Mac were acting like Cliff Richard and Una Stubbs in *Summer Holiday* and were irritating me by holding hands and looking happy. I just mooched around the house looking grumpy. Our mum thought I was ill and made me take two Phensics but, luckily, I avoided having to swallow a lump of Vaseline Jelly or pour peroxide into my ears. Our dad got up in time to cycle to the club and pub to see a man about a dog before dinner, which meant that we couldn't start eating until he staggered home after two o'clock. I checked the chocolates which all had teeth marks. I put the television on to watch *The Red Stallion*, which was billed as a Western turned out to be a soppy film about horses and no baddies or Indians were killed, so I turned it off and mooned around again. Eventually our Mum told me to get myself a beer and cheer up, so I sat in the dining room, drinking warm light ale, puffing away on my Woodbines and sighing a lot until dinner. Finally, after an interminable long morning, our dad came home and we could have dinner. Even then, our mum gave Mac a drumstick, because he was a guest. Our dad and I always shared the drumsticks and the unfairness added to my woes. Even our dad's joke about rearing a chicken with four drumsticks as an experiment which failed because no-one could catch the chicken, didn't make me laugh. And everyone else seemed to be enjoying themselves, which made it worse.

I waited for our dad to get back from the club again on Boxing Day, having spent the morning in bed and being force-fed Phensics. As unhappy and depressed as I was, I looked forward to the now annual ritual of our dad's war stories to cheer me up. Our dad was sipping a pint of cider, port and gin with a dash of lemonade in the dining room after dinner and the washing up now, thankfully, taken over by our Rae and Mac. Our mum and nana were watching wrestling on ITV. I stayed in the dining room with our dad.

"We used to live next door to the Perrins in Telford Road before the war," he began. "Their boy Ronnie was younger than me, so I didn't really know 'im that well, but 'e seemed a nice enough lad. Then one day in 1945, somewhere in Italy I think…the war was as good as over… Jerry was on the run. I gets a letter from Mrs. Perrin to say that her Ronnie's joined up and was in our lot because I was sort of 'is 'ero and our mam used to let 'im read all my letters 'ome. Anyway, she says could I keep a look out for 'im and look after 'im cos 'e's only eighteen. Just a boy really. I knew that the chances was next to nuthin' that I'd ever see 'im but kept a look out anyway. One day, reinforcements arrived, fresh over on the boat so we was told, so I say's to some of 'em, anyone know a Ronnie Perrin? Finally, one young bloke says yes, so I says you seen 'im lately and 'e says yes. When? I says. Two days ago, 'e says, got 'it by a mortar bomb. Nothing left of 'im, mate. Sorry."

There were tears in our dad's eyes and I had never seen that before. "Nothin' I could do, see. Eighteen years old. I couldn't look after 'im, could I? Nothin' I could do, was there?"

Our dad went to bed. I went into the garden for a cigarette. Our mum, our nana, our Rae and Mac were watching the wrestling.

Chapter 10 – January – September 1964

- Cassius Clay beat Sonny Liston to become World Heavyweight Champion
- Top of the Pops first aired by the BBC
- Mod/Rocker riots at Brighton
- Radio Caroline pirate radio station begins transmission

Before returning to school, I went into town with the Paines boys, shopping with money that I had saved, borrowed and stolen from our dad's pocket when he was asleep after going to the pub. I was going to buy some new, trendy shoes in the January sales. The first shop I visited was Stead and Simpson's where, prominently displayed in the window, was a pair of dark red winkle-pickers with double buckles on the outsides. The shop assistant told me that the colour was ox-blood and the shoe box was included, which removed any doubts that I may have had about their value, and I handed over my £1/19/11. There was no need to visit any other shops and we walked home via the British Rail factory tunnel and Ferndale recreation ground, with me proudly clutching my new purchase.

We waited in our classroom for Holy Joe to turn up as Form Master in the normal noisy and rambunctious way. Clewey, Bernie, Moggie and I were laughing at a particularly smutty joke in the corner when the door opened and the classroom fell immediately silent. Standing in the doorway, arms folded and reviewing the mild mayhem with apparent disdain stood Stephenson. The class shuffled immediately to their places and stood meekly behind their desks as Stephenson strode to the teacher's desk in the corner. He reviewed his vassals as I imagine a Roman Emperor would survey defeated gladiators before turning his thumbs down to signify death.

"Sit!" Stephenson spoke in with such authority that the whole class had their bums on chairs almost before the word was finished. My head swam and I began to think that I had indeed done something to vex the Gods and was reaping the rewards of a sinful past. I was never popular with teachers but had only ever really fallen out with three: By playing up Rackham in the third year before he became my form teacher in the fourth (although he turned out to be a good influence): Arguing over religion with Holy Joe in the fourth year before he became form teacher in the fifth and now Stephenson. The man who had constantly criticized me in games lessons, had tried to cheat me out of my Duke of Edinburgh's bronze award and had committed the unspeakable and heinous crime of refusing to allow me into the first fifteen team photograph. No teacher ever changed classes half-way through a school year until now but, we learned, Holy Joe was ill over the Christmas and was ordered to take life a little easier so handed over control of form 5M to my nemesis Stephenson. I didn't believe the reason for the substitution: it was divine providence and if ever there was doubt about the existence of a forgiving and benevolent god, this surely proved He could not exist.

Stephenson began the term with the customary inspirational homily about the need for hard work and I went through my customary self-analysis. I was determined to improve my performance for this, my final term, at Headlands. It had been drummed into me that I was privileged to receive the education offered at grammar school and I should grasp the opportunity to claw myself from the gutter of despair suffered by those poor, less fortunate souls at Secondary Moderns. We would have only one shot at GCEs and the whole of my future would depend upon the results. A good clutch of passes and the world became my oyster, offering a golden path to a dazzling life of success and riches. Anything less than half a dozen passes would commit me to a life of eternal damnation and failure with a premature death in the cold confines of the workhouse. The only way to obtain this passport to paradise was to give up my wayward ways, behave sensibly, work hard, concentrate in class and study intensely. As Stephenson droned on, I was suddenly awakened from my daydream of skipping along the Yellow Brick Road towards the Emerald City, holding hands with Judy Garland. Chairs scraped on the floor, desks opened and closed as the bustle of my classmates surrounded me. They left the classroom on their way to the first lesson of the new term and I had no idea what the lesson was or where we were going. So much for concentration.

At the end of the day, we filtered out of school in dribs and drabs and I called in to the tobacconist shop next to the school gates for a pack of four Dominoes. I left the shop and bumped into a small group of boys excitedly looking at Gareth Davies' feet. Naturally, I looked too.

He was wearing strange footwear which appeared to be winkle-pickers with the points cleanly cut off. "Chisel points," he said proudly, "They're the in thing at the moment, and look." He lifted his trouser leg enough to show that they were elastic sided. The other lads were full of admiration and I began to wonder if my ox-blood winkle-pickers with double buckles may just have been a reckless, impulse buy.

Later that week, I sat at home struggling to grasp the complexities of French verb conjugation, becoming increasingly frustrated. As I understood *Présent Indicatif,* I would immediately forget the *Imparfait sunjonctif* or confuse the two to create a hybrid verb which made no sense. At the same time, Maurice Chevalier was singing *Thank 'eaven for leedle girls* in my head which was not particularly helpful. I considered taking the positive step of abandoning any efforts to learn French and possibly History and perhaps English Literature, all of which took a disproportionate amount of my allocated study time. I reasoned that this brave and radical approach would allow me to concentrate on the remaining four subjects, which I was more confident of passing, English Language, Mathematics, Physics with Chemistry and Biology. I considered the strategy carefully and even drew up a small chart with two columns headed "FOR" and AGAINST", allowing me to compare various strategies. At the end of the exercise, I gave up the radical plan, having identified more "AGAINST" than "FOR" and went to bed leaving French and History homework unfinished.

Despite renewed determination to succeed, I was still struggling to manage my time. Weekends were a particular problem, with sport again taking up much of my leisure hours. My schedule was full. Football for the school Under 16 team on Saturday mornings: visits to the County Ground on Saturday afternoons: a walk to Bradley's Corner for my Football Pink and reading every word from cover to cover in the early evenings: well-deserved relaxation hanging around with my mates and a relaxing smoke later in the evening. Hence, Saturdays were a write-off as far as schoolwork was concerned. Sundays seemed to disappear with an equal lack of productive labour: up early to clean up sick on Sunday mornings before rushing home to read The People and Sunday Express to study every football score, the scorers, the league positions and next week's games. By the time that this study was complete and Sunday lunch eaten, I barely had time to visit mates or play football down the brook before it was evening. After tea, I would retire to my bedroom, determined to complete a weekend's homework in a couple of hours but, by the time I had unloaded my satchel, reviewed my homework diary, decided the order of play, neatly laid out the books in the order required and looked out of the window, the theme music of Sunday Night at the London Palladium would drift upstairs. No-one ever missed

Sunday Night at the London Palladium, especially when Alma Cogan, Dusty Springfield or the Beverley Sisters were on. By the time the programme was finished and I had had my usual two Weetabix for supper, there was no time for homework. I easily slipped back into my routine of plagiarism or inaction.

Our awards for the Duke of Edinburgh scheme took place at Drove Road School in mid-January and all the participants turned up at the ceremony in their best bib and tucker. Many parents had turned up to proudly support their offspring, but our mum was too busy and I knew that it wasn't worth asking our dad. Every effort to catch Trish's eye failed and I was thwarted when I tried to manoeuvre my way into the seat next to her. I was embarrassed but immensely proud to receive my award and was now the majestic owner of a certificate and a lapel badge that proclaimed that I been awarded the Duke of Edinburgh's Bronze Award. At the end of the awards evening, the participants were encouraged to enter the next phase in the scheme, in my case the Silver Award but, for reasons lost in time, I never signed up. As we left the school, I again tried to catch Trish's eye, but to no avail, yet felt sure that our paths in life were interlinked and would cross in the future, possibly leading to a blissful and fulfilling relationship. I felt that there was something drawing us together, something ethereal and magical that could not be denied. After that evening, I never saw her again.

Some of my mates, including Derek Windslow had formed a rock group, and began spending many evenings and some weekends practicing in the church hall at Penhill. Derek's mum and dad were relatively well off as his mum worked full time, and they were able to buy him a real electric guitar. Robin Hapgood played the drums and two boys from the sixth form made up the ensemble. Geoff Peaple was very keen to join the group but, like most of us, buying expensive instruments was no more than a pipedream, so he assumed the unofficial role as roadie. The group played mainly instrumental numbers, copying the Tornadoes and the Shadows, even perfecting the Shadows walk. They decided that they would be called the Dandylions.

I was waiting for a chance to flaunt my new modern look with my newly acquired ox-blood shoes and second-hand clothes. An opportunity was offered when Derek, with whom I had remained very friendly despite the fact that he didn't smoke and spent most of his time practicing with the Dandylions, remarked that there was a dance to be held at Saint Barnabus's Church hall in Gorse Hill on Saturday and it offered a good opportunity to see a professional group in action. Several of us agreed that we would grace the event with our presence – Derek, Geoff, the other Dandylions and I arranged to meet at Derek's house at six thirty and walk across the allotments and the horses' field to Gorse Hill for an exciting evening of music, dancing and chatting up the local talent. I was resplendent in my new ensemble, selecting a black shirt under a maroon shaggy pullover, ice blue jeans with four-inch turn ups and, of course, my new ox-blood, double-buckled winkle pickers. I needed my nearly new donkey jacket to keep out the cold but reasoned that this would be abandoned in the dance hall, so its lack of coolness would not be an issue. I was babbling excitedly and strutting like a peacock as we paid our half-crowns and entered the church hall. It was all but empty with just a few young girls seated around the walls of the room and a pop group warming up their guitars on stage. I remembered my disaster night in the cave at Hastings but stood in a corner and tried to look cool, imagining that I was Kookie Byrnes from 77 Sunset Strip. I even took my comb from my back pocket and combed my hair a few times but refrained from calling the girls "Ginchy". In the hall was a small hatch where a large, jolly lady and a small, miserable man were dispensing Coco Cola, tea and crisps, so we drifted self-consciously towards the hatch and bought a coke each, before returning to our corner and standing there looking anything but cool. Thankfully the hall began to fill and the musicians began to play, covering numbers from the new groups that had risen to prominence on the back of the Beatles – *Glad All Over* by the Dave Clarke Five, *The Hippy Shake* by the Swingin' Blue Jeans and *Sugar and Spice* by the Searchers were well received but, as usual, instrumentals like the Shadows' *Geronimo* were considered uncool and met with derision by the local lads. As the girls began to dance around their handbags and the boys looked on, I felt a little out of place. It was obvious that many of the boys there had adapted the new mode of dress with their hair combed forward into a fringe and attired in Beatle boots, some even wearing smart suits with Beatle collars. The music was OK, but I still preferred real rock and roll and wondered why the group did not play Chuck Berry, Roy Orbison or Elvis (I had given up on Johnny Kidd and the Pirates at this time, as they had become traitors to the cause and were now making records which sounded just like the modern beat groups). I didn't particularly like Coca Cola either but felt that Kookie Burns would not stand in a dance hall whilst a group murdered chart hits and lights flashed on girls in gyrating in mini-skirts, whilst holding a nice cup of tea and dunking a Peek Frean's custard cream. And I was too shy to speak to the girls - and I couldn't dance anyway.

We walked home through the unlit horses' field and allotments, our breath billowing white clouds in the moonlight, as my mates extolled the brilliance of the music. I naturally agreed that the sound was fab, much as I thought that they would have been better singing romantic numbers like Roy Orbison's *Blue Bayou* or even hiring a lady singer to mimic Brenda Lee singing *As Usual*. I was sure that such romantic ballads would have encouraged me ask a mini-skirted dolly-bird to smooch. The conversation came around to the Dandylions and Derek stated that the group needed to update its image from a purely instrumental ensemble modelled on Cliff Richard's Shadows, and convert to the modern Liverpool sound. I couldn't help thinking that they had missed the boat by now and that this short-lived phenomenon would be over by the time that their conversion was complete.

A few weeks' later, chatting in Tony Duggan's dad's shed, Tony and I decided that we should have another night out on the beer. The sickness and hangover from four months' before were now distant memories and so we decided to try our luck and go for a pub crawl in town, identifying by reputation the Greyhound and the Glue Pot as likely venues that would not ask too many questions about age.

Again, I dressed to kill in the same clothes that I wore to the dance, and Tony wore his best imitation leather jacket. We set off to walk the two miles into town, selecting the Greyhound as our first stop. It was a small, traditional beer house on a junction to the west of Swindon and was one of half a dozen pubs crowded into the Westcott area. We entered the almost empty, yet smoke-filled, public bar and made our way to the bar, Tony again taking the lead.

"Two pints of beer please." He politely requested of a tubby barman who was wrapped in a large, stained apron.

The barman looked down and smiled. "What sort of beer, mate?" he asked.

This apparently easy question stumped us, but Tony quickly retorted, "What sort you got?"

The Barman's smile grew wider and the two or three tubby locals at the bar turned and stared at us with what I thought were looks of amusement tinged with pity. "We got bitter, best bitter, mild, light and brown,"

Tony looked at me in bewilderment. "Brown," I blurted, "We always have brown."

After all, the beer we had seen being quaffed by the locals was a brownish colour, if a very pale brownish, so it seemed a good choice: especially as we didn't want anything too bitter or too mild and had no idea what light meant.

To our surprise the barman opened two bottles and poured two almost black pints, rather than draw them from the pumps, but we had our beer and found a small table where we sat and lit up first Bristol of the night. The beer was sweeter than our previous experiment and left a bitter taste as it hit the throat, I thought it was a little like burnt toast, a taste I knew well. But, overall, it was not unpleasant, so we ordered another. The pub was now filling up and yet another tubby man took his seat at the piano and began tickling the ivories, except rather than tickle them, he crashed his fingers down on them – I had a feeling that he may have been the second half of the Symbolics, who were playing at the Christmas punch up a few years before. That said, he managed to belt out songs which the customers recognised and began singing along. The songs were new to Tony and me, but we attempted to look less conspicuous by joining in. The beer was, by now, most agreeable. We ordered another.

We sang, *Where be that blackbird be? I know where 'e be, 'E be up in yonder bush and I be after 'e*, which I particularly liked. Tony preferred, *That's my brother Silvest. 'E's got a row of forty medals on 'is chest!* but we both agreed that the one with a chorus which said, *The fly, the fly, the fly be on me turnip. The more I try, the buggered be I, to keep they off me turnip,* was our favourite. Somewhere amongst these songs were choruses where we bellowed out, *Over the 'ills, with a bloody gert stick in me 'and*, and, *Be I Wiltshire, be I buggery*, but we were unsure into which song this chorus fitted, if any. We sang along anyway, thoroughly enjoying the atmosphere, as the crowd grew and became more and more raucous. Then I felt sick and we had to leave.

I wasn't keen on calling in at another pub, but Tony insisted. We had agreed to go to the Glue Pot to make it a proper pub crawl and he insisted that you can't have a pub crawl in one pub. I reluctantly accepted this logic and we staggered along Faringdon Road towards our next venue. The Glue Pot had a reputation as being a scrumpy house and the hardest pub in town with fights a regular occurrence. It was situated in the old railway village, designed and built by Isambard Kingdom Brunel to house and provide recreation for the workers in the Great Western Railway factory. It was owned by the Devenish brewery from Weymouth and, if the rumours were to be believed, the brewery gave permission to sell one barrel of scrumpy per week, and a barrel was 288 pints. The pub was reportedly selling thirty barrels each week or over 8,000 pints. For a small pub which could probably house no more than fifty customers, each lunchtime and evening. I reckoned that this would mean each customer at each session drinking about a dozen pints. This seems ridiculously high, but then, cider can be a little moreish.

The spit and sawdust public bar was quiet, with just half a dozen old timers sitting around, their rosacea faces glowing red to illuminate the gloom. It was like sitting in a room hosting a W C Fields look-alike competition. Tony ordered two pints of scrumpy and the barman indicated a lonely corner. "Sit there lads," he ordered in a dry, croaking voice, "And if the police comes in, run out the back door and keep runnin'."

This command added to the sense of daring we were feeling, even though there was no-one else under seventy in the place and we were unlikely to witness the bar room brawl we had eagerly anticipated. The cider was a dull, cloudy yellow and very sweet with a bitter aftertaste. It was awful, but Tony took long swigs, smacking his lips after each drink and saying, "Mmm, that's good," so I was compelled to follow suit. We finally finished our pints, said goodnight to the W C Fields convention and left the pub. I felt exceptionally well as we stepped joyfully into the fresh air of Emlyn Square. Then I vomited. Bending over and projecting what felt like gallons of bitter puke into the gutter. I trembled, sweated and vomited again. I felt a little better and we started on our homeward trek. I stumbled and fell over. I swayed a little before missing my step and crashing down in the gutter. Tony lifted me up and we re-started our long walk home via London Street, Sheppard Street and Station Road, past Swindon Junction station to the White House, along Whitehouse Road, St. Mary's Grove and Pinehurst Road, across the allotments and through Tin Town to reach home. Before we reached London Street, I fell into the gutter again. I was reminded of one of my favourite seaside postcards and slurred to Tony, "Have I been walking with one foot in the gutter?"

"Yeah."

"Thank God. I thought I'd gone lame."

This caused us both to giggle uncontrollably as we staggered onward.

I had forgotten that our dad was on lates and one of his watchman posts was at the GWR entrance in Sheppard Street. If he was guarding Sheppard Street entrance, if he was not on his rounds, if he was not asleep and if he was looking out to the street, I was in big trouble. Our dad scored four out of four and intercepted our unsteady journey.

"Where you two been?" he asked.

"Just out for a drink. Greyhound and Gluepot," Tony answered. I smiled somewhat stupidly.

"Beer and scrumpy?" our dad asked.

Tony and I nodded.

"Always remember this," he said, "Never mix your drinks. It can make you ill," tapped the side of his nose and returned inside to leave us to stumble home. The matter was never spoken of again.

I was trying to work hard in the classroom and at home but was still being distracted by too many outside interests. Our mum always said that I was easily led when I was in trouble, and this seemed to be the case: except that I was often the one doing the leading. I had given up trying to drink in pubs with Tony because of the expense (beer was 1/10d a pint and cider 1/6d, so a night out would cost me up to five bob) and I was always violently ill, which seemed a waste of money and beer. Tony was spending more and more time with his non-girlfriend Julie and Pete and Dawn had disappeared altogether, cocooned in their private love-world. Derek, Geoff and the Dandylions were busy practicing their versions of Billy J Kramer, Brian Poole and Dave Clarke hits. My old Pinehurst mates had left school at fifteen and were working, many as apprentices in the GWR, and were forming new relationships with fellow apprentices. Moggie Widdows had been given a Lambretta LD scooter and spent much of his time with other scooter riders and had become a mod. I began spending more and more time with Bernie Wirdnam. We had always been the best of mates in school, seeking new and challenging ways of annoying teachers, but now became almost inseparable out of school. We spent much of our leisure hours in Bernie's front room listening in to the police messages on his radio and drinking beer and cider. Bernie had been buying cider for his dad for many years from the outdoor beer house attached to the Rodbourne Arms, across the road from his house and was never questioned about his age or eligibility to purchase alcohol. Bernie's favourite tipple was the recently introduced Strongbow cider, soon to become the refreshment of choice for vagrants everywhere, whilst my evening at the Glue Pot had put me off any apple-based drink for life. Bernie would take a two-pint jug from his kitchen and buy a quart of draft bitter for me and a bottle of Strongbow for himself. With a pack of Bristol cigarettes and the radio, this made for a very sociable evening.

One evening, the police transmission called for assistance and an ambulance to attend a serious accident at the Rodbourne Arms. Naturally, Bernie and I rushed out to see the carnage and were shocked to see a Lambretta scooter on its side under a bus and the parka-clad body of Moggie lying in the road. He was being attended to by various passers-by and appeared to be alive, so we called out and waved at him as a gesture of support and companionship, even offering an encouraging thumbs-up. But he didn't respond too positively, offering just a pained grin and a weak wave. An ambulance appeared within minutes and Moggie was rolled onto a stretcher, loaded up and transported away with blue light flashing and siren blaring. The scooter was loaded onto a truck and that, too, was taken away. Bernie and I returned to his front room and our drink, agreeing that it had been an excellent evening's entertainment.

A number of major events shaped my final term at Headlands Grammar School. The first was that news began filtering through that Pete Griffin had been expelled. This was an extremely rare occurrence at the school and was, in fact, the only time that any of us could remember an expulsion. The reason was unclear at first, but we soon learnt that it was because Dawn was pregnant. The full story unfolded, and it appeared that Dawn was well into her pregnancy and was being sent away to a home for wayward girls, where she would be forced to scrub floors for the weeks leading to the birth. The baby would be given up for adoption. The reason for this drastic sentence was that her parents were strong, church-going Christians and that is how very religious people handled carnal sin. The irony was not lost on us, even then. There was a rumour that Pete was not expelled for fathering the child but had exploded when confronted with his wickedness at school, with one version of events suggesting that he had threatened the Boss. We were shocked but not surprised. There had long been rumours that they had *done it*, rumours generated from the girls' camp. Pete said nothing. All this time when I had been feeling one breast under layers of clothing and thinking that I was a bit of a lad, one of my best mates had actually been *doing it*. I was determined to find a girlfriend who would let me do it too.

It had been agreed that Pete could return to school to take his 'O' Levels but at no other time would he be allowed past the school gates. He also refused all invitations to return to the companionship of his old acquaintances, stating that he would now study really hard, pass as many "O" Levels as possible and that would show the bastards. That is exactly what he did.

During last term and this, the whole of the year had reached their sixteenth birthdays. For most pupils, this birthday came and went with little fuss. I was given twenty cigarettes by our mum and another ten by our nana and our Rae and that was my sixteenth birthday done and dusted. A few of our contemporaries were given parties in their homes and I occasionally received an invitation. This was not greeted with great enthusiasm as it usually meant sitting in someone's front room whilst the parents and various aunts and uncles asked questions like, "How are your studies going?" or, "Are you staying on in the sixth form?" As I did little studying and was not staying on, the conversations tended to be very short.

There was some excitement when some of the class received invitations to Gareth Davies' birthday party, as he promised that his parents would be going out for the evening and we would be left alone: and he was inviting an equal number of boys and girls. I'm fairly sure that he only invited me because he felt superior after our fight, because he didn't see me as a threat with the girls and because he could laugh at my ox-blood winkle pickers with the double buckles. I chose my outfit carefully and included a nearly new, striped pullover from the would-be Swindon Town footballer via our nana. I cycled with Tony to Gareth's house in Old Walcott, a tidy, typically middle-class suburb with neat gardens and garages, bow windows and house names like The Firs, Belle Vue and even a ubiquitous Dunroamin. I joined the other teenagers in the sitting room, which Gareth called the lounge, and was happy that I knew most of the other guests. Indeed, all but one from our year at school and included Julie but no Jane who, I sadly realised, was too busy doing whatever she did with Big Dougie. Gareth's new and very attractive girlfriend was sitting quietly in the corner, seemingly distant from the chatter of the other girls. She was called Laura and was in the year above us, which made a most unusual relationship. Relationships where the girl was older than the boy were virtually unknown. I had a feeling of foreboding when we were welcomed into the house by Gareth's elder brother, a prefect at school and known to be an arrogant bully, there to keep an eye on us youngsters. My dreams of an orgy immediately dissipated, the disappointment offset a little by the fine array of food available, each plate of which was carefully labelled. There were a variety sandwiches, some even made with brown bread which was unusual, and they had the crusts cut off, which our mum would have considered a waste of good food. The fillings looked a little exotic and mysterious for my simple tastes. There was tuna and mayonnaise, ox tongue and tomato and liver sausage, none of which I had ever tasted and certainly wasn't about to start now. I was intrigued by tiny cubes of cheese and pineapple threaded on little matchsticks and stuck into a grapefruit. Equally fascinating were strange filled little pies labelled *vol au vents,* which were obviously French and which I had no intention of eating. There was even a bowl of salad which struck me as odd as it wasn't Sunday teatime. When the order came to tuck in, I concentrated on the white bread ham sandwiches and crisps before moving on to the puddings. These were also most unusual and seemed to consist solely of different coloured blancmanges in large wine glasses, but tasted quite nice, although I thought that a slab of spotted dick or bread pudding would not have gone amiss. I was also disappointed to find that no alcohol was provided but satisfied myself with lashings of orange squash.

The room was very warm and that, buoyed by an excess of sandwiches, crisps and squash encouraged me to abandon my striped pullover, which I tossed casually onto a chair and carried on with the blancmanges. The repast was brought to sudden and, to me, untimely conclusion as Gareth's brother called us all together and said that we were to have a game of postman's knock, a favourite with all the boys and only tolerated, I suspect, by the girls. Quite what our rules were, I am unsure, but the game involved one boy and one girl being selected to retire to the entrance hall where they were expected to snog before the next couple were selected. In the unwritten rules, it was also normal for the boy to move his hand over the girl's breast during the kiss, albeit over her clothes, thus feeling her up. Gareth's brother seemed a little over-enthusiastic in his organisation and timed each kiss for, he said, exactly one minute before bursting into the hall and breaking up the coupling.

After all those present had had a fair share of exchanging saliva, Gareth's brother introduced a new game. He began arranging the dining chairs into two facing semi-circles. It did not auger well when he found my new striped pullover on one chair. Held it aloft and shouted, "Who's left this old rag here?", leaving me to shamefacedly raise my hand to claim my nearly new pullover.

The girls were seated in one semicircle, the boys facing them in the other. The gist of the game was that a boy should wink at a girl and that girl crossed the floor and kissed the boy before returning to her seat to wink at a boy of her choice. Tony and I sat patiently waiting for a wink as the other guests winked and snogged and snogged and winked *ad nauseum*. Finally, someone winked at Tony and, after the snog, Tony winked at Julie who finished the snog and winked at me. I strutted across the room and snogged Julie, a little repulsed that I was probably tasting saliva not only from Julie, but from Tony's leftovers too. I had to concentrate to stop my right hand from automatically adopting feeling-up mode, before returning to my place. The opportunity was too great to miss and I fixed my gaze on Laura. Then I tried to wink, before remembering that I could not wink. I found it impossible to close my right eye without the left eye joining in. I tried to close my left with similar effect as my face screwed itself into unnatural poses which must have appeared that I had attempting to replicate Charles Laughton's Quasimodo. Laura was finally forced to accept that my gurn was a wink and crossed the floor for the kiss. As our lips met, I was shocked to find her tongue in my mouth and the others must have spotted the blatant attempt at seduction as they cheered and whooped. I was embarrassed and aroused but the noisy support from the room made me want to laugh which I tried to suppress. My mouth locked onto Laura's, the laugh had to be released and I snorted a loud, pig-like nasal exhalation. I pulled away immediately and was horrified to see a string of snot from my nose attached to Lara's cheek. I quickly raised my arm and wiped the snot in my sleeve before Laura dashed into the kitchen. The room fell silent, the game finished.

I could do no more than explain that I had to be leaving. I grabbed my striped pullover and donkey jacket and left, listening to the laughing and jolly throng as I closed the front door and mounted my bike. I began the slow ride home and Tony soon caught me, explaining that the party was finishing anyway, and everyone was going home. We reached the allotments and stopped as Tony gleefully pulled a bag of ham sandwiches and crisps from his saddle bag and we scoffed the feast before going home. All in all, and one string of snot excluded, we agreed that it wasn't a bad Saturday night out.

My previously successful athletics career came to an abrupt and ignominious end. As fifth formers, we were classed as seniors and had to compete with those pupils in the sixth and seventh years for places in the sports teams. Although I confidently entered the trials for the house athletics team, I was simply not fast enough and failed to make the relay team, let alone the individual sprints. I still chose athletics over cricket for games lessons, but this was more to do with avoiding Anderson's lethal bowling than any aspirations as an athlete. And I was still able to watch the girls' buttocks in their navy-blue knickers at close quarters. During the school sports day, where previously I had been competing in at least four events, I was left wandering the sports field aimlessly. Bernie and I managed to sneak off for a cigarette a couple of times, but the day was generally a wash out. That is, until we drifted over to the shot-put circle where Rackham was doing a fine job as the sole administrator and judge. It was a close event, with two or three of the big seventh formers in keen competition. The favourite was Big Dougie Watkins, but he was lying in third place, hampered by a slight shoulder strain. Dougie took up his position for his third and last throw with a look of fierce determination set on his rugged face, his body like a taught spring as he tucked the shot under his chin. He exploded backwards, twisted and released the shot at the perfect angle, with a grunt of pain. Just as the shot was released, Bernie tapped Rackham on the shoulder. "Who's winning, Sir," He asked innocently.

Rackham turned around spontaneously and was staring at Bernie open-mouthed as the shot thudded into the turf. He turned back to see the shot lying motionless and Dougie holding his shoulder but grinning through gritted teeth. Rackham looked like a rabbit in headlights and his face flushed a deep red as he looked from one person to another for help. None came.

"Oh dear." He said, "I missed that Watkins. Er…where did the shot land?"

"About three feet beyond everyone else's, Sir," said Dougie confidently.

Still in a state of embarrassed shock, Rackham stuttered, "Well, I'm afraid that I didn't see it Watkins. You'll have to take it again."

"Can't sir. My shoulder's gone completely this time," Dougie explained.

Bernie and I beat a rapid retreat as Rackham and Dougie debated the Amateur Athletic Association rules of shot putting where the sole adjudicator is looking the wrong way.

Our sister Rae and Mac had wanted to get married for the last year but our dad said that she had to wait until she was eighteen. He said that it was for the best and people would talk if they got married before that, which never seemed to me to be a very convincing argument, but no-one argued with our dad. On Wednesday, June the third, 1964, our Rae's eighteenth birthday, she went with Mac to see the vicar at Saint Mary's church and arranged her wedding to take place two months later on August eighth. I was asked to be best man, a request I was honoured to accept. The happy couple were left to plan almost everything alone and, amongst the rushed arrangements, was the reception to be organised, they had managed to hire Pinehurst Community Centre on The Circle for the celebration but were worried about supplying the music. I gave this a moment's thought and offered the services of the Dandylions, an offer which was accepted with some relief and more than a little trepidation, but I assured them all would be well.

I approached Derek, pleased that I was able to offer the group their first professional engagement, but Derek was a little apprehensive. He explained that the group's transition from a Shadows or Tornados style musical group to include vocals was difficult. They had recruited a local Penhill lad as singer and he had a great voice, but thus far they had not mastered any hit songs completely. Never mind, I assured him, you've got nine weeks.

I attended several practice sessions in the church hall and must admit to some nervousness as the only songs that the whole ensemble seemed confident in performing from start to finish were *It's over* by Roy Orbison and *Don't throw your Love Away* by the Searchers, neither of which seemed quite apt for a wedding reception.

Apart from my new role as a popular music impresario, I decided over the last few weeks of term that I really should knuckle down and concentrate on studying for the forthcoming GCE "O" Levels, the results of which would decide whether I would lead a life of wealth and luxury or be forever damned to a life of poverty and misery...apparently. I was registered to taker seven "O" Levels: English Language, English Literature, Mathematics, Physics with Chemistry, Biology, History and French. I was confident that Maths and English Language would be a breeze and fairly happy that my knowledge of the internal sexual components of rabbits would see me through Biology, providing that I didn't confuse the bits with human organs from Micky Millmore's mum's book and which had formed much of my extracurricular studies. I hoped that a good understanding of Physics would carry me through my less than adequate familiarity with Chemistry. The three subjects that would require extra revision were, therefore, French, History and English Literature. It was no coincidence that these involved a great deal of study and retention of information, neither attribute of which was a strength of mine. I was determined to overcome my lethargy and work hard to achieve my target, a minimum of five passes.

Staying on at school to take "A" Levels was never an option for me. Our dad always said that book learning was a waste of time and he was more than somewhat miffed that I had not left school at fifteen and secured employment in the British Rail factory. As he said, "I never had any school exams and look at me. With your brains, you could get a job inside - in the offices." GCE "A" levels were really of any use only as an entrance qualification to university, and kids from Pound Lane didn't go to university.

The school sent out a note saying that parents of all pupils who did not intend to stay on into the sixth form had the opportunity to attend a career interview with the experienced school careers officer. I was somewhat surprised and a trifle apprehensive when our mum said that she was attending. Her only previous intended attendance two years previously had been cancelled because of Z Cars. A date and time were agreed, and I made my way apprehensively and reluctantly to Merv Comrie's office at the appointed hour. In addition to being a fine English and History teacher, guardian of the English Language and keeper of the hippo, Merv was also the boys' career master. For a man who had spent his whole life in the academic and educational arena, his personal experience was limited, and so what he was going to recommend for me, I had no idea. I just hoped that it wasn't a job in the British Rail offices. At the specified time, I approached Merv's office and saw our mum sitting nervously outside, her face lighting up as I joined her. She was resplendent in a new coat and shoes and was even wearing lipstick. She patted the seat next to her and smiled. I grunted. Our dad never came of course. "Waste of time." he declared emphatically, "Won't make no difference anyway."

Our mum opened her bag, withdrew a pack of Tipped Woodbines and began to take out a cigarette. "Mum, you can't

Page 250

smoke in here," I whispered in panic and our mum looked genuinely puzzled. I don't think that she had ever been anywhere before where she couldn't smoke but put the cigarette back in her bag anyway.

After a few minutes of embarrassed silence, two parents emerged from the office and Merv called out "Next please." our mum and I entered. It was difficult to say who was the most nervous.

"No Mister Trueman?" Merv asked rhetorically.

"No. I'm afraid he's not with us now," our mum replied almost coyly.

"Oh dear," Merv sympathised, "I had no idea. Um...how long is it since he...er...passed?"

Our mum looked confused, then realised what Merv had surmised. "Oh no," she said, "He's not, you know, it's just that he's inside and can't be here."

Merv again looked at our mum compassionately. "I'm terribly sorry Mrs. Trueman," he said, "I...er...didn't know. Let's get on to young John's future then shall we."

I realised that Merv, despite his years in Headlands, had never grasped the fact that men working in the British Rail Factory in Swindon were always talked of as being "inside".

I had never seen Merv so kind and considerate as at that interview. At one point, he opened the office window before offering our mum a cigarette. They both sat puffing happily and our mum looked at me and nodded smugly as if to say *Told you so.* They then discussed what a fine young man I was and, after twenty minutes and two cigarettes, Merv announced that the only career path he could see for me was to join the services, possibly as an officer recruit in the army if I achieved the necessary number of "O" levels. Our mum shook his hand and smiled sweetly before thanking him for his help and almost bowing as we left his office. "You're not joining the army," she said when we were alone,

"Your dad'll never sign the papers," and off she set down the stairs. She never mentioned anything about a services career, or indeed any other employment issue, again.

A couple of weeks later, I was summoned to Merv's office. I was unaware of any misconduct I had perpetrated but was nervous, nonetheless. Merv called me in and pushed a piece of paper in front of me. He again seemed very agreeable and said, "I have arranged an interview for you for this job. Next Friday morning at Plessey on the Rodbourne Trading Estate. Accounts Trainee. Starting in August. It looks just your sort of thing, Trueman."

I glanced at the piece of paper, which did indeed look just my sort of thing. It required *good "O" Level passes including Mathematics and English Language* without specifying exactly what constituted *good* and the Trading Estate was within a twenty-minute walk of our house.

As I left Merv's office clutching the piece of paper, he said, "I've not recommended anyone else for this position, Trueman. Don't let me down," and patted me on the shoulder. "And Trueman," he added, "You must try to lose this barrack room lawyer mentality." I had no idea what he meant but nodded and replied that I would. It certainly seemed to pay off having our dad "inside".

The interview went smoothly and I was offered the job there and then providing I passed Maths and English 'O' Level. Nothing more was required and the offer, with all the relevant information, would be sent to me by post. I was excited. Just a few weeks left at school then I would leave and become an Accounts Trainee and be earning the small fortune of £4/2/6 a week. Four pounds two shillings and sixpence each week: every week. I would be rich.

All pupils taking GCEs were given two weeks' leave before the examinations began for home study and we cycled home on the final Friday in buoyant mood. For all practical purposes, we had left school. We had to return only for the examinations and on the final day of term to collect belongings and officially cut all ties with the school. Only Bernie had decided to stay on to take his "A" Levels. Tony had decided to join the navy, Derek had been offered a job as a draughtsman, Geoff just wanted to leave at all costs and Pete would not be welcomed back after his expulsion. We all agreed that we should still find time over the next two weeks to meet during some evenings and weekends but that we would all study hard during the normal working day. I was determined that nothing could stop me now and this was my last opportunity to make up for the time wasted in the past and to study as never before.

I was too busy to start studying during the first weekend. I had recently discovered the joys of snooker and every Saturday morning was spent in the Lucania Billiards Temperance Society above Burtons tailors in the town centre with the Paines boys. Although the football season had finished (Swindon Town had finished a creditable fourteenth in the second division), I was still meeting mates down the brook for games on Saturday afternoons. Saturday evenings were still spent with Bernie drinking Cider and listening to Radio Luxemburg or the police transmissions and on Sunday mornings I was busy cleaning sick from shop doorways. The rest of Sunday included sleeping, eating and generally resting in preparation for the travails to come in the following week.

I arose early on the first Monday determined that I would make the most of my limited time available. I laid out a series of exercise and textbooks before deciding what to study first. It was not an easy exercise, so I decided that that I needed a proper schedule to ensure that each subject was allocated sufficient and appropriate time. I reasoned that I could split each day into four sessions, two in the morning and two in the afternoon. This would provide twenty sessions each week, forty sessions over the fortnight study period. As I had seven subjects to study, this would allow six sessions on each subject if I squeezed in one more session each weekend, which should be achievable. I carefully drew up a calendar for the two weeks before adding the subjects to be studied. There was a false start when I forgot the weekend stint, so restarted the chart, studied the subjects and began filling in the calendar. This was not straightforward. I began by arranging the subjects in alphabetical order and starting on Monday, period one. Day one (Monday) was, therefore, Biology and English Language in the morning with English Literature and French in the afternoon. Day two (Tuesday) was History and Maths in the Morning and Physics with Chemistry in the afternoon. This left a spare slot on Tuesday afternoon which, by rights, belonged to Biology. I thought, however, that it may be easier to keep the same subjects to the same time of day, so reserved Tuesday afternoon as a rest period. In fact, I was so impressed with the notion of a rest period that I decided to keep it in for each day. I scrapped the chart and began again, this time leaving the last period each day as a rest period. This, of course, meant that I only had thirty sessions over the two weeks or four for each subject, leaving two sessions spare for emergencies and no weekend sessions. Then our mum called me for dinner, so I decided to start again after dinner.

Dinnertime at school had always lasted two hours and I saw no reason to alter this tradition, so dawdled upstairs to restart my chart at two o'clock. As I drew up the new matrix, I realised that there was a glaring error in my logic: the two morning sessions were one and a half hours each (from nine until twelve) but the two afternoon sessions were only one hour each (from two until four). I rethought the process and concluded that I should make each session one hour, thus enabling three equal study periods and one rest period each day. Over the fortnight, this still gave thirty sessions. I scrapped all previous attempts, re-drew the chart carefully blanking out my rest period with hatching and, as it was almost three o'clock and my rest period, I decided that I would begin filling in the subjects on Tuesday.

Tuesday began well as I re-gathered my thoughts. Four periods of one hour each day including a rest period. Three work periods times ten days equals thirty study sessions. Seven subjects equal four sessions to each subject, offering two emergency sessions and allowing weekends to be excluded. I scrapped the chart and re-drew it without weekends, filled in the subjects which took until almost dinnertime, so I finished early and waited for dinner.

As I took up my position ready for my first study session, an awful realisation struck me. I had been so intent on creating a logical and attractive timetable that I had quite missed the obvious – that almost two days had passed which invalidated the schedule. I decided that this stupid and unforgivable error was due to stress and exhaustion so took the afternoon off and cycled to Bernie's house for a cigarette.

On Wednesday, I began again with renewed vigour, allowing for lost time and postponing the starting session until Thursday. The chart looked splendid, albeit reduced to twenty-one sessions (three per day times the seven remaining days) which conveniently gave each subject three sessions of one hour each, somewhat short of my original plan of six sessions of one and a half hours each, but nonetheless sufficient if I studied as hard as I was determined to do. I was then hit by another obvious flaw in my planning. Although the exams began on the Monday after next, they took place over a two-week period, leaving several free days and hours for study between trips to the school. As each of the seven exams took half a day, we would spend only three and a half out of ten days (I had still excluded weekends as rest periods) being tested leaving six and half days, or thirteen half-days, free for study.

But, of course, the use of that free time for study needed to be intertwined within the exam schedule to ensure that each subject received its fair share of attention. This was now becoming a very complex matrix, so I decided to leave it until the following Monday and went to Bernie's house for cigarettes and cider.

For the preceding five years, it had been drummed into all pupils that these two weeks of GCE "O" Level exams would be the most important of our young lives, the fulcrum upon which our future would depend. It is odd, then, that I have no recollection of the time at all. Whether I did any swotting or not, what happened between exams, where the exams took place or what form the tests took are wiped forever from my memory banks. From my results, I guess that I did the minimum of revision or maybe I was just unable to cope. The fact that I had accepted the job offer at Plessey, which depended only on achieving passes in Maths and English Language may have added to my lethargy, but I do remember that I eventually produced a magnificently detailed and intricate revision schedule which I probably never followed.

I considered my final report irrelevant and, although I duly collected the document on my last day, was never shown to our mum. It contained the usual bland and futile comments, but was, perhaps surprisingly, much more positive that I had been used to. The strangest comment came from a largely anonymous English teacher who mysteriously wrote *His written work lacks polish*. How I was supposed to polish my written work was left unexplained.

A few weeks later, the results of the GCE 'O' Level examinations were issued and I had achieved a disappointing three passes, in Pure Mathematics and English, both of which I found easy, and Biology, in no small part due to my expert knowledge of rabbit penises and vaginas. No one at home or at work ever asked me about the results. No one. Ever.

I had been working as a trainee in the Accounts Department, Wiring and Connectors Division, The Plessey Company for five or six weeks when it was my seventeenth birthday. I was now a wealthy young man with my regular wages amounting to £3/10/- after tax and National Insurance. Thirty bob went to our mum for housekeeping leaving the grand sum of two pounds for me to spend as I saw fit. Our dad said that I was almost eighteen and now old enough to accompany him to the pub, but I had to buy my round, an important social practice. We set out one evening to the Southbrook Inn, strolling across the brook and through the allotments to Southbrook Street in silence. We stopped facing the pub. "Always remember this," our dad announced with dramatic gravity, "Never trust a landlord that don't drink his own beer," and tapped the side of his nose sagely.

It was probably the best advice that he'd ever given me.

EPILOGUE

Headlands Grammar School was established in 1952 following the Butler Act of 1944. It became a comprehensive school in the 1970's with the introduction of non-selective secondary school education. The Headlands Comprehensive School was closed on 31 August 2004 and on 1 September 2004 Headlands School was born. Swindon Academy opened in September 2007, replacing Headlands School, Pinehurst Junior School and Pinehurst Infant School.

The school buildings were demolished in December 2009.

The Grammar School headmaster, the feared but highly venerated Thomas Symmons Magson MA, moved on with the closure of the Grammar School to become a vicar in nearby Highworth. The majority of the school teaching staff left to find pastures new or to enjoy retirement.

Despite its reputation for hard work and tough discipline, I am yet to meet any Old Headlandian who has anything but respect for the regime.

Of my Grammar School mates:

Bernie Wirdnam became a lifelong friend. We remained close mates until his untimely death in 2008. We remained friends with Bob Francome for many years, following his amorous activities with interest. Bob and I have now lost touch.

I kept in touch with Mickie Millmore, Brian Mason, Derek Windslow and Geoff Peaple for a couple of years after we left school, until we made our different ways in the world. I have no idea where they now are.

I lost touch with Pete Griffin almost immediately after his expulsion. He sadly died in 2017.

Moggie Widdows and Richard Clewlow remained my mates for a number of years, until we lost contact when marriage and children changed our priorities. Clewey died in 2014.

Tony Duggan joined the navy from school. I have met him once since, around the turn of the century, and we went for a pint. We had nothing in common and the reunion never developed.

I have seen or heard nothing of Gareth Davies or Derek Wall since School.

I met Dougie Watkins occasionally over the years in the pub that he ran in Wroughton near Swindon. I read of his death in the Adver in 2014.

I would sporadically bump into one of the girls from Headlands but have no idea how their lives panned out or where they are now.

Of my Pinehurst mates:

The Paines Boys, Mick and John remained friends for many years before we lost touch. John sadly died in 2014.

Mick Kell and I were close mates for several years and still occasionally meet for a beer.

Spuddy Taylor remains a good friend and we still get into trouble together.

Of my family:

Our Rae and Mac wed on the 8th August 1964 and remain happily married. The Dandelions were considered a triumph by all present, undoubtedly helped by the fact that all guests were well-oiled.

Printed in Poland
by Amazon Fulfillment
Poland Sp. z o.o., Wrocław

50444653R00153